PENGUIN UNIVERSITY BOOKS

AN INQUIRY INTO MEANING AND TRUTH

Bertrand Russell was born in 1872 and educated at Trinity College, Cambridge, of which he was a Fellow. In 1910 he published with A. N. Whitehead the first volume of *Principia Mathematica*, a landmark in the history of mathematics, and in 1914 his reputation in philosophical circles was greatly increased by *Our Knowledge of the External World*. He published in 1917 his *Principles of Social Reconstruction*, and *Mysticism and Logic* appeared in 1918 and later became a Pelican.

Between the two world wars his output was prolific in many fields. In 1931 he succeeded his brother as the third Earl Russell, and at the beginning of 1941 he was appointed Professor of Philosophy at the Barnes Foundation, Philadelphia, for three years. Possibly the crowning achievement of his life's work was *A History of Western Philosophy* (1946). In 1949 he published the first Reith Lectures, *Authority and the Individual*, and in 1952 *The Impact of Science on Society*.

Bertrand Russell, who in 1961 published *Has Man a Future?*, was an active campaigner for nuclear disarmament, and played a leading role in the protest movement against America's actions in Vietnam. He was an F.R.S., and was awarded the O.M. in 1949 and the Nobel Prize for Literature in 1950. The first volume of his autobiography was published in 1967, and the third and final volume in 1969. Bertrand Russell died in 1970.

AN INQUIRY INTO
MEANING AND TRUTH

—

THE WILLIAM JAMES LECTURES
FOR 1940
DELIVERED AT HARVARD UNIVERSITY
BY

BERTRAND RUSSELL

PENGUIN BOOKS

Penguin Books Ltd, Harmondsworth, Middlesex, England
Penguin Books Inc., 7110 Ambassador Road, Baltimore, Maryland 21207, U.S.A.
Penguin Books Australia Ltd, Ringwood, Victoria, Australia

—

First published by Allen & Unwin 1940
Published in Pelican Books 1962
Reprinted 1963, 1965, 1967, 1970
Reissued in Penguin University Books 1973

—

Made and printed in Great Britain
by Fletcher & Son Ltd, Norwich,
Set in Monotype Plantin

—

CONTENTS

PREFACE

THIS book has developed gradually over a period of years, culminating in a series of academic appointments. In 1938 I treated part of the subject in a course of lectures on 'Language and Fact' at the University of Oxford. These lectures formed the basis for seminar courses at the University of Chicago in 1938-9 and the University of California at Los Angeles in 1939-40. The discussions at the two seminars did much to widen my conception of the problems involved and to diminish the emphasis which I originally placed on the linguistic aspects of the subject. I have to express a collective obligation to those, both Professors and pupils, who by detailed friendly criticism, helped (I hope) in the avoidance of errors and fallacies. More especially at Chicago, where the seminar was often attended by Professors Carnap and Morris, and where some of the graduate students showed great philosophic ability, the discussions were models of fruitful argumentative cooperation. Mr Norman Dalkey, who attended both seminars, has since read the whole book in manuscript, and I am greatly indebted to him for his careful and stimulating criticism. Finally, during the summer of 1940, I prepared these William James Lectures partly from accumulated material, and partly from a reconsideration of the whole subject.

As will be evident to the reader, I am, as regards method, more in sympathy with the logical positivists than with any other existing school. I differ from them, however, in attaching more importance than they do to the work of Berkeley and Hume. The book results from an attempt to combine a general outlook akin to Hume's with the methods that have grown out of modern logic.

INTRODUCTION

THE present work is intended as an investigation of certain problems concerning empirical knowledge. As opposed to traditional theory of knowledge, the method adopted differs chiefly in the importance attached to linguistic considerations. I propose to consider language in relation to two main problems, which, in preliminary and not very precise terms, may be stated as follows:

I. What is meant by 'empirical evidence for the truth of a proposition'?

II. What can be inferred from the fact that there sometimes is such evidence?

Here, as usually in philosophy, the first difficulty is to see that the problem is difficult. If you say to a person untrained in philosophy, 'How do you know I have two eyes?' he or she will reply, 'What a silly question! I can see you have.' It is not to be supposed that, when our inquiry is finished, we shall have arrived at anything radically different from this unphilosophical position. What will have happened will be that we shall have come to see a complicated structure where we thought everything was simple, that we shall have become aware of the penumbra of uncertainty surrounding the situations which inspire no doubt, that we shall find doubt more frequently justified than we supposed, and that even the most plausible premisses will have shown themselves capable of yielding unplausible conclusions. The net result is to substitute articulate hesitation for inarticulate certainty. Whether this result has any value is a question which I shall not consider.

As soon as we take our two questions seriously, difficulties crowd upon us. Take the phrase 'empirical evidence for the truth of a proposition'. This phrase demands that we should define the words 'empirical', 'evidence', 'truth', 'proposition', unless we conclude, after examination, that our question has been wrongly worded.

Let us begin with 'proposition'. A proposition is something

9

which may be said in any language: 'Socrates is mortal' and 'Socrate est mortel' express the same proposition. In a given language it may be said in various ways: the difference between 'Caesar was killed on the Ides of March' and 'it was on the Ides of March that Caesar was killed' is merely rhetorical. It is thus possible for two forms of words to 'have the same meaning'. We may, at least for the moment, define a 'proposition' as 'all the sentences which have the same meaning as some given sentence'.

We must now define 'sentence' and 'having the same meaning'. Ignoring the latter for the moment, what is a sentence? It may be a single word, or, more usually, a number of words put together according to the laws of syntax; but what distinguishes it is that it expresses something of the nature of an assertion, a denial, an imperative, a desire, or a question. What is more remarkable about a sentence, from our point of view, is that we can understand what it expresses if we know the meaning of its several words and the rules of syntax. Our investigation must therefore begin with an examination first of words, and then of syntax.

Before entering upon any detail, a few general remarks as to the nature of our problem may help us to know what is relevant.

Our problem is one in the theory of knowledge. What is the theory of knowledge? Everything that we know, or think we know, belongs to some special science; what, then, is left over for theory of knowledge?

There are two different inquiries, both important, and each having a right to the name 'theory of knowledge'. In any given discussion, it is easy to fall into confusions through failure to determine to which of the two inquiries the discussion is intended to belong. I will therefore, at the outset, say a few words in explanation of both.

In the first form of theory of knowledge, we accept the scientific account of the world, not as certainly true, but as the best at present available. The world, as presented by science, contains a phenomenon called 'knowing', and theory of knowledge, in its first form, has to consider what sort of phenomenon this is. Viewed from the outside, it is, to begin with, a characteristic of living organisms, which is (broadly speaking) increasingly displayed as the organism becomes more complex. It is clear that knowing is a relation of the organism to something else or to a part of itself. Still taking an outside observer's point of view, we may distinguish perceptive awareness from habit-knowledge. Perceptive awareness is a species of 'sensitivity', which is not confined to living organisms, but is also displayed by scientific instruments, and to some degree by everything. Sensitivity consists in behaving, in the presence of a stimulus of a certain kind, in a way in which the animal or thing does not behave in its absence.

A cat has a characteristic behaviour in the presence of a dog; this makes us say that the cat 'perceives' the dog. But a galvanometer has a characteristic behaviour in the presence of an electric current, and yet we do not say that it 'perceives' the electric current. The difference between the two cases has to do with 'habit-knowledge'.

An inanimate thing, so long as its physical constitution remains unchanged, makes always the same response to the same stimulus. An animal, on the contrary, when presented repeatedly with a stimulus to which, from the first, it makes *some* response, will gradually alter the character of the response until it reaches a point of (at least temporary) stability. When this point has been reached, the animal has acquired a 'habit'. Every habit involves what, from a behaviourist point of view, might count as belief in a general law, or even (in a sense) as knowledge of such a law, if the belief happens to be true. For example, a dog that has learnt to sit up and beg for food might be said by a behaviourist to believe the general law: 'the smell of food plus begging is followed by food; the smell of food alone is not'.

What is called 'learning by experience', which is characteristic of living organisms, is the same thing as the acquisition of habits. A dog learns by experience that human beings can open doors, and therefore, if his master is present when he wants to go out, barks round him instead of scratching at the door. 'Signs' depend, as a rule, upon habits learnt by experience. His master's voice is, to a dog, a sign of the master. We may say that A is a 'sign' of B if it promotes behaviour that B would promote, but that has no appropriateness to A alone. It must be admitted, however, that some signs are not dependent upon experience for their efficacy: animals respond to certain smells in a manner appropriate to the objects emitting the smells, and sometimes can do so even when they have never experienced the objects in question. The precise definition of a 'sign' is difficult, both on this account, and because there is no satisfactory definition of 'appropriate' behaviour. But the general character of what is meant is fairly clear, and it will be seen that language is a species of the genus 'sign'.

As soon as the behaviour of an organism is influenced by signs, it is possible to trace the beginnings of the distinction between 'subjective' and 'objective', and also between 'knowledge' and 'error'. Subjectively, A is a sign of B for an organism O if O behaves in the presence of A in a manner appropriate to B. Objectively, A is a sign of B if, in fact, A is accompanied or followed by B. Whenever A is subjectively a sign of B for the organism O, we may say that, speaking behaviouristically, O 'believes' the general proposition 'A is always accompanied or followed by B', but this belief is only 'true' if A is objectively a sign of B. Animals can be deceived by mirrors or scents. Such instances make it clear that, from our present point of view, the distinctions 'subjective-objective' and 'knowledge-error' begin at a very early stage in animal behaviour. Both knowledge and error, at this stage, are observable relations between the behaviour of the organism and the facts of the environment.

Within its limitations, theory of knowledge of the above sort is legitimate and important. But there is another kind of theory of knowledge which goes deeper and has, I think, much greater importance.

When the behaviourist observes the doings of animals, and decides whether these show knowledge or error, he is not thinking of himself as an animal, but as an at least hypothetically inerrant recorder of what actually happens. He 'knows' that animals are deceived by mirrors, and believes himself to 'know' that *he* is not being similarly deceived. By omitting the fact that *he* – an organism like any other – is observing, he gives a false air of objectivity to the results of his observation. As soon as we

remember the possible fallibility of the observer, we have introduced the serpent into the behaviourist's paradise. The serpent
whispers doubts, and has no difficulty in quoting scientific scripture for the purpose.

Scientific scripture, in its most canonical form, is embodied
in physics (including physiology). Physics assures us that the
occurrences which we call 'perceiving objects' are at the end
of a long causal chain which starts from the objects, and are not
likely to resemble the objects except, at best, in certain very
abstract ways. We all start from 'naïve realism', i.e., the doctrine
that things are what they seem. We think that grass is green,
that stones are hard, and that snow is cold. But physics assures us
that the greenness of grass, the hardness of stones, and the
coldness of snow, are not the greenness, hardness, and coldness
that we know in our own experience, but something very different. The observer, when he seems to himself to be observing a
stone, is really, if physics is to be believed, observing the effects
of the stone upon himself. Thus science seems to be at war with
itself: when it most means to be objective, it finds itself plunged
into subjectivity against its will. Naïve realism leads to physics,
and physics, if true, shows that naïve realism is false. Therefore
naïve realism, if true, is false; therefore it is false. And therefore
the behaviourist, when he thinks he is recording observations
about the outer world, is really recording observations about
what is happening in him.

These considerations induce doubt, and therefore lead us to a
critical scrutiny of what passes as knowledge. This critical
scrutiny is 'theory of knowledge' in the second of the two senses
mentioned above, or 'epistemology', as it is also called.

The first step in such a scrutiny is the arrangement of what
we think we know in a certain order, in which what comes later
is known (if it is known) because of what comes earlier. This
conception, however, is not so clear as it might seem to be. It is
not identical with logical order, nor yet with order of discovery,
though it has connexions with both. Let us illustrate by some
examples.

In pure mathematics, after the elements, logical order and
order of knowledge are identical. In a treatise (say) on Theory of

Functions, we believe what the author says because he deduces it from simpler propositions which are already believed; that is to say, the cause of our beliefs is also their logical ground. But this is not true at the beginning of mathematics. Logicians have reduced the necessary premises to a very small number of highly abstract symbolic propositions, which are difficult to understand, and which the logicians themselves only believe because they are found to be logically equivalent to a large number of more familiar propositions. The fact that mathematics can be deduced from *these* premises is emphatically not the reason for our belief in the truth of mathematics.

What epistemology requires of mathematics, though it is not the logical order, is also not the psychological cause of our beliefs. Why do you believe that $7 \times 8 = 56$? Have you ever verified this proposition? Certainly I never have. I believe it because I was told it in childhood, and have since seen it repeated by reputable authors. But when I am engaged in an epistemological investigation of mathematical knowledge, I ignore these historical causes of my belief that $7 \times 8 = 56$. The problem for epistemology is not 'why *do* I believe this or that?' but 'why *should* I believe this or that?' In fact, the whole subject is a product of Cartesian doubt. I observe that men err, and I ask myself what I must do to avoid error. Obviously one thing that I must do is to reason correctly, but I must also have premises from which to reason. In a perfected epistemology, the propositions will be arranged in *a* logical order, though not in the logical order that a logician would prefer.

Take the case of astronomy. In the mathematical theory of planetary motions, the logical order starts from the law of gravitation, but the historical order starts from the observations of Tycho Brahe, which led to Kepler's Laws. The epistemological order is similar to the historical order, but not identical, since we cannot be content with old observations. If we are to use them, we must first find evidence of their trustworthiness, which we can only do by means of observations of our own.

Or, again, take history. If there were a science of history, its facts would be deduced from general laws, which would come first in the logical order. In the epistemological order, most of us are content to believe, about (say) Julius Caesar, what we find in reliable books. But the critical historian must go to manuscripts and inscriptions; his data are certain shapes, of which the interpretation may sometimes be very difficult. In the case of cuneiform inscriptions, for example, the interpretation depends upon very elaborate inductions; to set out why we should believe what we do about Hamurabi is a complicated matter. For the critical historian, the essential premisses are that he sees certain shapes on certain tablets; for us, that he says he does, together with whatever reasons we may have for believing him to be truthful, which must consist in a comparison of his statements with our own experiences.

Epistemology must arrange all our beliefs, both those of which we feel convinced, and those that seem to us only more or less probable, in a certain order, beginning with those that, on reflection, appear to us credible independently of any argument in their favour, and indicating the nature of the inferences (mostly not strictly logical) by which we pass from these to derivative beliefs. Those statements about matters of fact that appear credible independently of any argument in their favour may be called 'basic propositions'.* These are connected with certain non-verbal occurrences which may be called 'experiences'; the nature of this connexion is one of the fundamental questions of epistemology.

Epistemology involves both logical and psychological elements. Logically, we have to consider the inferential relation (usually not that of strict deduction) between basic propositions and those that we believe because of them; also the logical relations which often subsist between different basic propositions, causing them, if we accept certain general principles, to fit into a system which, as a whole, strengthens the probability of each of its constituents; also the logical character of basic propositions themselves. Psychologically, we have to examine the relation of basic propositions to experiences, the degree of doubt or certainty that we feel in regard to any of them, and the methods of diminishing the former and increasing the latter.

I shall, throughout this book, try to avoid the consideration of

* This is the expression used by Mr Ayer.

logical and mathematical knowledge, which does not raise the problems that I wish to discuss. My main problem, throughout, will be the relation of basic propositions to experiences, i.e., of the propositions that come first in the epistemological order to the occurrences which, in *some* sense, are our grounds for accepting these propositions.

The subject with which I shall be concerned is different from that discussed, for instance, in Carnap's *Logical Syntax of Language*, though at many points the discussions in that book and others dealing with similar topics are relevant. I am concerned with what makes empirical propositions true, and with the definition of 'truth' as applied to such propositions. Empirical propositions, except when their subject-matter happens to be linguistic, are true in virtue of occurrences which are not linguistic. In considering empirical truth, therefore, we are concerned with a relation between linguistic and non-linguistic events, or rather, with a series of relations of gradually increasing complexity. When we see a shooting star and say 'look', the relation is simple; but the relation of the law of gravitation to the observations upon which it is based is exceedingly complex.

Empiricism, in agreement with common sense, holds that a verbal statement may be confirmed or confuted by an observation, provided it is a statement which is significant and is not one of logic. Now the 'observation', in such a case, is supposed to be something non-verbal which we 'experience'. But if an observation is to confirm or confute a verbal statement, it must itself give ground, in some sense, for one or more verbal statements. The relation of a non-verbal experience to a verbal statement which it justifies is thus a matter which empiricism is bound to investigate.

The general course of my argument will be as follows.

In the first three chapters, I am concerned with an informal and introductory discussion of words, sentences, and the relation of an experience to a sentence which (partially) describes it. One of the difficulties of the subject is that we have to use common words in precise technical senses which they do not commonly bear; in these opening chapters, I have avoided such technical definitions, while preparing the ground for them by showing the nature of the problem for the sake of which they are needed. What is said in these chapters, accordingly, has not the degree of precision sought in later chapters.

Chapters 4–7 are concerned with certain problems in the analysis of language. One of the results that have emerged most clearly from the logical study of language is that there must be a hierarchy of languages, and that the words 'true' and 'false', as applied to the statements in any given language, are themselves words belonging to a language of higher order. This entails, as a consequence, the existence of a language of lowest order, in which the words 'true' and 'false' do not occur. So far as logical considerations are concerned, this language might be constructed in many ways; its syntax and vocabulary are not determined by the logical conditions, except that it should not allow apparent variables, i.e., it should not contain the words 'all' and 'some'. Proceeding psychologically, I construct a language (not *the* language) fulfilling the logical conditions for the language of lowest type; I call this the 'object-language' or the 'primary language'. In this language, every word 'denotes' or 'means' a sensible object or set of such objects, and, when used alone, asserts the sensible presence of the object, or of one of the set of objects, which it denotes or means. In defining this language, it is necessary to define 'denoting' or 'meaning' as applied to object-words, i.e., to the words of this language. Words in languages of higher orders 'mean' in other and much more complicated ways.

We pass from the primary to the secondary language by adding what I call 'logical words', such as 'or', 'not', 'some', and 'all', together with the words 'true' and 'false' as applied to sentences in the object-language. The development of languages of higher order than the second is a matter for the logician, since it raises no new problems as to the relation between sentences and non-linguistic occurrences.

Chapters 6 and 7 are concerned with syntactical questions, namely 'proper names' and 'egocentric particulars' – i.e., words such as 'this', 'I', 'now', which have a meaning relative to the speaker. The theory of proper names which is suggested is important if true, in particular in connexion with space and time.

The next four chapters are concerned with perceptive knowledge, and more particularly with 'basic propositions', i.e., with those propositions which most directly report knowledge derived from perception.

We said that it is the business of epistemology to arrange the propositions which constitute our knowledge in a certain logical order, in which the later propositions are accepted because of their logical relation to those that come before them. It is not necessary that the later propositions should be logically deducible from the earlier ones; what is necessary is that the earlier ones should supply whatever grounds exist for thinking it likely that the later ones are true. When we are considering empirical knowledge, the earliest propositions in the hierarchy, which give the grounds for all the others, are not deduced from other propositions, and yet are not mere arbitrary assumptions. They have grounds, though their grounds are not propositions, but observed occurrences. Such propositions, as observed above, I shall call 'basic' propositions; they fulfil the function assigned by the logical positivists to what they call 'protocol propositions'. It is, to my mind, one of the defects of the logical positivists that their linguistic bias makes their theory of protocol propositions vague and unsatisfactory.

We pass next to the analysis of 'propositional attitudes', i.e., believing, desiring, doubting, etc., that so-and-so is the case. Both for logic and for theory of knowledge, the analysis of such occurrences is important, especially in the case of belief. We find that believing a given proposition does not necessarily involve words, but requires only that the believer should be in one of a number of possible states defined, mainly if not wholly, by causal properties. When words occur, they 'express' the belief, and, if true, 'indicate' a fact other than the belief.

The theory of truth and falsehood which naturally results from such considerations as I have been suggesting is an epistemological theory, that is to say, it only affords a definition of 'true' and 'false' where there is some method of obtaining such knowledge as would decide the alternative. This suggests Brouwer and his denial of the law of excluded middle. It accordingly becomes necessary to consider whether it is possible to give a non-epistemological definition of 'true' and 'false', and so preserve the law of excluded middle.

Finally there is the question: how far, if at all, do the logical categories of language correspond to elements in the non-linguistic world that language deals with? Or, in other words: does logic afford a basis for any metaphysical doctrines? In spite of all that has been said by the logical positivists, I incline to answer this question in the affirmative; but it is a difficult matter, as to which I have not the audacity to be dogmatic.

There are three theses which I regard as specially important in what follows.

I. It is argued that, on the basis of a single experience, a number of verbal statements are justified. The character of such statements is investigated, and it is contended that they must always be confined to matters belonging to the biography of the observer; they can be such as 'I see a canoid patch of colour', but not such as 'there is a dog'. Statements of this latter kind always involve, in their justification, some element of inference.

II. In every assertion, two sides must be separated. On the subjective side, the assertion 'expresses' a state of the speaker; on the objective side, it intends to 'indicate' a 'fact', and succeeds in this intention when true. The psychology of belief is concerned only with the subjective side, the question of truth or falsehood also with the objective side. It is found that the analysis of what a sentence 'expresses' renders possible a psychological theory of the meaning of logical words, such as 'or', 'not', 'all', and 'some'.

III. Finally, there is the question of the relation between truth and knowledge. Attempts have been made to define 'truth' in terms of 'knowledge', or of concepts, such as 'verifiability', which involve 'knowledge'. Such attempts, if carried out logically, lead to paradoxes which there is no reason to accept. I conclude that 'truth' is the fundamental concept, and that 'knowledge' must be defined in terms of 'truth', not vice versa. This entails the consequences that a proposition may be true although we can see no way of obtaining evidence either for or against it. It involves also a partial abandonment of the complete metaphysical agnosticism that is favoured by the logical positivists.

INTRODUCTION

It appears from our analysis of knowledge that, unless it is much more restricted than we suppose, we shall have to admit principles of non-demonstrative inference which may be difficult to reconcile with pure empiricism. This problem emerges at various points, but I have refrained from discussing it, partly because it would require for its treatment a book as large as the present work, but mainly because any attempt at solution must be based upon an analysis of the matters considered in the following chapters, and the disinterestedness of this analysis might be jeopardized by premature investigation of its consequences.

CHAPTER I

WHAT IS A WORD?

I COME now to a preliminary consideration of the question: 'what is a word?' But what I have to say now will be supplemented by detailed discussions at later stages.

Words, from the earliest times of which we have historical records, have been objects of superstitious awe. The man who knew his enemy's name could, by means of it, acquire magic powers over him. We still use such phrases as 'in the name of the Law'. It is easy to assent to the statement 'in the beginning was the Word'. This view underlies the philosophies of Plato and Carnap and of most of the intermediate metaphysicians.

Before we can understand language, we must strip it of its mystical and awe-inspiring attributes. To do this is the main purpose of the present chapter.

Before considering the meaning of words, let us examine them first as occurrences in the sensible world. From this point of view, words are of four sorts: spoken, heard, written, and read. It will do no harm to assume a common-sense view of material objects, since we can always subsequently translate what has been said in common-sense terms into whatever philosophical language we may prefer. It is therefore possible to amalgamate written and read words, substituting for each a material object – a mound of ink, as Neurath says – which is a written or printed word according to circumstances. The distinction between writing and reading is of course important, but almost everything that needs to be said about it can be said in connexion with the difference between speaking and hearing.

A given word, say 'dog', may be uttered, heard, written, or read by many people on many occasions. What happens when a man says a word I shall call a 'verbal utterance'; what happens when a man hears a word I shall call a 'verbal noise'; the physical object which consists of a word written or printed I shall call a 'verbal shape'. It is of course obvious that verbal utterances, noises, and shapes are distinguished from other utterances, noises, and shapes by psychological characteristics – by 'intention' or 'meaning'. But for the moment I wish, as far as may be, to leave these characteristics on one side, and consider only the status of words as part of the world of sense.

The spoken word 'dog' is not a single entity: it is a class of similar movements of the tongue, throat, and larynx. Just as jumping is one class of bodily movements, and walking another, so the uttered word 'dog' is a third class of bodily movements. The word 'dog' is a universal, just as *dog* is a universal. We say, loosely, that we can utter the same word 'dog' on two occasions, but in fact we utter two examples of the same species, just as when we see two dogs we see two examples of the same species. There is thus no difference of logical status between *dog* and the word 'dog': each is general, and exists only in instances. The word 'dog' is a certain class of verbal utterances, just as *dog* is a certain class of quadrupeds. Exactly similar remarks apply to the heard word and to the written word.

It may be thought that I have unduly emphasized a very obvious fact in insisting that a word is a universal. But there is an almost irresistible tendency, whenever we are not on our guard, to think of a word as one thing, and to argue that, while there are many dogs, the one word 'dog' is applicable to them all. Hence we come to think that dogs all have in common a certain canine essence, which is what the word 'dog' really means. And hence we arrive at Plato and the dog laid up in heaven. Whereas what we really have is a number of more or less similar noises which are all applicable to a number of more or less similar quadrupeds.

When we attempt to define the spoken word 'dog', we find that we cannot do so without taking account of intention. Some people say 'dawg', but we recognize that they mean 'dog'. A German is apt to say 'dok'; if we hear him say 'De dok vaks hiss tail ven pleasst', we know that he has uttered an instance of the word 'dog', though an Englishman who had made the same noise would have been uttering an instance of the word 'dok'. As regards the written word, similar considerations apply to people whose handwriting is bad. Thus while similarity to a standard noise or shape – that of a B.B.C. announcer or copy-book calligraphist – is essential in defining an instance of a word, it is not sufficient, and the necessary degree of similarity to the standard cannot be precisely defined. The word, in fact, is a family,* just as dogs are a family, and there are doubtful inter-mediate cases, just as, in evolution, there must have been be-tween dogs and wolves.

In this respect print is preferable. Unless the ink is faded, it can hardly be doubtful, to a person of normal eyesight, whether the word 'dog' is printed at a certain place or not. In fact, print is an artefact designed to satisfy our taste for classification. Two instances of the letter A are closely similar, and each very differ-ent from an instance of the letter B. By using black print on white paper, we make each letter stand out sharply against its background. Thus a printed page consists of a set of discrete and easily classified shapes, and is in consequence a logician's para-dise. But he must not delude himself into thinking that the world outside books is equally charming.

Words, spoken, heard, or written, differ from other classes of bodily movements, noises, or shapes, by having 'meaning'. Many words only have meaning in a suitable verbal context – such words as 'than', 'or', 'however', cannot stand alone. We cannot begin the explanation of meaning with such words, since they presuppose other words. There are words, however – in-cluding all those that a child learns first – that can be used in isolation: proper names, class-names of familiar kinds of animals, names of colours, and so on. These are what I call 'object-words', and they compose the 'object-language', as to which I shall have much to say in a later chapter. These words have various peculiarities. First: their meaning is learnt (or can be learnt) by confrontation with objects which are what they mean, or in-stances of what they mean. Second: they do not presuppose other words. Third: each of them, by itself, can express a whole proposition; you can exclaim 'fire!', but it would be pointless to exclaim 'than!' It is obviously with such words that any ex-planation of 'meaning' must begin; for 'meaning', like 'truth'

* I owe this way of putting the matter to Wittgenstein.

and 'falsehood', has a hierarchy of meanings, corresponding to the hierarchy of languages.

Words are used in many ways: in narrative, in request, in command, in imaginative fiction, and so on. But the most elementary use of object-words is the demonstrative use, such as the exclamation 'fox' when a fox is visible. *Almost* equally primitive is the vocative: the use of a proper name to indicate desire for the presence of the person named; but this is not *quite* so primitive, since the meaning of an object-word must be learnt in the presence of the object. (I am excluding such words as are learnt through verbal definitions, since they presuppose an already existing language.)

It is obvious that knowing a language consists in using words appropriately, and acting appropriately when they are heard. It is no more necessary to be able to say what a word means than it is for a cricketer to know the mathematical theory of impact and of projectiles. Indeed, in the case of many object-words, it must be strictly impossible to *say* what they mean, except by a tautology, for it is with them that language begins. You can only explain (say) the word 'red' by pointing to something red. A child understands the heard word 'red' when an association has been established between the heard word and the colour red; he has mastered the spoken word 'red' when, if he notices something red, he is able to say 'red' and has an impulse to do so.

The original learning of object-words is one thing; the use of speech, when the instrument has been mastered, is another. In adult life, all speech, like the calling of a name, though less obviously, is, in intention, in the imperative mood. When it seems to be a mere statement, it should be prefaced by the words 'know that'. We know many things, and assert only some of them; those that we assert are those that we desire our hearers to know. When we see a falling star and say simply 'look!' we hope that this one word will cause the bystander to see it too. If you have an unwelcome visitor, you may kick him downstairs, or you may say 'get out!' Since the latter involves less muscular exertion, it is preferable if equally effective.

It follows that when, in adult life, you use a word, you do so, as a rule, not only because what the word 'denotes' is present to sense or imagination, but because you wish your hearer to do something about it. This is not the case with a child learning to speak, nor is it *always* the case in later years, because the use of words on interesting occasions becomes an automatic habit. If you were to see suddenly a friend whom you had falsely believed to be dead, you would probably utter his name even if neither he nor anyone else could hear you. But such situations are exceptional.

In the meaning of a sentence, there are three psychological elements: the environmental causes of uttering it, the effects of hearing it, and (as part of the causes of utterance) the effects which the speaker *expects* it to have on the hearer.

We may say, generally, that speech consists, with some exceptions, of noises made by persons with a view to causing desired actions by other persons. Its indicative and assertive capacities, however, remain fundamental, since it is owing to them that, when we hear speech, it can cause us to act in a manner appropriate to some feature of the environment which is perceived by the speaker but not by the hearer, or which the speaker remembers from past perceptions. In leading a visitor out of your house at night, you may say 'here there are two steps down', which causes him to act as if he saw the steps. This, however, implies a certain degree of benevolence towards your visitor. To state fact is by no means always the purpose of speech; it is just as possible to speak with a view to deceit. 'Language was given us to enable us to conceal our thoughts.' Thus when we think of language as a means of stating facts we are tacitly assuming certain desires in the speaker. It is interesting that language *can* state facts; it is also interesting that it *can* state falsehoods. When it states either, it does so with a view to causing some action in the hearer; if the hearer is a slave, a child, or a dog, the result is achieved more simply by using the imperative. There is, however, a difference between the effectiveness of a lie and that of the truth: a lie only produces the desired result so long as the truth is expected. In fact, no one could learn to speak unless truth were the rule: if, when your child sees a dog, you say 'cat', 'horse', or 'crocodile', at random, you will not be able to deceive him by saying 'dog' when it is not a dog. Lying is thus a derivative activity, which presupposes truth-speaking as the usual rule.

It thus appears that, while most sentences are primarily imperative, they cannot fulfil their function of causing action in the hearer except in virtue of the indicative character of object-words. Suppose I say 'run!' and the person addressed consequently runs; this happens only because the word 'run' indicates a certain type of action. This situation is seen in its simplest form in military drill: a conditioned reflex is established, so that a certain kind of noise (the word of command) produces a certain kind of bodily movement. We may say, in this case, that the kind of noise in question is the name of the kind of movement in question. But words which are not names of bodily movements have a less direct connexion with action.

It is only in certain cases that the 'meaning' of a verbal utterance can be identified with the effect that it is intended to have on the hearer. The word of command and the word 'look!' are such cases. But if I say 'look, there's a fox', I not only seek to produce a certain action in the hearer, but I give him a motive for action by describing a feature of the environment. In the case of narrative speech, the distinction between 'meaning' and intended effect is even more evident.

Only sentences have intended effects, whereas meaning is not confined to sentences. Object-words have a meaning which does not depend upon their occurring in sentences.

At the lowest level of speech, the distinction between sentences and single words does not exist. At this level, single words are used to indicate the sensible presence of what they designate. It is through this form of speech that object-words acquire their meaning, and in this form of speech each word is an assertion. Anything going beyond assertions as to what is sensibly present, and even some assertions which do not do so, can only be effected by means of sentences; but if sentences contain object-words, what they assert depends upon the meaning of the object-words. There are sentences containing no object-words; they are those of logic and mathematics. But all empirical statements contain object-words, or dictionary words defined in terms of them. Thus the meaning of object-words is fundamental in the theory of empirical knowledge, since it is through them that language is connected with non-linguistic occurrences in the way that makes it capable of expressing empirical truth or falsehood.

CHAPTER 2

SENTENCES, SYNTAX, AND
PARTS OF SPEECH

SENTENCES may be interrogative, optative, exclamatory, or imperative; they may also be indicative. Throughout most of the remainder of our discussions, we may confine ourselves to indicative sentences, since these alone are true or false. In addition to being true or false, indicative sentences have two other properties which are of interest to us, and which they share with other sentences. The first of these is that they are composed of words, and have a meaning derivative from that of the words that they contain; the second is that they have a certain kind of unity, in virtue of which they are capable of properties not possessed by their constituent words.

Each of these three properties needs investigation. Let us begin with the unity of a sentence.

A single grammatical sentence may not be logically single. 'I went out and found it was raining' is logically indistinguishable from the two sentences: 'I went out', 'I found it was raining'. But the sentence 'when I went out I found it was raining' is logically single: it asserts that two occurrences were simultaneous. 'Caesar and Pompey were great generals' is logically two sentences, but 'Caesar and Pompey were alike in being great generals' is logically one. For our purposes, it will be convenient to exclude sentences which are not logically single, but consist of two assertions joined by 'and' or 'but' or 'although' or some such conjunction. A single sentence, for our purposes, must be one which says something that cannot be said in two separate simpler sentences.

Consider next such a sentence as 'I should be sorry if you fell ill'. This cannot be divided into 'I shall be sorry' and 'you will fall ill'; it has the kind of unity that we are demanding of a sentence. But it has a complexity which some sentences do not have; neglecting tense, it states a relation between 'I am sorry' and 'you are ill'. We may interpret it as asserting that at any time when the second of these sentences is true, the first is also true. Such sentences may be called 'molecular' in relation to their constituent sentences, which, in the same relation, may be called 'atomic'. Whether any sentences are 'atomic' in a non-relative sense, may, for the present, be left an open question; but whenever we find a sentence to be molecular, we shall do well, while we are considering what makes the unity of sentences, to transfer our attention, in the first place, to its atoms. Roughly an atomic sentence is one containing only one verb; but this would only be accurate in a strictly logical language.

This matter is by no means simple. Suppose I say first 'A' and then 'B'; you may judge: 'the sound "A" preceded the sound "B"'. But this implies 'the sound "A" occurred' and 'the sound "B" occurred', and adds that one occurrence was earlier than the other. Your statement, therefore, is really analogous to such a statement as 'after I went out I got wet'. It is a molecular statement whose atoms are 'A occurred' and 'B occurred'. Now what do we mean by 'A occurred'? We mean that there was a noise of a certain class, the class called 'A'. Thus when we say 'A preceded B' our statement has a concealed logical form, which is the same as that of the statement: 'first there was the bark of a dog, and then the neigh of a horse'.

Let us pursue this a little further. I say 'A'. Then I say 'what did I say?' Then you reply 'you said "A"'. Now the noise you make when saying 'A' in this reply is different from the noise I originally made; therefore, if 'A' were the name of a particular noise, your statement would be false. It is only because 'A' is the name of a *class* of noises that your statement is true; your statement classifies the noise I made, just as truly as if you had said 'you barked like a dog'. This shows how language forces us into generality even when we most wish to avoid it. If we want to speak about the particular noise that I made, we shall have to give it a proper name, say 'Tom'; and the noise that you made when you said 'A' we will call 'Dick'. Then we can say 'Tom and Dick are As'. We can say 'I said Tom' but not 'I said "Tom"'. Strictly, we ought not to say 'I said "A"'; we ought to say 'I said an "A"'. All this illustrates a general principle, that when we use a general term, such as 'A' or 'man', we are not having in our minds a universal, but an instance to which the present instance is similar. When we say 'I said "A"', what we really mean is 'I made a noise closely similar to the noise I am now about to make: "A"'. This, however, is a digression.

We will revert to the supposition that I say first 'A' and then 'B'. We will call the particular occurrence which was my first utterance 'Tom', and that which was my second utterance 'Harry'. Then we can say 'Tom preceded Harry'. This was what we really meant to say when we said 'the sound "A" preceded the sound "B"'; and now, at last, we seem to have reached an atomic sentence which does not merely classify.

It might be objected that, when I say 'Tom preceded Harry', this implies 'Tom occurred' and 'Harry occurred', just as when I said 'the sound "A" preceded the sound "B"', that implied '"A" occurred' and '"B" occurred'. This, I think, would be a logical error. When I say that an unspecified member of a class occurred, my statement is significant provided I know what class is meant; but in the case of a true proper name, the name is meaningless unless it names something, and if it names something, that something must occur. This may seem reminiscent of the ontological argument, but it is really only part of the definition of 'name'. A proper name names something of which there are not a plurality of instances, and names it by a convention *ad hoc*, not by a description composed of words with previously assigned meanings. Unless, therefore, the name names something, it is an empty noise, not a word. And when we say 'Tom preceded Harry', where 'Tom' and 'Harry' are names of particular noises, we do not presuppose 'Tom occurred' and 'Harry occurred', which are both strictly meaningless.

In practice, proper names are not given to single brief occurrences, because most of them are not sufficiently interesting. When we have occasion to mention them, we do so by means of descriptions such as 'the death of Caesar' or 'the birth of Christ'. To speak for the moment in terms of physics, we give proper names to certain continuous stretches of space-time, such as Socrates, France, or the moon. In former days, it would have been said that we give a proper name to a substance or collection of substances, but now we have to find a different phrase to express the object of a proper name.

A proper name, in practice, always embraces many occurrences, but not as a class-name does: the separate occurrences are *parts* of what the name means, not *instances* of it. Consider, say, 'Caesar died'. 'Death' is a generic word for a number of occurrences having certain resemblances to each other, but not necessarily any spatio-temporal interconnexion; each of these is *a* death. 'Caesar', on the contrary, stands for a series of occurrences, collectively, not severally. When we say 'Caesar died', we say that one of the series of occurrences which was Caesar was a member of the class of deaths; this occurrence is called 'Caesar's death'.

From a logical point of view, a proper name may be assigned to any continuous portion of space-time. (Macroscopic continuity suffices.) Two parts of one man's life may have different names; for instance, Abram and Abraham, or Octavianus and Augustus. 'The universe' may be regarded as a proper name for the whole of space-time. We *can* give a proper name to very small portions of space-time, provided they are large enough to be noticed. If I say 'A' once at 6 p.m. on a given date, we can give a proper name to this noise, or, to be still more particular, to the auditory sensation that some one person present has in hearing me. But even when we have arrived at this degree of minuteness, we cannot say that we have named something destitute of structure. It may therefore be assumed, at least for the present, that every proper name is the name of a structure, not of something destitute of parts. But this is an empirical fact, not a logical necessity.

If we are to avoid entanglement in questions that are not linguistic, we must distinguish sentences, not by the complexity which they may happen to have, but by that implied in their form. 'Alexander preceded Caesar' is complex owing to the complexity of Alexander and Caesar; but 'x preceded y' does not, by its form, imply that x and y are complex. In fact, since

Alexander died before Caesar was born, every constituent of Alexander preceded every constituent of Caesar. We may thus accept 'x precedes y' as an atomic *form* of proposition, even if we cannot actually mention an x and a y which give an atomic proposition. We shall say, then, that a *form* of proposition is atomic if the fact that a proposition is of this form does not logically imply that it is a structure composed of subordinate propositions. And we shall add that it is not logically necessary that a proper name should name a structure which has parts.

The above discussion is a necessary preliminary to the attempt to discover what constitutes the essential unity of a sentence; for this unity, whatever its nature may be, obviously exists in a sentence of atomic form, and should be first investigated in such sentences.

In every significant sentence, some connexion is essential between what the several words mean – omitting words which merely serve to indicate syntactical structure. We saw that 'Caesar died' asserts the existence of a common member of two classes, the class of events which was Caesar and the class of events which are deaths. This is only one of the relations that sentences can assert; syntax shows, in each case, what relation is asserted. Some cases are simpler than 'Caesar died', others are more complex. Suppose I point to a daffodil and say 'this is yellow'; here 'this' may be taken as the proper name of a part of my present visual field, and 'yellow' may be taken as a class-name. This proposition, so interpreted, is simpler than 'Caesar died', since it classifies a given object; it is logically analogous to 'this is a death'. We have to be able to know such propositions before we can know that two classes have a common member, which is what is asserted by 'Caesar died'. But 'this is yellow' is not so simple as it looks. When a child learns the meaning of the word 'yellow', there is first an object (or rather a set of objects) which is yellow by definition, and then a perception that other objects are similar in colour. Thus when we say to a child 'this is yellow', what (with luck) we convey to him is: 'this resembles in colour the object which is yellow by definition'. Thus classificatory propositions, or such as assign predicates, would seem to be really propositions asserting similarity. If so, the simplest propositions are relational.

There is, however, a difference between relations that are symmetrical and those that are asymmetrical. A relation is symmetrical when, if it holds between x and y, it also holds between y and x; it is asymmetrical if, when it holds between x and y, it cannot hold between y and x. Thus similarity is symmetrical, and so is dissimilarity; but 'before', 'greater', 'to the right of', and so on, are asymmetrical. There are also relations which are neither symmetrical nor asymmetrical; 'brother' is an example, since, if x is the brother of y, y may be the sister of x. These and asymmetrical relations are called non-symmetrical. Non-symmetrical relations are of the utmost importance, and many famous philosophies are refuted by their existence.

Let us try to state what exactly are the linguistic facts about non-symmetrical relations. The two sentences 'Brutus killed Caesar' and 'Caesar killed Brutus' consist of the same words, arranged, in each case, by the relation of temporal sequence. Nevertheless, one of them is true and the other false. The use of order for this purpose is, of course, not essential; Latin uses inflexions instead. But if you had been a Roman schoolmaster teaching the difference between nominative and accusative, you would have been compelled, at some point, to bring in non-symmetrical relations, and you would have found it natural to explain them by means of spatial or temporal order. Consider for a moment what happened when Brutus killed Caesar: a dagger moved swiftly from Brutus into Caesar. The abstract scheme is 'A moved from B to C', and the fact with which we are concerned is that this is different from 'A moved from C to B'. There were two events, one A-being-at-B, the other A-being-at-C, which we will name x and y respectively. If A moved from B to C, x preceded y; if A moved from C to B, y preceded x. Thus the ultimate source of the difference between 'Brutus killed Caesar' and 'Caesar killed Brutus' is the difference between 'x precedes y' and 'y precedes x', where x and y are events. Similarly in the visual field there are the spatial relations above-and-below, right-and-left, which have the same property of asymmetry. 'Brighter', 'louder', and comparatives generally, are also asymmetrical.

The unity of the sentence is peculiarly obvious in the case of asymmetrical relations: 'x precedes y' and 'y precedes x' consist of the same words, arranged by the same relation of temporal succession; there is nothing whatever in their ingredients to distinguish the one from the other. The sentences differ as wholes, but not in their parts; it is this that I mean when I speak of a sentence as a unity.

At this point, if confusions are to be avoided, it is important to remember that words are universals.* In the two sentential utterances 'x precedes y' and 'y precedes x', the two symbols 'x' are not identical, no more are the two symbols 'y'. Let S_1 and S_2 be proper names of these two sentential utterances; let X_1 and X_2 be proper names of the two utterances of 'x', Y_1 and Y_2 of those of 'y', and P_1 and P_2 of those of 'precedes'. Then S_1 consists of the three utterances X_1, P_1, Y_1 in that order, and S_2 consists of the three utterances Y_2, P_2, X_2 in that order. The order in each case is a fact of history, as definite and unalterable as the fact that Alexander preceded Caesar. When we observe that the order of words can be changed, and that we can say 'Caesar killed Brutus' just as easily as 'Brutus killed Caesar', we are apt to think that the words are definite things which are capable of different arrangements. This is a mistake: the words are abstractions, and the verbal utterances can only have whichever order they do have. Though their life is short, they live and die, and they are incapable of resurrection. Everything has the arrangement it has, and is incapable of rearrangement.

I do not wish to be thought needlessly pedantic, and I will therefore point out that clarity on this matter is necessary for the understanding of *possibility*. We say it is *possible* to say either 'Brutus killed Caesar' or 'Caesar killed Brutus', and we do not realize that this is precisely analogous to the fact that it is possible for a man to be to the left of a woman on one occasion, and for another man to be to the right of another woman on another occasion. For: let β be the class of verbal utterances

---

* This does not imply that there are universals. It only asserts that the status of a word, as opposed to its instances, is the same as that of Dog as opposed to various particular dogs.

which is the spoken word 'Brutus'; let κ be the class of verbal utterances which is the spoken word 'killed'; and let γ be the class of verbal utterances which is the spoken word 'Caesar'. Then to say that we can say either 'Brutus killed Caesar' or 'Caesar killed Brutus' is to say that (1) there are occurrences x, P, y, such that x is a member of β, P is a member of κ, y is a member of γ, x is just before P, and P is just before y; (2) there, are occurrences x', P', y' fulfilling the above conditions as to membership of β, κ, γ but such that y' is just before P' and P' just before x'. I maintain that in all cases of possibility, there is a subject which is a variable, defined as satisfying some condition which many values of the variable satisfy, and that of these values some satisfy a further condition while others do not; we then say it is 'possible' that the subject may satisfy this further condition. Symbolically, if 'ϕx and ψx' and 'ϕx and not ψx' are each true for suitable values of x, then, given ϕx, ψx is possible but not necessary. (One must distinguish empirical and logical necessity; but I do not wish to go into this question.)

Another point is to be noted. When we say that the sentences 'x P y' and 'y P x' (where P is an asymmetrical relation) are incompatible, the symbols 'x' and 'y' are universals, since, in our statement, there are two instances of each; but they must be names of particulars. 'Day precedes night' and 'night precedes day' are both true. There is thus, in such cases, an absence of logical homogeneity between the symbol and its meaning: the symbol is a universal while the meaning is particular. This kind of logical heterogeneity is very liable to lead to confusions. All symbols are of the same logical type: they are classes of similar utterances, or similar noises, or similar shapes, but their meanings may be of any type, or of ambiguous type, like the meaning of the word 'type' itself. The relation of a symbol to its meaning necessarily varies according to the type of the meaning, and this fact is important in the theory of symbolism.

Having now dealt with the possible confusions that may arise through saying that the same word can occur in two different sentences, we can henceforth freely use this expression, just as we can say 'the giraffe is to be found in Africa and in the Zoo', without being misled into the belief that this is true of any particular giraffe.

In a language like English, in which the order of the words is essential to the meaning of the sentence, we can put the matter of non-symmetrical relations as follows: given a set of words which is capable of forming a sentence, it often happens that it is capable of forming two or more sentences of which one is true while the others are false, these sentences differing as to the order of the words. Thus the meaning of a sentence, at any rate in some cases, is determined by the *series* of words, not by the *class*. In such cases, the meaning of the sentence is not obtainable as an aggregate of the meanings of the several words. When a person knows who Brutus was, who Caesar was, and what killing is, he still does not know who killed whom when he hears the sentence 'Brutus killed Caesar'; to know this, he requires syntax as well as vocabulary, since the form of the sentence as a whole contributes to the meaning.*

To avoid unnecessary lengthiness, let us assume, for the moment, that there is only spoken speech. Then all words *have* a time order, and some words *assert* a time order. We know that, if 'x' and 'y' are names of particular events, then if 'x precedes y' is a true sentence, 'y precedes x' is a false sentence. My present problem is this: can we state anything equivalent to the above in terms which are not concerned with language, but with events? It would seem that we are concerned with a characteristic of temporal relations, and yet, when we try to state what this characteristic is, we appear to be driven to stating a characteristic of sentences about temporal relations. And what applies to temporal relations applies equally to all other asymmetrical relations.

When I hear the sentence 'Brutus killed Caesar', I perceive the time-order of the words; if I did not, I could not know that I had heard that sentence and not 'Caesar killed Brutus'. If I proceed to assert the time-order by the sentences ' "Brutus" preceded "killed" ' and ' "killed" preceded "Caesar" ', I must again be aware of the time-order of the words in these sentences. We must, therefore, be aware of the time-order of events in

---

* Sometimes there is ambiguity: cf. 'The muse herself that Orpheus bore.'

cases in which we do not assert that they have that time-order, for otherwise we should fall into an endless regress. What is it that we are aware of in such a case?

The following is a theory which might be suggested: when we hear the word 'Brutus', there is an experience analogous to that of the gradually fading tone of a bell; if the word was heard a moment ago, there is still now an akoluthic sensation, analogous to that of a moment ago, but fainter. Thus when we have just finished hearing the sentence 'Brutus killed Caesar', we are still having an auditory sensation which might be represented by

Brutus KILLED CAESAR;

whereas when we have just finished hearing 'Caesar killed Brutus', our sensation may be represented by

Caesar KILLED BRUTUS.

These are different sensations, and it is this difference – so it may be contended – that enables us to recognize order in time. According to this theory, when we distinguish between 'Brutus killed Caesar' and 'Caesar killed Brutus', we are distinguishing, not between two wholes composed of exactly similar parts which are successive, but between two wholes composed of somewhat dissimilar parts which are simultaneous. Each of these wholes is characterized by its constituents, and does not need the further mention of an arrangement.

In this theory there is, no doubt, an element of truth. It seems clear, as a matter of psychology, that there are occurrences, which may be classed as sensations, in which a present sound is combined with the fading ghost of a sound heard a moment ago. But if there were no more than this, we should not know that past events have occurred. Assuming that there are akoluthic sensations, how do we know their likeness to and difference from sensations in their first vigour ? If we only knew present occurrences which are in fact related to past occurrences, we should never know of this relationship. Clearly we do sometimes, in some sense, know the past, not by inference from the present, but in the same direct way in which we know the present. For if this were not the case, nothing in the present could lead us

37

to suppose that there was a past, or even to understand the supposition.

Let us revert to the proposition: 'if x precedes y, y does not precede x'. It *seems* clear that we do not know this empirically, but it does not *seem* to be a proposition of logic.* Yet I do not see how we can say that it is a linguistic convention. The proposition 'x precedes y' can be asserted on the basis of experience. We are saying that, if this experience occurs, no experience will occur such as would lead to 'y precedes x'. It is obvious that, however we restate the matter, there must always be a negation somewhere in our statement; and I think it is also fairly obvious that negation brings us into the realm of language. When we say 'y does not precede x', it might seem that we can only mean: 'the sentence "y precedes x" is false'. For if we adopt any other interpretation, we shall have to admit that we can perceive negative facts, which *seems* preposterous, but perhaps is not, for reasons to be given later. I think something similar may be said about 'if': where this word occurs, it must apply to a sentence. Thus it seems that the proposition we are investigating should be stated: 'at least one of the sentences "x precedes y" and "y precedes x" is false, if x and y are proper names of events'. To carry the matter further demands a definition of falsehood. We will therefore postpone this question until we have reached the discussion of truth and falsehood.

Parts of speech, as they appear in grammar, have no very intimate relation to logical syntax. 'Before' is a preposition and 'precedes' is a verb, but they mean the same thing. The verb, which might seem essential to a sentence, may be absent in many languages, and even in English in such a phrase as 'more haste, less speed'. It is possible, however, to compose a logical language with a logical syntax, and to find, when it has been constructed, certain suggestions in ordinary language which lead up to it.

The most complete part of logic is the theory of conjunctions. These, as they occur in logic, come only between whole sentences; they give rise to molecular sentences, of which the atoms

---

* To decide this question, we need a discussion of proper names, to which we shall come later.

are separated by the conjunctions. This part of the subject is so fully worked out that we need waste no time on it. Moreover, all the earlier problems with which we are concerned arise in regard to sentences of atomic form.

Let us consider a few sentences: (1) this is yellow; (2) this is before that; (3) A gives a book to B.

(1) In 'this is yellow', the word 'this' is a proper name. It is true that, on other occasions, other objects are called 'this', but that is equally true of 'John': when we say 'here's John', we do not mean 'here is some member of the class of people called "John"'; we regard the name as belonging to only one person. Exactly the same is true of 'this'.* The word 'men' is applicable to all the objects called severally 'a man', but the word 'these' is not applicable to all the objects severally called 'this' on different occasions.

The word 'yellow' is more difficult. It seems to mean, as suggested above, 'similar in colour to a certain object', this object being yellow by definition. Strictly, of course, since there are many shades of yellow, we need many objects which are yellow by definition: but one may ignore this complication. But since we can distinguish similarity in colour from similarity in other respects (e.g. shape), we do not avoid the necessity of a certain degree of abstraction in arriving at what is meant by 'yellow'.† We cannot see colour without shape, or shape without colour; but we can perceive the difference between the similarity of a yellow circle to a yellow triangle and the similarity of a yellow circle to a red circle. It would seem, therefore, that sensible predicates, such as 'yellow', 'red', 'loud', 'hard', are derived from the perception of kinds of similarity. This applies also to very general predicates such as 'visual', 'audible', 'tactile'. Thus to come back to 'this is yellow', the meaning seems to be 'this has colour-similarity to that', where 'this' and 'that' are proper-names, the object called 'that' is yellow by definition, and colour-similarity is a dual relation which can be perceived. It will be observed that colour-similarity is a

---

* The word 'this' will be discussed in the chapter on 'Egocentric Particulars'.

† But consider Carnap's *Logischer Aufbau*; yellow =(by defiintion) a group all similar to this and each other, and not all similar to anything outside the group. This subject will be discussed in Chapter 6.

symmetrical relation. That is the reason which makes it possible to treat 'yellow' as a predicate, and to ignore comparison. Perhaps, indeed, what has been said about the comparison applies only to the *learning* of the word 'yellow'; it may be that, when learnt, it is truly a predicate.*

(2) 'This is before that' has already been discussed. Since the relation 'before' is asymmetrical, we cannot regard the propo ition as assigning a common predicate to this and that. And if we regard it as assigning different predicates (e.g., dates) to this and that, these predicates themselves will have to have an asymmetrical relation corresponding to 'before'. We may, formally, treat the proposition as meaning 'the date of this is earlier than the date of that', but 'earlier' is an asymmetrical relation just as 'before' was. It is not easy to find a logical method of manufacturing asymmetry out of symmetrical data.†

The word 'before', like the word 'yellow', may be derived from comparison. We may start from some very emphatic case of sequence, such as a clock striking twelve, and, by taking other cases of sequence which have no other obvious resemblance to the striking clock, gradually lead to a concentration of attention on sequence. It seems clear, however – whatever may be the case in regard to 'yellow' – that in regard to 'before' this only applies to the learning of the word. The meaning of such words as 'before' or 'colour-similarity' cannot always be derived from comparison, since this would lead to an endless regress. Comparison is a necessary stimulus to abstraction, but abstraction must be possible, at least as regards similarity. And if possible in regard to similarity, it seems pointless to deny it elsewhere.

To say that we understand the word 'before' is to say that, when we perceive two events A and B in a time-sequence, we know whether to say 'A is before B' or 'B is before A', and concerning one of these we know that it describes that we perceive.

* This question has no substance. The object is to construct a minimum vocabulary, and in this respect it can be done in two ways.

† As to this, Dr Sheffer has a way of distinguishing between the couple *x*-followed-by-*y* and the couple *y*-followed-by-*x* which shows that it is technically possible to construct asymmetry out of symmetrical materials. But it can hardly be maintained that it is more than a technical device.

Another way of dealing with asymmetry will be considered in a later chapter.

(3) 'A gives a book to B.' This means: 'there is an x such that A gives x to B and x is bookish' – using 'bookish', for the moment, to mean the defining quality of books. Let us concentrate on 'A gives C to B', where A, B, C are proper names. (The questions raised by 'there is an x such that' we will consider presently.) I want to consider what sort of occurrence gives us evidence of the truth of this statement. If we are to know its truth, not by hearsay, but by the evidence of our own senses, we must see A and B, and see A holding C, moving C towards B, and finally giving C into B's hands. (I am assuming that C is some small object such as a book, not an estate or a copyright or anything else of which possession is a complicated legal abstraction.) This is logically analogous to 'Brutus killed Caesar with a dagger'. What is essential is that A, B, and C should all be sensibly present throughout a finite period of time, during which the spatial relations of C to A and B change. Schematically, the geometrical minimum is as follows: first we see three shapes A_1, B_1, C_1, of which C_1 is close to A_1; then we see three very similar shapes A_2, B_2, C_2, of which C_2 is close to B_2. (I am omitting a number of niceties.) Neither of these two facts alone is sufficient; it is their occurrence in quick succession that is asserted. Even this is not really sufficient: we have to believe that A_1 and A_2, B_1 and B_2, C_1 and C_2 are respectively appearances of the same material objects, however these may be defined. I will ignore the fact that 'giving' involves intention; but even so the complications are alarming. At first sight, it would seem that the minimum assertion involved must be something like this: 'A_1, B_1, C_1 are appearances of three material objects at one time; A_2, B_2, C_2 are appearances of the "same" objects at a slightly later time; C_1 touches A_1 but not B_1; C_2 touches B_2 but not A_2'. I do not go into the evidence required to show that two appearances at different times are appearances of the 'same' object; this is ultimately a question for physics, but in practice and the law-courts grosser methods are tolerated. The important point, for us, is that we have apparently been led to an atomic form involving six terms, namely: 'the proximity of C_1 to A_1 and its comparative remoteness from B_1 is an occurrence slightly anterior to the proximity of C_2 to B_2 and its comparative

remoteness from A_2'. We are tempted to conclude that we cannot avoid an atomic form of this degree of complexity if we are to have sensible evidence of such a matter as one person handing an object to another person.

But perhaps this is a mistake. Consider the propositions: C_1 is near A_1, C_1 is far from B_1, A_1 is simultaneous with B_1, B_1 is simultaneous with C_1, A_1 is slightly anterior to A_2, A_2 is simultaneous with B_2, B_2 is simultaneous with C_2, C_2 is near B_2, C_2 is far from A_2. This set of nine propositions is logically equivalent to the one proposition involving A_1, B_1, C_1, A_2, B_2, C_2. The one proposition, therefore, can be an inference, not a datum. There is still a difficulty: 'near' and 'far' are relative terms; in astronomy, Venus is near the earth, but not from the point of view of a person handing something to another person. We can, however, avoid this. We can substitute 'C_1 touches A_1' for 'C_1 is near A_1', and 'something is between C_1 and B_1' for 'C_1 is far from B_1'. Here 'touching' and 'between' are to be visual data. Thus the three-term relation 'between' seems the most complex datum required.

The importance of atomic forms and their contradictories is that – as we shall see – all propositions, or at least all non-psychological propositions justified by observation without inference, are of these forms. That is to say, if due care is taken, all the sentences which embody empirical physical data will assert or deny propositions of atomic form. All other physical sentences can theoretically be either proved or disproved (as the case may be), or rendered probable or improbable, by sentences of these forms; and we ought not to include as a datum anything capable of logical proof or disproof by means of other data. But this is merely by way of anticipation.

In a sentence of atomic form, expressed in a strictly logical language, there are a finite number of proper names (any finite number from one upwards), and there is one word which is not a proper name. Examples are: 'x is yellow', 'x is earlier than y', 'x is between y and z', and so on. We can distinguish proper names from other words by the fact that a proper name can occur in every form of atomic sentence, whereas a word which is not a proper name can only occur in an atomic sentence which has the appropriate number of proper names. Thus 'yellow' demands one proper name, 'earlier' demands two, and 'between' demands three. Such terms are called predicates, dyadic relations, triadic relations, etc. Sometimes, for the sake of uniformity, predicates are called monadic relations.

I come now to the parts of speech, other than conjunctions, that cannot occur in atomic forms. Such are 'a', 'the', 'all', 'some', 'many', 'none'. To these, I think, 'not' should be added; but this is analogous to conjunctions. Let us start with 'a'. Suppose you say (truly) 'I saw a man'. It is obvious that 'a man' is not the sort of thing one can see; it is a logical abstraction. What you saw was some particular shape, to which we will give the proper name A; and you judged 'A is human'. The two sentences 'I saw A' and 'A is human' enable you to deduce 'I saw a man', but this latter sentence does not imply that you saw A, or that A is human. When you tell me that you saw a man, I cannot tell whether you saw A or B or C or any other of the men that exist. What is known is the truth of some proposition of the form:

'I saw x and x is human'.

This form is not atomic, being compounded of 'I saw x' and 'x is human'. It can be deduced from 'I saw A and A is human'; thus it can be proved by empirical data, although it is not the sort of sentence that expresses a perceptual datum, since such a sentence would have to mention A or B or C or whoever it was that you saw. *Per contra*, no perceptual data can *disprove* the sentence 'I saw a man'.

Propositions containing 'all' or 'none' can be disproved by empirical data, but not proved except in logic and mathematics. We can prove 'all primes except 2 are odd', because this follows from definitions; but we cannot prove 'all men are mortal', because we cannot prove that we have overlooked no one. In fact, 'all men are mortal' is a statement about everything, not only about all men; it states, concerning every x, that x is either mortal or not human. Until we have examined everything, we cannot be sure but that something unexamined is human but immortal. Since we cannot examine everything, we cannot *know* general propositions empirically.

No proposition containing *the* (in the singular) can be strictly proved by empirical evidence. We do not know that Scott was *the* author of *Waverley*; what we know is that he was *an* author of *Waverley*. For aught we know, somebody in Mars may have also written *Waverley*. To prove that Scott was *the* author, we should have to survey the universe and find that everything in it either did not write *Waverley* or was Scott. This is beyond our powers.

Empirical evidence can prove propositions containing 'a' or 'some', and can disprove propositions containing 'the', 'all', or 'none'. It cannot disprove propositions containing 'a' or 'some', and cannot prove propositions containing 'the', 'all', or 'none'. If empirical evidence is to lead us to disbelieve propositions about 'some' or to believe propositions about 'all', it must be in virtue of some principle of inference other than strict deduction – unless, indeed, there should be propositions containing the word 'all' among our basic propositions.

CHAPTER 3

SENTENCES DESCRIBING EXPERIENCES

ALL persons who have learnt to speak can use sentences to describe events. The events are the evidence for the truth of the sentences. In some ways, the whole thing is so obvious that it is difficult to see any problem; in other ways, it is so obscure that it is difficult to see any solution. If you say 'it is raining', you may know that what you say is true because you see the rain and feel it and hear it; this is so plain that nothing could be plainer. But difficulties arise as soon as we try to analyse what happens when we make statements of this sort on the basis of immediate experience. In what sense do we 'know' an occurrence independently of using words about it? How can we compare it with our words, so as to know that our words are right? What relation must subsist between the occurrence and our words in order that our words may be right? How do we know, in any given case, whether this relation subsists or not? Is it perhaps possible to know that our words are right without having any non-verbal knowledge of the occurrence to which they apply?

Let us consider the last point first. It *might* happen that, on certain occasions, we utter certain words, and feel them to be right, without having any independent knowledge of the causes of our utterances. I think this does sometimes happen. You may, for instance, have been making strenuous efforts to like Mr A., but suddenly you find yourself exclaiming 'I hate Mr A.', and you realize that this is the truth. The same sort of thing, I imagine, happens when one is analysed by a psychoanalyst. But such cases are exceptional. In general, where present sensible facts are concerned at any rate, there is *some* sense in which we can know them without using words. We may notice that we are hot or cold, or that there is thunder or lightning, and if we proceed to state in words what we have noticed, we merely register what we already know. I am not maintaining that this pre-verbal stage always exists, unless we mean, by 'knowing' an experience, no more than that we have the experience; but I do maintain that such pre-verbal knowledge is very common. It is necessary, however, to distinguish between experiences that we notice, and others that merely happen to us, though the distinction is only one of degree. Let us illustrate by some examples.

Suppose you are out walking on a wet day, and you see a puddle and avoid it. You are not likely to say to yourself: 'there is a puddle; it will be advisable not to step into it'. But if some-body said 'why did you suddenly step aside?' you would answer 'because I didn't wish to step into that puddle'. You know, retrospectively, that you had a visual perception, to which you reacted appropriately; and in the case supposed, you express this knowledge in words. But what would you have known, and in what sense, if your attention had not been called to the matter by your questioner?

When you were questioned, the incident was over, and you answered by memory. Can one remember what one never knew? That depends upon the meaning of the word 'know'.

The word 'know' is highly ambiguous. In most senses of the word, 'knowing' an event is a different occurrence from the event which is known; but there is a sense of 'knowing' in which, when you have an experience, there is no difference be-tween the experience and knowing that you have it. It might be maintained that we always know our present experiences; but this cannot be the case if the knowing is something different from the experience. For, if an experience is one thing and knowing it is another, the supposition that we always know an experience when it is happening involves an infinite multiplica-tion of every event. I feel hot; this is one event. I know that I feel hot; this is a second event. I know that I know that I feel hot; this is a third event. And so on *ad infinitum*, which is absurd. We must therefore say either that my present experience is indistinguishable from my knowing it while it is present, or that, as a rule, we do not know our present experiences. On the whole, I prefer to use the word 'know' in a sense which implies that the knowing is different from what is known, and to accept the consequence that, as a rule, we do not know our present experiences.

We are to say, then, that it is one thing to see a puddle, and another to know that I see a puddle. 'Knowing' *may* be defined as 'acting appropriately'; this is the sense in which we say that a dog knows his name, or that a carrier pigeon knows the way home. In this sense, my knowing of the puddle consisted of my stepping aside. But this is vague, both because other things might have made me step aside, and because 'appropriate' can only be defined in terms of my desires. I might have wished to get wet, because I had just insured my life for a large sum, and thought death from pneumonia would be convenient; in that case, my stepping aside would be evidence that I did *not* see the puddle. Moreover, if desire is excluded, appropriate reaction to certain stimuli is shown by scientific instruments, but no one would say that the thermometer 'knows' when it is cold.

What must be done with an experience in order that we may know it? Various things are possible. We may use words describing it, we may remember it either in words or in images, or we may merely 'notice' it. But 'noticing' is a matter of degree, and very hard to define; it seems to consist mainly in isolating from the sensible environment. You may, for instance, in listening to a piece of music, deliberately notice only the part of the cello. You hear the rest, as is said, 'unconsciously' – but this is a word to which it would be hopeless to attempt to attach any definite meaning. In one sense, it may be said that you 'know' a present experience if it rouses in you any emotion, however faint – if it pleases or displeases you, or interests or bores you, or surprises you or is just what you were expecting.

There is an important sense in which you *can* know anything that is in your present sensible field. If somebody says to you 'are you now seeing yellow?' or 'do you hear a noise?' you can answer with perfect confidence, even if, until you were asked, you were not noticing the yellow or the noise. And often you can be sure that it was already there before your attention was called to it.

It seems, then, that the most immediate knowing of which we have experience involves sensible presence *plus* something more, but that any very exact definition of the more that is needed is likely to mislead by its very exactness, since the matter is essentially vague and one of degree. What is wanted may be called 'attention'; this is partly a sharpening of the appropriate sense-organs, partly an emotional reaction. A sudden loud noise is almost sure to command attention, but so does a very faint sound that has emotional significance.

Every empirical proposition is based upon one or more sensible occurrences that were noticed when they occurred, or immediately after, while they still formed part of the specious present. Such occurrences, we shall say, are 'known' when they are noticed. The word 'know' has many meanings, and this is only one of them; but for the purposes of our inquiry it is fundamental.

This sense of 'know' does not involve words. Our next problem is: when we notice an occurrence, how can we formulate a sentence which (in a different sense) we 'know' to be true in virtue of the occurrence?

If I notice (say) that I am hot, what is the relation of the occurrence that I notice to the words 'I am hot'? We may leave out 'I', which raises irrelevant problems, and suppose that I merely say 'there is hotness'. (I say 'hotness', not 'heat', because I want a word for what can be felt, not for the physical concept.) But as this phrase is awkward, I shall go on saying 'I am hot', with the above proviso as to what is meant.

Let us be clear as to our present problem. We are no longer concerned with the question: 'how can I know that I am hot?' This was our previous question, which we answered – however unsatisfactorily – by merely saying that I notice it. Our question is not about knowing that I am hot, but about knowing, when I already know this, that the words 'I am hot' express what I have noticed, and are true in virtue of what I have noticed. The words 'express' and 'true', which occur here, have no place in mere noticing, and introduce something radically new. Occurrences may be noticed or not noticed, but they cannot be noticed if they do not occur; therefore, so far as mere noticing is concerned, truth and falsehood do not come in. I do not say that they come in *only* with words, for a memory which is in images may be false. But this may be ignored for the present, and in the case of a statement purporting to express what we are noticing, truth and falsehood first make their appearance with the use of words.

When I am hot, the word 'hot' is likely to come into my mind. This might seem to be the reason for saying 'I am hot'. But in that case what happens when I say (truly) 'I am not hot'? Here the word 'hot' has come into my mind although my situation is not of the kind that was supposed to have this effect. I think we may say that the stimulus to a proposition containing 'not' is always partly verbal; some one says 'are you hot?' and you answer 'I am not'. Thus negative propositions will arise when you are stimulated by a word but not by what usually stimulates the word. You hear the word 'hot' and you do not feel hot, so you say 'no' or 'I am not hot'. In this case the word is stimulated partly by the word (or by some other word), partly by an experience, but not by the experience which is what the word means.

The possible stimuli to the use of a word are many and various. You may use the word 'hot' because you are writing a poem in which the previous line ends with the word 'pot'. The word 'hot' may be brought into your mind by the word 'cold', or by the word 'equator', or, as in the case of the previous discussion, by the search for some very simple experience. The particular experience which is what the word 'hot' means has some connexion with the word over and above that of bringing the word to mind, since it shares this connexion with many other things. Association is an essential part of the connexion between being hot and the word 'hot', but is not the whole.

The relation between an experience and a word differs from such other associations as have been just mentioned, in the first place, by the fact that one of the associated items is not a word. The association between 'hot' and 'cold', or between 'hot' and 'pot', is verbal. This is one important point, but I think there is another, suggested by the word 'meaning'. To mean is to intend, and in the use of words there is generally an intention, which is more or less social. When you say 'I am hot', you give information, and as a rule you intend to do so. When you give information, you enable your hearer to act with reference to a fact of which he is not directly aware; that is to say, the sounds that he hears stimulate an action, on his part, which is appropriate to an experience that you are having but he is not. In the case of 'I am hot', this aspect is not very noticeable, unless you are a visitor and your words cause your host to open the window although he is shivering with cold; but in such a case as 'look out, there's a car coming', the dynamic effect on the hearer is what you intend.

An utterance which expresses a present sensible fact is thus, in some sense, a bridge between past and future. (I am thinking of such utterances as are made in daily life, not of such as philosophers invent.) The sensible fact has a certain effect upon A, who is aware of it; A wishes B to act in a manner which is rendered appropriate by this fact; therefore A utters words which 'express' the fact, and which, he hopes, will cause B to act in a certain way. An utterance which truly expresses a present sensible fact enables the hearer to act (to some extent) as he would if the fact were sensible to him.

The hearer who is relevant to the truth of a statement may be a hypothetical hearer, not necessarily an actual one. The statement may be made in solitude, or to a deaf man, or to a man who does not know the language used, but none of these circumstances affects its truth or falsehood. The hearer is assumed to be a person whose senses and linguistic habits resemble those of the speaker. We may say, as a preliminary rather than a final definition, that a verbal utterance truly expresses a sensible fact when, if the speaker had heard the utterance without being sensible of the fact, he would have acted as a result of the utterance as he did act as a result of the sensible fact.

This is unpleasantly vague. How do we know how the man would have acted? How do we know what part of his actual action is due to one feature of the environment and what to another? Moreover it is by no means wholly true that words produce the same effects as what they assert. 'Queen Anne is dead' has very little dynamic power, but if we had been present at her deathbed the fact would probably have produced vigorous action. This example may, however, be ruled out, since we are concerned with the verbal expression of *present* facts, and historical truth may be left to be considered at a later stage.

I think intention is only relevant in connexion with sentences, not with words, except when they are used as sentences. Take a word like 'hot', of which the meaning is sensible. It may be maintained that the *only* non-verbal stimulus to this word is something hot. If, in the presence of something hot, the word 'cold' comes into my mind, that will be because the word 'hot' has come first, and has suggested the word 'cold'. It may be that every time I see a fire I think of the Caucasus, because of the lines:

> Can one hold a fire in his hand
> By thinking on the frosty Caucasus?

But the intermediate verbal association is essential, and I shall not be led into the error of supposing that 'Caucasus' means 'fire'. We may, then, say: if certain situations suggest a certain word without any verbal intermediary, the word means those situations, or something that they have in common. And in such a case the hearing of the word will suggest some situation of the kind in question. When I speak of a word 'suggesting' a situation, I mean something not very definite, which may be an image or an action or an incipient action.

A sentence, we shall say, differs from a word by having an intention, which may be only that of communicating information. But it is from the meanings of words that it derives its power of fulfilling an intention. For when a man utters a sentence, it is owing to the meanings of the words that it has power to influence the hearer's actions, which is what the speaker intends it to do.

Sentences that describe experiences must contain words that have that kind of direct relation to sense that belongs to such a word as 'hot'. Among such words are the names of colours, the names of simple and familiar shapes, loud, hard, soft, and so on. Practical convenience mainly determines what sensible qualities shall have names. In any given case, a number of words are applicable to what we experience. Suppose we see a red circle in a blue square. We may say 'red inside blue' or 'circle inside square'. Each is an immediate verbal expression of an aspect of what we are seeing; each is completely verified by what we are seeing. If we are interested in colours we shall say the one, and if in geometry the other. The words that we use never exhaust all that we could say about a sensible experience. What we say is more abstract than what we see. And the experience that justifies our statement is only a fraction of what we are experiencing at the moment, except in cases of unusual concentration. As a rule we are aware of many shapes, noises, and bodily sensations in addition to the one that justifies our statement.

Many statements based upon immediate experience are much more complex than 'I am hot'. This is illustrated by the above example of 'circle inside square' or 'red inside blue' or 'red circle inside blue square'. Such things can be asserted as direct expressions of what we see. Similarly we can say 'this is hotter than that' or 'this is louder than that', as the direct result of observation; and 'this is before that' if both are within one specious present. Again: if A is a circular patch of blue, B a circular patch of green, and C a circular patch of yellow, all within one visual field, we can say, as expressing what we see, 'A is more like B than like C'. There is, so far as I know, no theoretical limit to the complexity of what can be perceived. When I speak of the complexity of what can be perceived, the phrase is ambiguous. We may, for instance, observe a visual field, first as a whole, and then bit by bit, as would be natural in looking at a picture in a bad light. We gradually discover that it contains four men, a woman, a baby, an ox, and an ass, as well as a stable. In a sense we saw all these things at first; certainly we can say, at the end, that the picture has these parts. But there may be no moment when we are analytically aware, in the way of sense-perception, of all these parts and their relations. When I speak of complexity in the datum, I mean more than what happens in such a case: I mean that we are noticing several inter-related things as several and as interrelated. The difference is most obvious in the case of music, where one may hear a total sound or be aware of the separate instruments and of the ingredients that make up the total effect. It is only in the latter case that I should speak of complexity in the auditory datum. The complexity that I am interested in is measured by the logical form of the judgement of perception; the simplest is a subject-predicate proposition, e.g. 'this is warm'; the next is e.g. 'this is to the left of that'; the next e.g. 'this is between that and the other'; and so on. Composers and painters probably go furthest in capacity for this kind of complexity.

The important point is that such propositions, however complex they may become, are still directly based on experience, just as truly and completely as 'I am warm'. This is quite a different matter from *Gestalt* as dealt with in Gestalt-psychology. Take (say) perception of the ten of clubs. Any person used to cards sees at once that it is the ten of clubs, and sees it by a perception of *Gestalt*, not analytically. But he *can* also see that it consists of ten similar black patterns on a white ground. This would be a remarkable feat, but in the case of the two or the three it would be easy. If, looking at the two of clubs, I say 'this surface consists of two similar black patterns on a white ground', what I say is not merely an analysis of a visual datum, but is itself an expression of a visual datum; that is to say, it is a proposition which I can know by the use of my eyes, without any need of inference. It is true that the proposition *can* be inferred from 'this is a black pattern on a white ground', 'so is that' and 'this is similar to that', but in fact it need not be so inferred.

There is, however, an important distinction between propositions which cannot be inferred and propositions which could be but are not. Sometimes it is very difficult to know to which class a proposition belongs. Take again the two of clubs, and the proposition 'this is similar to that' applied to the two pippets. We may give a name to the shape, and call it 'clover-shaped'. Thus we can say 'this is clover-shaped' and 'that is clover-shaped'; also 'this is black' and 'that is black'. We may infer 'this and that are similar in shape and colour'. But this is, in some sense, an inference from the similarity of the two verbal utterances 'clover-shaped' and the two verbal utterances 'black'. Thus a proposition of the form 'this is similar to that', if not itself an expression of a sensible datum, must, it would seem, be derived from premisses of which at least one is of the same form. Suppose, for example, that you are conducting experiments in which it is important to record colour. You observe black, and speak the word 'black' into your dictaphone. On a subsequent day you do the same thing again. You may then, on a third occasion, cause your dictaphone to repeat the two utterances 'black', which you observe to be similar. You infer that the colours you saw on two different days were similar. Here the dictaphone is inessential. If you see two black patches in quick succession, and say, in each case, 'this is black', you may, immediately afterwards, remember your words but have no visual memory of the patches; in that case, you infer the similarity of the patches from that of the two utterances 'black'. Thus language affords no escape from similarity to identity.

In such cases, the question as to what is inference and what is not is one that has, psychologically, no one definite answer.

In theory of knowledge, it is natural to attempt to reduce our empirical premisses to a minimum. If there are three propositions p, q, r, all of which we assert on the basis of direct experience, and if r can be logically inferred from p and q, we shall dispense with r as a premiss in theory of knowledge. In the above instance, we see 'those are both black'. But we *can* see 'this is black' and 'that is black' and infer 'those are both black'. But this matter is not so simple as it looks. Logic deals, not with verbal or sentential utterances, but with propositions, or at least sentences. From the standpoint of logic, when we know the two propositions 'this is black' and 'that is black', the word 'black' occurs in both. But as an empirical psychological fact, when we utter the two sentences, verbal utterances occur which are two different instances of the word 'black', and in order to infer 'this and that are black' we need a further empirical premiss; 'the first utterance "black" and the second utterance "black" are both instances of the word "black".' But in each case I can only utter an instance of the word, not the word itself, which remains immovably in a Platonic heaven.

Logic, and the whole conception of words and sentences as opposed to verbal and sentential utterances, is thus incurably Platonic. When I say 'this is black' and 'that is black', I *want* to say the same thing about both, but I fail to do so; I only succeed when I say 'this and that are black', and then I say something different from either of the things I had previously said about this and about that. Thus the sort of generality that *seems* to be involved in the repeated use of the word 'black' is an illusion; what we really have is similarity. To perceive the similarity of two utterances of the word 'black' is the same kind of thing as to perceive the similarity of two black patches. But in fact, when we use language, it is not necessary to *perceive* similarity. One black patch causes one verbal utterance 'black', and another causes another; the patches are similar, and their verbal effects are similar, and the effects of the two verbal utterances are similar. These similarities *can* be observed, but *need* not be; all that is necessary is that they should in fact exist. The importance of the question is in connexion with logic and the theory of universals. And it shows how complicated are the psychological presuppositions of the doctrine, which logic takes for granted, that the same word can occur on different occasions, in different sentential utterances and even in different sentences. This, if we are not careful, may be just as misleading as it would be to infer that an okapi may be simultaneously in London and New York, on the ground that 'an okapi is now in London' and 'an okapi is now in New York' may be both true.

To return from this excursion into logic, let us consider further what happens when we pass from a Gestalt-perception to an analytic perception, e.g. from 'there is the two of clubs', when we perceive the whole shape as a unity, to 'there are two similar black marks on a white ground', where we see the parts of the shape and their interrelations. Familiarity with one kind of sensible material affects such analytic judgements. You are aware that a pack of cards contains thirteen clubs and four twos, and you have the habit of the twofold classification of cards. This, however, works both ways. It enables you to recognize a ten by the pattern, whereas a person unfamiliar with cards might have to count up to ten – not in order to see that the pattern is different from a nine or an eight, but in order to give it its name.

It is easy to exaggerate what is necessary, for instance in counting. If you have to count a heap of nuts and you possess the motor habit of saying 'one, two, three . . .' in the right order, you can drop the nuts one by one into a bag, saying a number each time, and at the end you will have counted them without any need of memory or of apprehending numbers except as a string of sounds coming in a certain order as the result of habit. This illustrates how much more words seem to know than is known by the person who uses them. In like manner, a black object may cause you to say 'this is black' as a result of a mere mechanism, without any realization of the meaning of your words. Indeed, what is said in this thoughtless way is perhaps more likely to be true than what is said deliberately; for if you know English there is a causal connexion between a black object and the word 'black' which there is not between the same object and the name of a different colour. This is what gives such a high probability of truth to sentences stimulated by the presence of the objects to which they refer.

When you see a black object and say 'this is black', you are not, as a rule, noticing that you say these words; you know the thing is black, but you do not know that you say it is. I am using 'know' in the sense of 'notice', explained above. You *can* notice yourself speaking, but you will only do so if, for some reason, your speaking interests you as much as the object does – if, e.g., you are learning the language or practising elocution. If you are – as we are – studying the relation of language to other facts, you will notice a connexion between your words and the black object, which you might express in the sentence: 'I said "this is black" because it is black'. This 'because' demands close scrutiny. I have discussed this question in 'The Limits of Empiricism', *Proceedings of the Aristotelian Society*, 1935-6. At present I shall confine myself to a brief repetition of the relevant parts of that paper.

We are concerned here with the relations of three propositions:

'There is a black patch', which we will call 'p';

'I said "there is a black patch"', which we will call 'q';

'I said "there is a black patch" because a black patch is there', which we will call 'r'.

In regard to r two questions arise: first, how do I know it? second, what is the meaning of the word 'because' as it occurs in this proposition?

As to the first question, I do not see how to escape from the view that we know r, as we know p and q, because it is a sentence expressing an experience. But before we can adequately consider this view, we must be a little more definite about q, which may mean merely that I made certain noises, or may mean that I made an assertion. The latter says more than the former, since it states that the noises were made with a certain intention. I might have said 'there is a black patch', not because I wished to assert it, but because it is part of a poem. In that case, r would have been untrue. Therefore, if r is to be true, it is not sufficient that I should make the noises which constitute a sentential utterance of q, but I must make them with the intention of making an assertion about a present sensible fact.

But this is somewhat too definite and explicit. 'Intention' suggests something conscious and deliberate, which ought not to be implied. Words may result from the environment just as directly as the sound 'ow' when I am hurt. If someone asks 'why did you say "ow"?' and I reply 'because I had a twinge of toothache', the 'because' has the same meaning as in our proposition r: in each case it expresses an observed connexion between an experience and an utterance. We can use a word correctly without observing this connexion, but it is only by observing the connexion that we can explicitly know the meaning of a word, providing the word is not one which has a verbal definition, but one which we learn by confrontation with what it means. The difference between a cry of pain and the word 'black' is that the former is an unconditioned reflex, which the latter is not; but this difference does not involve a difference in the word 'because'. People who have learnt a certain language have acquired an impulse to use certain words on certain occasions, and this impulse, when it has been acquired, is strictly analogous to the impulse to cry when hurt.

We may have various reasons for uttering the sentence 'there is a black patch'. The fact may be so interesting that we exclaim without thought; we may wish to give information; we may wish to attract someone's attention to what is happening; we may wish to deceive; we may, as in reciting poetry, be uttering the words without asserting anything. We can know, if we choose, which of these was our reason for uttering the words, and we know this by observation – the kind of observation that is called introspection. In each case we have an observed connexion between two experiences. The simplest case is that in which the sight of the black patch is the reason for the exclamation 'there is a black patch!' This is the case contemplated in our proposition *r*. But the further discussion of the 'because' which occurs in the proposition *r* must be postponed until we have considered propositional attitudes.

CHAPTER 4

THE OBJECT-LANGUAGE

TARSKI, in his important book *Der Wahrheitsbegriff in den form-
alisierten Sprachen*, has shown that the words 'true' and 'false',
as applied to the sentences of a given language, always require
another language, of higher order, for their adequate definition.
The conception of a hierarchy of languages is involved in the
theory of types, which, in some form, is necessary for the solution of the paradoxes; it plays an important part in Carnap's
work as well as in Tarski's. I suggested it in my introduction to
Wittgenstein's *Tractatus*, as an escape from his theory that
syntax can only be 'shown', not expressed in words. The
arguments for the necessity of a hierarchy of languages are over-
whelming, and I shall henceforth assume their validity.*

The hierarchy must extend upwards indefinitely, but not
downwards, since, if it did, language could never get started.
There must, therefore, be a language of lowest type. I shall

* These arguments are derived from the paradoxes; their applicability to the words
'true' and 'false' is derived from the paradox of the liar.

My inference from the paradox of the liar was, in outline, as follows; A man says
'I am lying', i.e. 'there is a proposition p such that I assert p and p is false'. We may,
if we like, make the matter more precise by supposing that, at 5.30, he says 'between
5.29 and 5.31 I make a false statement', but that throughout the rest of the two
minutes concerned he says nothing. Let us call this statement 'q'. If q is true, he
makes a false statement during the crucial two minutes; but q is his only statement in
this period: therefore q must be false. But if q is false, then every statement that he
makes during the two minutes must be true, and therefore q must be true, since he
makes it during the two minutes. Thus if q is true it is false, and if it is false it is true.

Let '$A(p)$' mean 'I assert p between 5.29 and 5.31'. Then q is 'there is a proposition
p such that $A(p)$ and p is false'. The contradiction emerges from the supposition that
q is the proposition p in question. But if there is a hierarchy of meanings of the word
'false' corresponding to a hierarchy of propositions, we shall have to substitute for
q something more definite, i.e. 'there is a proposition p of order n, such that $A(p)$ and
p has falsehood of order n'. Here n may be any integer: but whatever integer it is, q
will be of order $n + 1$, and will not be capable of truth or falsehood of order n. Since
I make no assertion of order n, q is false, and, since q is not a possible value of p, the
argument that q is also true collapses. The man who says 'I am telling a lie of order
n' *is* telling a lie, but of order $n + 1$. Other ways of evading the paradox have been
suggested, e.g. by Ramsey, *Foundations of Mathematics*, p. 48.

define one such language, not the only possible one.* I shall call this sometimes the 'object-language', sometimes the 'primary language'. My purpose, in the present chapter, is to define and describe this basic language. The languages which follow in the hierarchy I shall call secondary, tertiary, and so on; it is to be understood that each language contains all its predecessors.

The primary language, we shall find, can be defined both logically and psychologically; but before attempting formal definitions it will be well to make a preliminary informal exploration.

It is clear, from Tarski's argument, that the words 'true' and 'false' cannot occur in the primary language; for these words, as applied to sentences in the nth language, belong to the $(n+1)^{th}$ language. This does not mean that sentences in the primary language are neither true nor false, but that, if 'p' is a sentence in this language, the two sentences 'p is true' and 'p is false' belong to the secondary language. This is, indeed, obvious apart from Tarksi's argument. For, if there is a primary language, its words must not be such as presuppose the existence of a language. Now 'true' and 'false' are words applicable to sentences, and thus presuppose the existence of language. (I do not mean to deny that a memory consisting of images, not words, may be 'true' or 'false'; but this is in a somewhat different sense, which need not concern us at present.) In the primary language, therefore, though we can make assertions, we cannot say that our own assertions or those of others are either true or false.

When I say that we make assertions in the primary language, I must guard against a misunderstanding, for the word 'assertion' is ambiguous. It is used, sometimes, as the antithesis of denial, and in this sense it cannot occur in the primary language. Denial presupposes a form of words, and proceeds to state that this form of words is false. The word 'not' is only significant when attached to a sentence, and therefore presupposes language. Consequently, if 'p' is a sentence of the primary language, 'not-p' is a sentence of the secondary language. It is easy to fall into confusion, since 'p', without verbal alteration, may

* My hierarchy of languages is not identical with Carnap's or Tarski's.

express a sentence only possible in the secondary language. Suppose, for example, you have taken salt by mistake instead of sugar, and you exclaim 'this is *not* sugar'. This is a denial, and belongs to the secondary language. You now use a different sprinkler, and say with relief 'this *is* sugar'. Psychologically, you are answering affirmatively the question 'is this sugar?' You are in fact saying, as unpedantically as you can: 'the sentence "this is sugar" is true'. Therefore what you mean is something which cannot be said in the primary language, although the same form of words can express a sentence in the primary language. The assertion which is the antithesis of denial belongs to the secondary language; the assertion which belongs to the primary language has no antithesis.

Just the same kind of considerations as apply to 'not' apply to 'or' and 'but' and conjunctions generally. Conjunctions, as their name implies, join other words, and have no meaning in isolation; they therefore presuppose the existence of a language. The same applies to 'all' and 'some'; you can only have all of something, or some of something, and in the absence of other words 'all' and 'some' are meaningless. This argument also applies to 'the'.

Thus logical words, without exception, are absent from the primary language. All of them, in fact, presuppose propositional forms: 'not' and conjunctions presuppose propositions, while 'all' and 'some' and 'the' presuppose propositional functions.

Ordinary language contains a number of purely syntactical words, such as 'is' and 'than', which must obviously be excluded from the primary language. Such words, unlike those that we have hitherto considered, are in fact wholly unnecessary, and do not appear in symbolic logical languages. Instead of 'A is earlier than B' we say 'A precedes B'; instead of 'A is yellow' a logical language will say 'yellow (A)'; instead of 'there are smiling villains' we say: it is false that all values of 'either x does not smile or x is not a villain' are false. 'Existence' and 'Being', as they occur in traditional metaphysics, are hypostatized forms of certain meanings of 'is'. Since 'is' does not belong to the primary language, 'existence' and 'being', if they are to mean anything, must be linguistic concepts not directly applicable to objects.

There is another very important class of words that must be at least provisionally excluded, namely such words as 'believe', 'desire', 'doubt', all of which, when they occur in a sentence, must be followed by a subordinate sentence telling what it is that is believed or desired or doubted. Such words, so far as I have been able to discover, are always psychological, and involve what I call 'propositional attitudes'. For the present, I will merely point out that they differ from such words as 'or' in an important respect, namely that they are necessary for the description of observable phenomena. If I want to see the paper, that is a fact which I can easily observe, and yet 'want' is a word which has to be followed by a subordinate sentence if anything significant is to result. Such words raise problems, and are perhaps capable of being analysed in such a way as to make them able to take their place in the primary language. But as this is not *prima facie* possible, I shall for the present assume that they are to be excluded. I shall devote a later chapter to the discussion of this subject.

We can now partially define the primary or object-language as a language consisting wholly of 'object-words',* where 'object-words' are defined, logically, as words having meaning in isolation, and, psychologically, as words which have been learnt without its being necessary to have previously learnt any other words. These two definitions are not strictly equivalent, and where they conflict the logical definition is to be preferred. They would become equivalent if we were allowed to suppose an indefinite extension of our perceptive faculties. We could not, in fact, recognize a chiliagon by merely looking at it, but we can easily imagine beings capable of this feat. On the other hand, it is clearly impossible that any being's knowledge of language should begin with an understanding of the word 'or', although the meaning of this word is not learnt from a formal definition. Thus in addition to the class of actual object-words, there is a class of possible object-words. For many purposes the class of

---

* There must be syntax, but it need not be rendered explicit by the use of syntactical words, such as 'is'.

actual and possible object-words is more important than the class of actual object-words.

In later life, when we learn the meaning of a new word, we usually do so through the dictionary, that is to say, by a definition in terms of words of which we already know the meaning. But since the dictionary defines words by means of other words, there must be some words of which we know the meaning without a verbal definition. Of these words, a certain small number do not belong to the primary language; such are the words 'or' and 'not'. But the immense majority are words in the primary language, and we have now to consider the process of learning what these words mean. Dictionary words may be ignored, since they are theoretically superfluous; for wherever they occur they can be replaced by their definitions.

In the learning of an object-word, there are four things to be considered: the understanding of the heard word in the presence of the object, the understanding of it in the absence of the object, the speaking of the word in the presence of the object, and the speaking of it in the absence of the object. Roughly speaking, this is the order in which a child acquires these four capacities.

Understanding a heard word may be defined behaviouristically or in terms of individual psychology. When we say that a dog understands a word, all that we have a right to mean is that he behaves in an appropriate manner when he hears it; what he 'thinks' we cannot know. Consider, for example, the process of teaching a dog to know his name. The process consists of calling him, rewarding him when he comes, and punishing him when he does not. We may imagine that, to the dog, his name means: 'either I shall be rewarded because I approach my master, or I shall be punished because I do not'. Which alternative is considered the more probable is shown by the tail. The association, in this case, is a pleasure-pain association, and therefore imperatives are what the dog understands most easily. But he can understand a sentence in the indicative, provided its content has sufficient emotional importance; for instance, the sentence 'dinner!' which means, and is understood to mean: 'you are now about to receive the nourishment that you desire.' When I

63

say that this is understood, I mean that, when the dog hears the word, he behaves very much as he would if you had a plate of food in your hand. We say the dog 'knows' the word, but what we ought to say is that the word produces behaviour similar to that which the sight or smell of a dinner out of reach would produce.

The meaning of an object-word can only be learnt by hearing it frequently pronounced in the presence of the object. The association between word and object is just like any other habitual association, e.g. that between sight and touch. When the association has been established, the object suggests the word, and the word suggests the object, just as an object seen suggests sensations of touch, and an object touched in the dark suggests sensations of sight. Association and habit are not specially connected with language; they are characteristics of psychology and physiology generally. How they are to be interpreted is, of course, a difficult and controversial question, but it is not a question which specially concerns the theory of language.

As soon as the association between an object-word and what it means has been established, the word is 'understood' in the absence of the object, that is to say, it 'suggests' the object in exactly the same sense in which sight and touch suggest one another.

Suppose you are with a man who suddenly says 'fox' because he sees a fox, and suppose that, though you hear him, you do not see the fox. What actually happens to you as a result of your understanding the word 'fox'? You look about you, but this you would have done if he had said 'wolf' or 'zebra'. You may have an image of a fox. But what, from the observer's standpoint, shows your understanding of the word, is that you behave (within limits) as you would have done if you had seen the fox.

Generally, when you hear an object-word which you understand, your behaviour is, up to a point, that which the object itself would have caused. This may occur without any 'mental' intermediary, by the ordinary rules of conditioned reflexes, since the word has become associated with the object. In the morning you may be told 'breakfast is ready', or you may smell the bacon. Either may have the same effect upon your actions.

The association between the smell and the bacon is 'natural', that is to say it is not a result of any human behaviour. But the association between the word 'breakfast' and breakfast is a social matter, which exists only for English-speaking people. This, however, is only relevant when we are thinking of the community as a whole. Each child learns the language of its parents as it learns to walk. Certain associations between words and things are produced in it by daily experience, and have as much the appearance of natural laws as have the properties of eggs or matches; indeed they are exactly on the same level so long as the child is not taken to a foreign country.

It is only some words that are learnt in this way. No one learns the word 'procrastination' by hearing it frequently pronounced on occasions when some one is dilatory. We learn, by direction association with what the word means, not only proper names of the people we know, class-names such as 'man' and 'dog', names of sensible qualities such as 'yellow', 'hard', sweet', and names of actions such as 'walk', 'run', 'eat', 'drink', but also such words as 'up' and 'down', 'in' and 'out', 'before' and 'after', and even 'quick' and 'slow'. But we do not learn in this way either complicated words such as 'dodeca-hedron' or logical words such as 'not', 'or', 'the', 'all', 'some'. Logical words, as we have seen, presuppose language; in fact, they presuppose what, in an earlier chapter, we spoke of as 'atomic forms'. Such words belong to a stage of language that is no longer primitive, and should be carefully excluded from a consideration of those ways of speaking which are most inti-mately related to non-linguistic occurrences.

What kind of simplicity makes the understanding of a word into an example of understanding an object-language? For it is to be observed that a sentence may be spoken in the object-language and understood in a language of higher order, or vice versa. If you excite a dog by saying 'rats!' when there are no rats, your speech belongs to a language of higher order, since it is not caused by rats, but the dog's understanding of it belongs to the object-language. A heard word belongs to the object-language when it causes a reaction appropriate to what the word means. If some one says 'hark, hark, the lark', you may listen, or you may say 'at heaven's gate sings'; in the former case, what you have heard belongs to the object-language, in the latter case, not. Whenever you doubt or reject what you are told, your hearing does not belong to the object-language; for in such a case you are lingering on the words, whereas in the object-language the words are transparent, i.e. their effects upon your behaviour depend only upon what they mean, and are, up to a point, identical with the effects that would result from the sensible presence of what they designate.

In learning to speak, there are two elements, first, the muscular dexterity, and second, the habit of using a word on appropriate occasions. We may ignore the muscular dexterity, which can be acquired by parrots. Children make many articulate sounds spontaneously, and have also an impulse to imitate the sounds made by adults. When they make a sound which the adults consider appropriate to the environment, they find the results pleasant. Thus, by the usual pleasure-pain mechanism which is employed in training performing animals, children learn, in time, to utter noises appropriate to objects that are sensibly present, and then, almost immediately, they learn to use the same noises when they desire the objects. As soon as this has happened, they possess an object-language: objects suggest their names, their names suggest them, and their names may be suggested, not only by the presence of the objects, but by the thought of them.

I pass now from the learning of an object-language to its characteristics when learnt.

We may, as we have seen, divide words into three classes: (1) object-words, of which we learn the meaning by directly acquiring an association between the word and the thing; (2) propositional words, which do not belong to the object-language; (3) dictionary words, of which we learn the meaning through a verbal definition. The distinction between (1) and (3) varies considerably from one person to another. 'Pentagram' is to most people a dictionary word, but to a child brought up in a house decorated with pentagrams it might be an object-word. 'Swastika' used to be a dictionary word, but is so no longer. It is important to note, however, that there must be object-words, since otherwise dictionary definitions could not convey any-thing.

Let us now consider how much, in the way of language, can be done by object-words alone. I shall assume, for this purpose, that the person considered has had every possible opportunity of acquiring object-words: he has seen Mount Everest and Popocatepetl, the anaconda, and the axolotl, he is acquainted with Chiang Kai-shek and Stalin, he has tasted birds' nests and shark's fins, and altogether has a wide experience of the sensible world. But he has been too busy seeing the world to acquire the use of such words as 'not', 'or', 'some', etc. If you say to him 'is there any country that you have not visited?' he will not know what you mean. The question is: what will such a person know, and what will he not know?

Can we say: 'he will know everything that can be known by observation alone, but nothing that needs inference'? Let us first alter our question, and ask, not what can he know, but what can he express in words?

To begin with: if he can put every observable fact into words, he must have as many words as facts; now some words are among facts; therefore the number of his words must be infinite. This is impossible; consequently there are facts he leaves unexpressed. The case is analogous to Royce's bottle with a label on which there was a picture of the bottle, including, of course, a picture on the label.

But although he must leave out some observable facts, there is not any one observable fact of which we can say 'he must leave this one out.' He is in the position of a man who wishes to pack three suits into a suit-case that will only hold two; he must leave one out, but there is not one that he must leave out. So our travelled friend, we will suppose, sees a man called Tom, and without difficulty he says: 'I see Tom'. This remark is itself an observable fact, so he says: 'I say that I see Tom'. This again is an observable fact, so he says: 'I say that I say that I see Tom'. There is no one definite point at which he must break off this series, but he must break it off somewhere, and at that point there is an observable fact which he does not express in words. It seems, therefore, that it is impossible for a mortal to give verbal expression to every observable fact, but that, nevertheless, every observable fact is such that a mortal could give verbal expression to it. This is not a contradiction.

We have thus two different totals to consider: first, the total of the man's actual statements, and secondly the total of possible statements out of which his actual statements must be chosen. But what is a 'possible' statement? Statements are physical occurrences, like thunderstorms or railway accidents; but at least a novelist or poet can describe a thunderstorm that never took place. But it is difficult to describe a statement without making it. In describing a political speech, you may remark: 'what Sir Somebody So-and-So did *not* say was ...' and then follows a statement; that is to say, in order to say that a statement was not made, we have to make it, except in the rare instances of statements that have names, such as the Coronation Oath.

There are, however, ways of avoiding this difficulty, the best of which is due to Gödel. We assume a completely formalized language, with an entirely explicit vocabulary and syntax. We assign numbers to the words of the vocabulary, and hence, by arithmetical rules, to all possible sentences in the language. If, as we are assuming, the initial vocabulary is finite, but there is no limit to the length of sentences (except that they must be finite), the number of possible sentences will be the same as the number of finite integers. Consequently, if n is any finite integer, there is one definite sentence which is the nth, and our rules will enable us to construct it, given n. We can now make all sorts of statements about Mr A's statements, without having actually to make his statements. We might say 'Mr A never makes a statement of which the number is divisible by 13', or 'all Mr A's statements have numbers which are prime'.

But there are still difficulties, of the kind emphasized by the finitists. We are used to thinking of the whole series of natural numbers as in some sense 'given', and we have utilized this idea to give definiteness to the theory of possible statements. But how about numbers which no one has ever mentioned or thought of? What is a number except something that occurs in a statement? And, if so, a number that has never been mentioned involves a possible statement, which cannot, without circularity be defined by means of such a number.

This subject cannot be pursued at present, since it would take us too deep into the subject of logical language. Let us see whether, ignoring such logical points, we can be a little more definite about the possibilities of a language which contains only object-words.

Among object-words, as we saw, are included a certain number of verbs, such as 'run', 'eat', 'shout', and even some prepositions such as 'in' and 'above' and 'before'. All that is essential to an object-word is some similarity among a set of phenomena, which is sufficiently striking for an association to be established between instances of the set and instances of the word for the set, the method of establishing the association being that, for some time, the word is frequently heard when a member of the set is seen. It is obvious that what can be learnt in this way depends upon psychological capacity and interest. The similarity between different instances of eating is likely to strike a child, because eating is interesting; but in order to learn in this way the meaning of the word 'dodecagon' a child would need a precocity of geometrical interest surpassing Pascal's and a superhuman capacity for perceiving *Gestalt*. Such gifts are, however, not logically impossible. But how about 'or'? You cannot show a child examples of it in the sensible world. You can say: 'will you have pudding or pie?' but if the child says yes, you cannot find a nutriment which is 'pudding-or-pie'. And yet 'or' has a relation to experience; it is related to the experience of choice. But in choice we have before us two possible courses of action, that is to say, two actual thoughts as to courses of action. These thoughts may not involve explicit sentences, but no change is made in what is essential if we supposed them to be explicit. Thus 'or', as an element of experience, presupposes sentences, or something mental related in a similar manner to some other fact. When we say 'this or that' we are not saying something directly applicable to an object, but are stating a relation between *saying* 'this' and *saying* 'that'. Our statement is about statements, and only indirectly about objects.

Let us consider, in like manner, negative propositions which seem to have an immediate relation to experience. Suppose you are told 'there is butter in the larder, but no cheese'. Although they seem equally based upon sensible experience in the larder, the two statements 'there is butter' and 'there is not cheese' are really on a very different level. There was a definite occurrence which was seeing butter, and which might have put the word 'butter' into your mind even if you had not been thinking of butter. But there was no occurrence which could be described as 'not seeing cheese' or as 'seeing the absence of cheese'.* You must have looked at everything in the larder, and judged, in each case, 'this is not cheese'. You *judged* this, you did not *see* it; you saw what each thing was, not what it was not. To judge 'this is not cheese', you must have the word 'cheese', or some equivalent, in your mind already. There is a clash between what you see and the associations of the word 'cheese', and so you judge 'this is not cheese'. Of course, the same sort of thing may happen with an affirmative judgement, if it answers a previous question; you then say 'yes, this *is* cheese'. Here you really mean 'the statement "this is cheese" is true'; and when you say 'this is not cheese' you mean 'the statement "this is cheese" is false'. In either case, you are speaking about a statement, which you are not doing in a direct judgement of perception. The man, therefore, who understands only object-words, will be able to tell you everything that *is* in the larder, but will be unable to infer that there is no cheese. He will, moreover, have no conception of truth or falsehood; he can say 'this is butter' but not 'it is true that this is butter'.

The same sort of considerations apply to 'all' and 'some'. Suppose our unphilosophical observer goes to a small Welsh village in which everyone is called Williams. He will discover that A is called Williams, B is called Williams, and so on. He may, in fact, have discovered this about everybody in the village, but he cannot know that he has done so. To know it, he would have to know 'A, B, C, . . . are all the people in this village'. But this is like knowing that there is no cheese in the larder; it involves knowing 'nobody in this village is neither A nor B nor C

---

* This subject will be discussed again in a later chapter, and what is said above will be at once amplified and guarded against a too literal interpretation.

nor . . .'. And this is plainly not to be known by perception alone.

The case of 'some' is a little less obvious.* In the above case, will not our friend know that 'some people in this village are called Williams'? I think not. This is like 'pudding-or-pie'. From the standpoint of perception, none of them are 'some people'; they are the people they are. It is only by a detour through language that we can understand 'some people'. Whenever we make a statement about *some* of a collection, there are alternative possibilities in our minds; in each particular case, the statement may be true or false, and we assert that it is true in certain cases but perhaps not in all. We cannot express alternatives without introducing truth and falsehood, and truth and falsehood, as we have seen, are linguistic terms. A pure object-language, therefore, cannot contain the word 'some' any more than the word 'all'.

We have seen that the object-language, unlike languages of higher orders, does not contain the words 'true' and 'false' in any sense whatever. The next stage in language is that in which we can not only speak the object-language, but can speak about it. In this second-type language, we can define what is meant by saying, of a sentence in the first-type language, that it is true. What is meant is that the sentence must *mean* something that can be *noticed* in a datum of perception. If you see a dog and say 'dog', you make a true statement. If you see a dog in a kennel and say 'dog in kennel', you make a true statement. There is no need of verbs for such sentences, and they may consist of single words.

One of the things that have seemed puzzling about language is that, in ordinary speech, sentences are true or false, but single words are neither. In the object-language this distinction does not exist. Every single word of this language is capable of standing alone, and, when it stands alone, means that it is applicable to the present datum of perception. In this language, when you say 'dog', your statement is false if it is a wolf that you are looking at. In ordinary speech, which is not sorted out into languages of different types, it is impossible to know, when the word 'dog' occurs by itself, whether it is being used as a word in the object-

* This topic, again, will be resumed in a later chapter.

language or in a linguistic manner, as when we say 'that is not a dog'. Obviously, when the word 'dog' can be used to deny the presence of a dog as well as to affirm it, the single word loses all assertive power. But in the object-language, upon which all others are based, every single word is an assertion.

Let us now restate the whole matter of the object-language.

An *object-word* is a class of similar noises or utterances such that, from habit, they have become associated with a class of mutually similar occurrences frequently experienced at the same time as one of the noises or utterances in question. That is to say, let A_1, A_2, A_3 ... be a set of similar occurrences, and let a_1, a_2, a_3 ... be a set of similar noises or utterances; and suppose that when A_1 occurred you heard the noise a_1, when A_2 occurred you heard the noise a_2, and so on. After this has happened a great many times, you notice an occurrence A_n which is like A_1, A_2, A_3 ..., and it causes you, by association, to utter or imagine a noise a_n which is like a_1, a_2, a_3 ... If, now, A is a class of mutually similar occurrences of which A_1, A_2, A_3 ... A_n are members, and a is a class of mutually similar noises or utterances of which a_1, a_2, a_3 ... a_n are members, we may say that a is a word which is the name of the class A, or 'means' the class A. This is more or less vague, since there may be several classes which satisfy the above conditions for A and a. A child learning the object-language applies Mill's Canons of Induction, and gradually corrects his mistakes. If he knows a dog called 'Caesar', he may think this word applies to all dogs. On the other hand, if he knows a dog whom he calls 'dog', he may not apply this word to any other dog. Fortunately many occurrences fit into natural kinds; in the lives of most children, anything that looks like a cat is a cat, and anything that looks like one's mother is one's mother. But for this piece of luck, learning to speak would be very difficult. It would be practically impossible if the temperature were such that most substances were gaseous.

If now, in a certain situation, you are impelled to say 'cat', that will be (so long as you are confined to the object-language) because some feature of the environment is associated with the word 'cat', which necessarily implies that this feature resembles the previous cats that caused the association. It may not resemble them sufficiently to satisfy a zoologist; the beast may be a lynx or a young leopard. The association between the word and the object is not likely to be 'right' until you have seen many animals that were not cats but looked rather as if they were, and many other animals that were cats but looked rather as if they were not. But the word 'right', here, is a social word, denoting correct behaviour. As soon as certain beasts suggest the word 'cat' to you and others do not, you possess a language, though it may not be correct English.

Theoretically, given sufficient capacity, we could express in the object-language every non-linguistic occurrence. We can in fact observe fairly complicated occurrences, such as 'while John was putting the horse in the cart, the bull rushed out and I ran away', or 'as the curtain was falling, there were cries of "fire" and a stampede'. This sort of thing can be said in the object-language, though it would have to be translated into a sort of pidgin English. Whether it is possible to express in the object-language such observable facts as desires, beliefs, and doubts is a difficult question, which I shall discuss at length in a later chapter. What is certain is that the object-language does not contain the words 'true' and 'false', or logical words such as 'not', 'or', 'some', and 'all'. Logical words will be the subject of my next chapter.

CHAPTER 5

LOGICAL WORDS

IN the present chapter I wish to consider certain words which occur in the secondary language and in all higher languages, but not in the object-language. The words in question are characteristic of logic. I shall especially consider 'true', 'false', 'not', 'or', 'some', and 'all'. We know from logic that these terms cannot all be defined, but that it is to a large extent optional which shall be defined in terms of which. Our problem being one of theory of knowledge, we are less concerned with the *definition* of these terms than with the way in which we come to know propositions in which they occur.

Let us begin with the words 'true', 'false', and 'not'. It is unnecessary to have the two words 'false' and 'not', for, if p is a proposition, 'p is false' and 'not-p' are strictly synonymous. The difference, in practice, is one of emphasis. If you are interested in the object you say 'not-p', but if in the statement you say 'p is false'. If you want butter and look in a cupboard and find cream cheese, you will say 'this isn't butter'; but if the dairyman offers for sale a substance labelled 'butter' which you find to be margarine, you will say 'you *say* this is butter, but that is false', because you are more interested in his wickedness than in his goods. Such rhetorical points, however, do not concern us, and we may safely treat 'false' and 'not' as synonyms.

In the secondary language, we are concerned with the words of the object-language, not simply as noises or bodily movements, for in that respect they belong to the object-language, but as having meaning. We are concerned, that is to say, with the relation between object-words and object-sentences on the one hand, and what they designate or assert on the other hand. 'Word' cannot occur in the object-language, but 'object-word' can occur in the secondary language. Assuming that logical words occur in the secondary language, 'logical word' will first occur in the tertiary language. If 'tertiary words' are defined as those that occur in the tertiary language but not in the primary or secondary language, then 'tertiary word' belongs to the quaternary language. And so on. It is to be understood that each language contains all the languages of lower orders. 'Word' is, itself, of ambiguous order, and has therefore no definite meaning; if this is forgotten, contradictions are apt to result. Take, e.g., the contradiction about 'heterological'. A predicate is 'heterological' when it cannot be predicated of itself; thus 'long' is heterological because it is not a long word, but 'short' is homological.* We now ask: is 'heterological' heterological? Either answer leads to a contradiction. To avoid such antinomies, the hierarchy of languages is essential.

The words 'true' and 'false', as we are to consider them in this chapter, are to be applied only to sentences in the primary language.

In practice, as opposed to philosophy, we only apply the words 'true' and 'false' to statements which we have heard or read or considered before we possessed the evidence that would enable us to decide which of the two words was applicable. Someone tells us that Manx cats have no tails, but as he has previously told you that Manx men have three legs, you do not believe him. When he shows you his Manx cat you exclaim, 'so what you said was true!' The newspapers, at one time, said that I was dead, but after carefully examining the evidence I came to the conclusion that the statement was false. When the statement comes first and the evidence afterwards, there is a process called 'verification', which involves confrontation of the statement with the evidence. In the case of a statement in the primary language, the evidence must consist of a sensible experience or of a set of such experiences. We have already considered sentences describing experiences. Speaking broadly, the process of verification is as follows: first you hear or read or consider a sentence S; then you have an experience E; then you observe that S is a sentence which describes E. In that case you say that S is 'true'. I do not mean that this is a definition of the word

* German, learned, beautiful, are heterological: English, erudite, ugly, are homological.

'true', but that it is a description of the process by which you come to know that this word is applicable to a given primary sentence. The word 'false' is much more difficult. But before considering this word there are some further things to be said about the word 'true'.

In the first place, the word 'true' may be applied to a sentential utterance, a sentence, or a proposition. Two sentential utterances which are instances of the same sentence, or two sentences which are instances of the same proposition, are either both true or both false. Thus in determining truth or falsehood, it is the proposition that is relevant.

In the second place, a sentence or proposition is known to be 'true' when it has a certain relation to an experience. In the case of 'verification', the sentence comes first and the experience after, but this is logically irrelevant; if the experience comes first, it equally proves the sentence to be true, provided the sentence 'describes' the experience. What is meant by this word 'describes' we have already considered, and I shall say no more about it at present.

In the third place, not all sentences in the primary language can be correctly said to describe a single experience. If you see something and say 'that is a dog', you are going beyond what can be seen at the moment. A dog has a past and a future, it has auditory and olfactory characteristics, and so on. All these are suggested by the word 'dog', which is a condensation of many inductions. Fortunately, animals fit into natural kinds. If your dog proceeded to mew like a cat, and to give birth to a mixed litter of puppies and kittens, words would fail you. In like manner the man who mistakes salt for sugar is making an induction: 'what looks like this tastes sweet'. In this case the induction is false. If he said merely 'this is white', he would not be making a mistake. Even if he said 'this is grey' because he meant by 'grey' what other people mean by 'white', he would not be making an intellectual error, but only using language in an unusual way. So long as a man avoids words which are condensed inductions, and confines himself to words that can describe a single experience, it is possible for a single experience to show that his words are true.

When I say that such a word as 'dog' embodies condensed inductions, I do not mean that such inductions are conscious or deliberate. Certain situations suggest the word 'dog' to you, and both they and the word rouse certain expectations. When you have said 'that is a dog', subsequent events may astonish you; but when you have said 'that is white', nothing in your statement gives any ground for surprise at what happens next, or for supposing that you were mistaken in saying that what you saw was white. So long as your words merely describe present experiences, the sole possible errors are linguistic, and these only involve socially wrong behaviour, not falsehood.

I come now to falsehood and negation, which raise some rather difficult problems.

We have agreed that when you do what a logician would call 'asserting not-p', you are saying 'p is false'. The question that I am concerned with at present is: how can experience show you that a proposition is false? Let us take some very simple negation, such as 'this is not white'. You say this, we will suppose, in the course of a discussion with the laundry. The phrase 'this is white' is in your mind, *this* is before your eyes, and 'this is grey' is a sentence describing your experience. But 'this is not white' is not a sentence describing what you see, and yet, on the basis of what you see, you are sure that it is true, in other words, that 'this is white' is false. It might be argued that you know the general proposition 'what is grey is not white', and that from this, together with 'this is grey', you infer 'this is not white'. Or it might be said that you can confront the word 'white' with what you see, and perceive an incompatibility. Either view has difficulties.

Let us first be clear on a point of logic. From premisses none of which contains the word 'not' or the word 'false' (or some equivalent) it is impossible logically to infer any proposition containing either of these words. Therefore, if there are negative empirical propositions, there must be, among basic propositions, either pure negations, such as 'this is not white', or implications of the form 'p implies not-q', e.g. 'if this is grey it is not white'. Logic allows no third possibility.

We certainly know – though it is difficult to say how we know

– that two different colours cannot coexist at the same place in one visual field. Position in the visual field is absolute, and may be defined by relation to the centre of the field by means of two angular coordinates which we may call θ, ϕ. I am saying that we know the following proposition: 'at a given time and in a given visual field, if the colour A is at the place θ, ϕ, no other colour B is at this place'. More simply: 'this is red' and 'this is blue' are incompatible.

The incompatibility is not logical. Red and blue are no more *logically* incompatible than red and round. Nor is the incompatibility a generalization from experience. I do not think I can *prove* that it is not a generalization from experience, but I think this is so obvious that no one, nowadays, would deny it. Some people say the incompatibility is grammatical. I do not deny this, but I am not sure what it means.

There are other sets of sensible qualities that have the same sort of incompatibility as colours have. A sensation of touch on the toe has a quality which enables us to refer it to the toe; a sensation of touch on the arm has a quality which which enables us to refer it to the arm. These two qualities are incompatible. 'Hot' and 'cold', 'hard' and 'soft', 'sweet' and 'sour', are similarly incompatible as applied to sensible experiences. In all these cases we 'see' the incompatibility. So much so that it requires some reflection to realize that an incompatibility such as that of 'white' and 'black' is not logical.

If we regard such incompatibilities as among basic propositions, we have to suppose that we know basic general propositions of the form: 'for all possible values of $x, \phi x$ implies not-ψx'. Here 'ϕx' may be 'x is blue', and 'ψx' may be 'x is red'. In that case, given a judgement of perception 'this is blue', we can infer 'this is not red'. We thus arrive at a negative empirical proposition, but by the help of a general proposition which is not empirical.

This is not a very plausible or satisfying theory. We may say, instead, that whenever we perceive 'this is blue', we can know, as a basic proposition, 'this is not red'. But I am not sure that this would help us much. For we must ask: how do we know that we can know this? It hardly seems to be an induction; it cannot be a logical inference. We shall therefore be driven to adopt a basic proposition even more complicated than the former one, namely: 'whoever sees red, and asks himself "is this blue?" knows that the answer is "no".'

I shall return to this problem in connexion with basic propositions. For the present, I will leave it unsolved.

I come now to the word 'or', and again I am concerned with the circumstances in which we know propositions containing this word, without knowing which alternative is the right one.

Disjunctions, as we have seen already, arise in practice in the form of a choice. You see a sign-post saying 'To Oxford', and presently you come to a fork in the road where there is no sign-post. You then believe the proposition 'Oxford is along the right-hand road or Oxford is along the left-hand road'. It is in situations of this sort that disjunctions occur in practice.

It is obvious that nothing in the non-linguistic or non-psychological world is 'indicated' by a disjunction. Suppose that, in fact, Oxford is to the right: this is not something verbal, it is a fact of geography, and if you go to the right you will get there. Similarly if, in fact, Oxford is to the left. There is not a third possible location, 'right-or-left'. Facts are what they are, without ambiguity. If a disjunction 'p or q' is true, it is true because p is true, or it is true because q is true; if p and q both belong to the primary language, 'p or q' is true in virtue of a fact which is 'expressed' by p, or in virtue of a fact which is 'expressed' by q. Thus 'or' lives in the world of propositions, and cannot form part of any language in which, as in the primary language, every word is directly related to an object, or to a set of objects, which is its meaning.

Psychologically, 'or' corresponds to a state of hesitation. A dog will wait at a fork in the road, to see which way you are going. If you put crumbs on the window-sill, you can see birds behaving in a manner which we should express by: 'shall I brave the danger or go hungry?' I once, to test the story of Buridan's ass, put a cat exactly half-way between her two kittens, both too young to move: for a time she found the disjunction paralysing. I think that animals in a state of hesitation, although they do not use words, have something more or less analogous to a 'propositional attitude', and I think any valid psychological explanation of the word 'or' must be applicable, with suitable adaptations, to any behaviour that shows hesitation.

Hesitation arises when we feel two incompatible impulses, and neither is strong enough to overcome the other.

> Thou'dst shun a bear,
> But if thy flight lay toward the raging sea,
> Thou'dst meet the bear i' the mouth.

But if the sea was not *very* raging, you might be left in complete doubt as to which was worse; you would have, one might say, a disjunction in your body, not only in your mind.

It will be remembered that we considered all speech to be fundamentally imperative: that is to say, it is designed to cause certain behaviour in the hearer. When 'those behind cried "forward", and those before cried "back"', the result upon people in the middle was a disjunction, in the sense in which animals may experience it, for instance tigers in a hunt when surrounded by beaters. It is not really necessary that there should be outsiders to cry 'forward' and 'back'. You can yourself have both motor impulses, and if you are used to words these impulses will suggest both words; you will then have a proper verbal disjunction. Inanimate matter, when subjected to two simultaneous forces, chooses a middle course, according to the parallelogram law; but animals seldom do this. No motorist, at a fork in the road, goes across the fields in the middle. As with motorists, so with other animals, either one impulse completely prevails, or there is inaction. But the inaction is quite different from that of a quiescent animal: it involves conflict and tension and discomfort; it is not genuine inaction, but search for some way of reaching a decision.

A disjunction is the verbal expression of indecision, or, if a question, of the desire to reach a decision.

Thus when someone asserts 'p or q', neither p nor q can be taken as saying something about the world, as would be the case if we asserted one of the alternatives; we have to consider the state of the person making the assertion. When we assert p, we are in a certain state; when we assert q, we are in a certain other state; when we assert 'p or q' we are in a state which is derivative from these two previous states, and we express this state, not something about the world. Our state is called 'true' if p is true, and also if q is true, but not otherwise; but this is a new definition.

But, it will be objected, if we know 'p or q', surely we know something about the world? To this question we may answer *yes* in one sense and *no* in another. To begin with the reasons for answering *no*: when we try to say what we know, we must use the word 'or' over again. We can say: in a world in which p is true, 'p or q' is true; similarly if q is true: in our illustration of the fork in the road, 'this road goes to Oxford' may express a geographical fact, and then 'this road or that goes to Oxford' is true; similarly if that road goes to Oxford; but there is no state of affairs in the non-linguistic world which is found when, and only when, this road *or* that goes to Oxford. Thus the straightforward correspondence theory of truth, which is valid in the primary language, is no longer available where disjunctions are concerned.

Here, however, there is a difficulty which must be examined, which brings us to the reasons for the opposite answer to our question. Often a single word is logically equivalent to a disjunction. The following conversation might occur between a medical logician and his wife. 'Has Mrs So-and-So had her child?' 'Yes.' 'Is it a boy or a girl?' 'Yes.' The last answer, though logically impeccable, would be infuriating. One may say 'a child is never a boy-or-girl, but only one of the alternatives'. For certain purposes, propositions containing the word 'child' are equivalent to the same propositions with the words 'boy or girl' substituted for 'child'; but for certain other purposes the equivalence fails. If I am told 'Mrs So-and-So has had a child', I can infer that she has had a boy or a girl. But if I then want to know whether she has had a boy or a girl, I do not want to know whether she has had a child, since I know this already.

In this question, it is necessary to separate psychology and logic. When, in daily talk, we use the word 'or', we do so, as a rule, because we are in doubt and wish to decide an alternative.

If we have no wish to decide the alternative, we shall be content with a generic word covering both possibilities. If you are to inherit Mrs So-and-So's money provided she dies childless, you will be interested in the question whether she has had a child, but only politeness will impel you to ask whether it is a boy or a girl. And clearly you know, in some sense, something about the world when you know a child has been born, even though you do not know its sex.

Is there any distinction, and if so what, between disjunctive predicates and others? If 'A' and 'B' are two predicates, 'A' is logically equivalent to 'A-and-B or A-and-not-B'. Thus so far as logic is concerned, any predicate can be replaced by a disjunction. From the psychological point of view, on the other hand, there is a clear distinction. A predicate is disjunctive if we feel a desire to decide alternatives which it leaves open; if not, it is not. But this is not quite adequate. The alternatives must be such as the predicate itself suggests, not irrelevant possibilities. Thus 'boy' is not to be considered disjunctive because it leaves open the question 'dark or fair?' Thus a predicate is only disjunctive if it *suggests* a question, and whether it does so or not depends solely upon the interests of the person concerned.

All our knowledge about the world, in so far as it is expressed in words, is more or less general, because every sentence contains at least one word that is not a proper name, and all such words are general. Consequently every sentence is logically equivalent to a disjunction, in which the predicate is replaced by the alternative of two more specific predicates. Whether a sentence gives us a *feeling* of knowledge or of doubt depends upon whether it leaves open alternatives calling for different actions and emotions or not. Every disjunction which is not logically exhaustive (i.e., not such as 'A or not-A') gives *some* information about the world, if it is true; but the information may leave us so hesitant as to what to do that it is *felt* as ignorance.

Owing to the fact that words are general, the correspondence of fact and sentence which constitutes truth is many-one, i.e., the truth of the sentence leaves the character of the fact more or less indeterminate. This indeterminateness can be diminished without limit; in the process of diminishing it, former single words are replaced by disjunctions. 'This is metal' may satisfy us for some purposes; for others, such a statement must be replaced by 'this is iron or copper or, etc.', and we must seek to decide which possibility is realized. There is no point in the growing precision of language beyond which we cannot go; our language can always be rendered less inexact, but can never become quite exact.

Thus the difference between a statement which is disjunctive and one which is not does not consist in any difference in the state of affairs which would make it true, but solely in the question whether the difference between the possibilities which our statement leaves open is interesting to us or not.

There is another situation in which a disjunction may arise in practice, and that is where there is imperfect memory. 'Who told you that?' 'Well, it was either Brown or Jones, but I can't remember which.' 'What is So-and-So's telephone number?' 'I know it is 514 or 541, but I can't be sure which is right without looking it up.' In such cases, there was originally an experience which gave rise to a judgement of perception, in which there was no disjunction; and if you were to set to work to find out the truth, you would prove one of the alternatives, and again there would be no disjunction. Basic propositions, when they are expressions of present experience, never contain the word 'or' unless the experience is verbal; but *memories* may be disjunctive.

We come now to propositions containing the word 'some' or the word 'all'. We considered these, in the previous chapter, to the extent required to satisfy ourselves that they could not be included in the primary language, but we want now to consider them more positively, and particularly to consider the circumstances that lead us to make use of such propositions.

Propositions about 'some' arise, in practice, in four ways: first, as generalizations of disjunctions; secondly, when, having come across an instance, we are interested in the compatibility of two general terms which might have been thought incompatible; thirdly, as steps on the way to a generalization; and fourthly, in cases of imperfect memory analogous to those that we considered in connexion with disjunction. Let us illustrate these successively.

In our former illustration of the road to Oxford, if, instead of a mere fork, we had come to a place where a great many roads branched off, we might have said: 'well, *some* road must lead to Oxford'. Here the alternatives can be enumerated, and we have merely an abbreviation of a disjunction 'p or q or r or . . .', where $p, q, r, \ldots$ can all be collected into one verbal formula.

The second kind of case is more interesting. It is illustrated by Hamlet, when he says: 'one may smile and smile and be a villain; at least I am sure it may be so in Denmark'. He has discovered a person (namely the King) who combines smiling with villainy, and has arrived at the proposition: 'at least one villain smiles'. The pragmatic value of the proposition is: 'next time I meet a man who smiles and smiles, I will suspect him of villainy'. He does so in the case of Rosencrantz and Gildenstern. Similar to this are the propositions 'some swans are black' and 'some blackbirds are white'; they are warnings against plausible generalizations. We make such propositions when the generalization is more interesting to us than the particular instance – though in Hamlet's case this is an ironical pretence.

The third kind of case arises when we are trying to prove an inductive generalization, and also when instances lead us to discover a general proposition in mathematics. These cases are similar, except that in the latter you arrive at certainty, and in the former only at probability. Let us take the latter case first. You observe that $1 + 3 = 2^2$, $1 + 3 + 5 = 3^2$, $1 + 3 + 5 + 7 = 4^2$, and you say to yourself: 'in some cases, the sum of the first n odd numbers is n^2; perhaps this is true in all cases'. As soon as this hypothesis has occurred to you, it is easy to prove that it is correct. In empirical material, a complete enumeration may sometimes be possible. You discover (say) that iron and copper, which are metals, are good conductors of electricity, and you suspect that this may be true of all metals. In this case, the generalization has the same degree of certainty as the instances. But when you argue: 'A, B, and C died, and were men, therefore some men are mortal; therefore perhaps all men are mortal', you cannot make your generalization as certain as its instances, both because you cannot enumerate men and because some have not yet died. Or take a cure for a disease which, so far, has only been tried in a few cases, but in all of them has proved beneficial; in this case a proposition about *some* is very useful as suggesting the possibility of a proposition about *all*.

In regard to imperfect memory, the instances are closely analogous to those of disjunctions. 'I know that book is somewhere in my shelves, because I saw it yesterday.' 'I dined with Mr B, who made a most admirable joke, but unfortunately I have forgotten it.' 'There are some very good lines in *The Excursion*, but I can't remember any of them.' Thus a great deal of what we know at any given time consists of propositions about *some* which we cannot, at the moment, deduce from propositions with singular subjects, nor yet from propositions about *all*.

A statement about *some* has, as our four kinds of instances have shown, three kinds of uses: it may be a step towards the proof of a proposition with a singular subject, or towards the proof of a general proposition, or it may be a refutation of a contrary generalization. In the first and fourth classes of cases, the proposition about *some* is intended to lead on to a proposition with a singular subject: '*this* is the road to Oxford' or '*here* is that book' (where I take *here* as the subject). There is this difference between the first and fourth classes of cases, that in the first the proposition about *some* is always an inference, whereas in the fourth it is not. In the second and third classes of cases, the proposition 'some S is P' is deduced from instances 'S_1 is P', 'S_2 is P', etc.; it tells us less than they do, but tells us the part that is useful for the purpose in hand.

What exactly do we know when we know a proposition of the form 'some S is P' without knowing either 'all S is P' or some proposition of the form 'S_1 is P'? Let us take as our example 'I know that book is somewhere in this room'. There are two circumstances which would logically justify you in saying this, though in neither case would you say it unless you were a professional logician. The first would be if the room were filled with that book – say a publisher's room, completely stacked with copies of a certain best seller. You could then say: 'every place in this room contains the book in question, therefore (since the room exists) some place contains it'. Or you might be seeing the book, and argue: 'this place contains it, therefore some place contains it'. But in fact, unless you were engaged in teaching logic, you would never argue in this way. When you say 'that book is *somewhere* in this room', you say so because you cannot be more definite.

It is obvious that 'the book is *somewhere* in the room' cannot be a judgement of perception; you cannot perceive *somewhere*, you can only perceive *there*. But a judgement of memory is different. You may remember 'I saw the book when I was in this room', or something of that kind. You may remember saying 'Oh there's that book' while you were in the room. Or you may have a pure verbal memory of saying 'I see I did put that book on a shelf'. These, however, are only the grounds for your judgement; they are not an analysis of it.

The analysis of such a judgement must be essentially similar to that of a disjunction. There is a state of mind in which you perceive 'the book is in this place', another in which you perceive 'the book is in that place', and so on. The state of mind when you judge 'the book is somewhere in the room' contains what all these have in common, together with perplexity. It is because of the absence of perplexity that you would not make the judgement in the above two cases in which it could be deduced from more definite judgements. To this, however, there is an exception: if you have doubted whether the book is in the room, and then you see it, you may say 'so the book *is* in the room'. This is no longer our present case, but that of the smiling villain.

In the case of a judgement about *some*, as in disjunction, we cannot interpret the words except in reference to a state of mind. We cannot, in fact, ever so interpret our words except in the primary language.

Most of what we have said about 'some' applies also to 'all'. There is, however, an important difference in regard to knowledge. We often know propositions about 'some', and they can be proved empirically, although they cannot express facts of direct observation. But propositions about 'all' are much more difficult to know, and can never be proved unless there are some such propositions among our premisses. Since there are no such propositions among judgements of perception, it might be thought that we must either forgo all general propositions or abandon empiricism. Yet this seems to contradict common sense. Take an instance we have already discussed, 'there is no cheese in the larder'. It seems preposterous to maintain that, if we accept statements of this sort, we abandon empiricism. Or take another instance we have already discussed, 'everyone in this village is called Williams', arrived at by complete enumeration. There is, however, a difficulty, which is illustrated by Hamlet's mother when he asks if she does not see the ghost:

HAMLET: Do you see nothing there?
QUEEN: Nothing at all; yet all that is I see.

I have always wondered how she knew she saw 'all that is'. But she was right in regarding this as a necessary premiss for her denial of the ghost; and so it is for the man who says there is no cheese in the larder, and nobody in the village not called Williams. Clearly the question of our knowledge of general propositions involves difficulties as yet unsolved.

I am not at all sure that empiricists are right when they reject from among basic propositions all extra-logical general statements. We have already considered the statement 'no visual place contains two different colours', which seems to be a case in point. Or, to take an even more inescapable instance, suppose you live in a remote country place, and you are expecting the arrival of a friend in a car. Your wife says 'do you hear anything?' and after listening for a moment you answer 'no'. Have you, in giving this answer, abandoned empiricism? You have committed yourself to a stupendous generalization, namely: 'everything in the universe is not a sound now heard by me'. And yet no one can maintain that experience does not justify your statement. I think, therefore, that apart from logic, we do know some general propositions otherwise than by inductive generalization. This, however, is a very large question. I shall return to it in a later chapter; for the moment, I only wish to enter a *caveat*.

The question arises: do logical words involve anything psychological? You may see something, and say 'this is yellow'; afterwards you may say 'it was yellow or orange, but I can't remember which'. One has a feeling that, in such a case, the yellow was a fact in the world, whereas 'yellow or orange' could only exist in someone's mind. It is extremely difficult to avoid confusion in considering this question, but I think what can be said is this: The non-mental world can be completely described without the use of any logical word, though we cannot, without the word 'all', *state* that the description is complete; but when we come to the mental world, there are facts which cannot be mentioned without the use of logical words. In the above instance, I remember that it was yellow or orange; in a complete description of the world, this recollection must be mentioned, and it cannot be mentioned without using the word 'or' or some equivalent. Thus while the word 'or' does not occur in the basic propositions of physics, it does occur in some of the basic propositions of psychology, since it is an observable fact that people sometimes believe disjunctions. And the same is true of the words 'not', 'some', and 'all'.

If this is true, it is important. It shows, for instance, that we cannot accept one possible interpretation of the thesis which Carnap calls 'physicalism', which maintains that all science can be expressed in the language of physics. It might, however, be contended that, in describing what happens when a man believes 'p or q', the 'or' that we must use is not the same as the 'or' of logic. It is possible to contend, more generally, that when we assert 'A believes p', the p is not the same as when we assert 'p', and that the difference ought to be indicated by writing 'A believes "p"'. If we were speaking of what A says, not of what he believes, we should certainly have to make this distinction. A says 'fire', and we say 'A says "fire"'. In what we say, 'fire' occurs as denoting a word, whereas in what A says it occurs as denoting an object. This whole question is a very difficult one, and I shall consider it in a later chapter in connexion with propositional attitudes. Meanwhile, we must bear in mind that, *prima facie*, logical words, though not necessary in describing physical facts, are indispensable for the description of certain mental facts.

CHAPTER 6

PROPER NAMES*

IT is customary in logic to divide words into categories: names, predicates, dyadic relations, triadic relations, etc. This is not the total of words; it does not include logical words, and it is doubtful whether it includes words for 'propositional attitudes', such as 'believe', 'desire', 'doubt', etc. There is also difficulty about 'egocentric particulars', i.e. 'I', 'this', 'now', 'here', etc. Propositional attitudes and egocentric particulars will be considered in due course. For the present, it is names that I wish to consider.

To avoid verbiage, I shall speak of predicates, when convenient, as 'monadic relations'. Thus we are concerned with the distinction between names and relations, in regard to which we have to ask two questions:

(1) Can we invent a language without the distinction of names and relations?

(2) If not, what is the minimum of names required in order to express what we know or understand? And, in connexion with this question, which of our ordinary words are to be considered names?

As to the first of these problems, I have very little to say. It may be possible to invent a language without names, but for my part I am totally incapable of imagining such a language. This is not a conclusive argument, except subjectively: it puts an end to my power of discussing the question.

It is my purpose, however, to suggest a view which might seem at first sight equivalent to the abolition of names. I propose to abolish what are usually called 'particulars', and be content with certain words that would usually be regarded as universals, such as 'red', 'blue', 'hard', 'soft', and so on. These words, I shall suggest, are names in the syntactical sense; I am not there-

* The subjects of this chapter and the next will be resumed in Chapter 24.

fore seeking to abolish names, but to suggest an unusual extension for the word 'name'.

Let us begin with the definition of the word 'name'. For this purpose we might first define 'atomic forms'.

A sentence is of atomic form when it contains no logical words and no subordinate sentence. It must not contain 'or', 'not', 'all', 'some' or any equivalent; nor must it be such as 'I think it will rain', because this contains the subordinate sentence 'it will rain'. Positively, a sentence is of atomic form if it contains one relation-word (which may be a predicate) and the smallest number of other words required to form a sentence. If R_1 is a predicate, R_2 a dyadic relation, R_3 a triadic relation, etc.

$$R_1(x), R_2(x, y), R_3(x, y, z), \ldots$$

will be sentences of atomic form, provided x, y, z are such words as make the sentences concerned significant.

If $R_n(x_1, x_2, x_3, \ldots x_n)$ is a sentence of atomic form, in which R_n is an n-adic relation, $x_1, x_2, x_3, \ldots x_n$ are *names*. We may define a 'name' as any word that can occur in any species of atomic sentence, i.e. in a subject-predicate sentence, a dyadic-relation sentence, a triadic-relation sentence, and so on. A word other than a name, if it can occur in an atomic sentence, can only occur in an atomic sentence of one species; e.g. if R_n is an n-adic relation, the only species of atomic sentence in which R_n can occur is $R_n(x_1, x_2, x_3 \ldots x_n)$. A name can occur in an atomic sentence containing any number of words; a relation can only occur in combination with a certain fixed number of other words appropriate to that relation.

This affords a syntactical definition of the word 'name'. It should be observed that no metaphysical assumptions are involved in the notion of 'atomic forms'. Such assumptions only appear if it is assumed that the names and relations appearing in an atomic sentence are incapable of analysis. In connexion with certain problems it may be important to know whether our terms can be analysed, but in connexion with names this is not important. The only way in which any analogous question enters into the discussion of names is in connexion with descriptions, which often masquerade as names. But whenever we have a sentence of the form

'The x satisfying ϕx satisfies ψx'

we presuppose the existence of sentences of the forms 'ϕa' and 'ψa', where 'a' is a name. Thus the question whether a given phrase is a name or a description may be ignored in a fundamental discussion of the place of names in syntax. For our purposes, unless reason should appear to the contrary, we may accept as a name whatever would ordinarily be considered as such: Tom, Dick, and Harry, the sun, the moon, England, France, etc. But as we proceed it will appear that, even though such words be names, they are for the most part not indispensable for the expression of what we know. *Per contra*, though some among indispensable words are, I believe, to be classed as names, these are, all of them, words not traditionally so classed.

Names, *prima facie*, are of two sorts: those that, like the names mentioned in the last paragraph, designate some continuous portion of space-time, and those that have an egocentric definition, such as 'I', 'you', 'this', 'that'. This latter class of words I propose to consider later; for the present, I shall ignore them. We are concerned only, therefore, with such names as designate, without ambiguity in principle, some definite continuous portion of space-time.

The first question to be considered is: how do we distinguish one region of space-time from another? This leads ultimately to such questions as: if there were in New York an Eiffel Tower exactly like the one in Paris, would there be two Eiffel Towers, or one Eiffel Tower in two places? If history repeated itself, would the world be in two exactly similar states on two different occasions, or would one and the same state occur twice, i.e., precede itself? The answers to such questions are only partly arbitrary; in any case, they are indispensable for the theory of names.

The theory of names has been neglected, because its importance is only evident to the logician, and to him names can remain purely hypothetical, since no proposition of logic can contain any actual name. For theory of knowledge, however, it is important to know what sort of objects can have names, assuming that there are names. One is tempted to regard 'this is red' as a subject-predicate proposition; but if one does so, one finds that 'this' becomes a substance, an unknowable something in which predicates inhere, but which, nevertheless, is not identical with the sum of its predicates. Such a view is open to all the familiar objections to the notion of substance. It has, however, certain advantages in relation to space-time. If 'this is red' is a proposition ascribing a quality to a substance, and if a substance is not defined by the sum of its predicates, then it is possible for *this* and *that* to have exactly the same predicates without being identical. This might seem essential if we are to say, as we should like to say, that the supposed Eiffel Tower in New York would not be identical with the one in Paris.

I wish to suggest that 'this is red' is not a subject-predicate proposition, but is of the form 'redness is here'; that 'red' is a name, not a predicate; and that what would commonly be called a 'thing' is nothing but a bundle of coexisting qualities such as redness, hardness, etc. If this view is adopted, however, the identity of indiscernibles becomes analytic, and the supposed Eiffel Tower in New York would be strictly identical with the one in Paris if really indiscernible from it. This requires, when analysed, that spatial and temporal relations, such as *to-the-left-of* or *before*, should not imply diversity. This causes difficulties in the construction of space-time as required in physics, and these difficulties must be overcome before the view that I am suggesting can be considered a possible one. I think they can be overcome, but only by admitting as empirical and doubtful certain propositions which have seemed certain, such as 'if A is to the left of B, A and B are not identical', where A and B are the nearest approach to 'things' that our theory allows.

Let us first establish a useful piece of vocabulary. Let us give the name 'qualities' to specific shades of colour, specific degrees of hardness, sounds completely defined as to pitch and loudness and every other distinguishable characteristic, and so on. Although we cannot, in perception, distinguish exact from approximate similarity, whether in colour or in any other kind of quality, we can, by experience, be led to the conception of exact similarity, since it is transitive, whereas approximate similarity is not. Given a visual area, we can define its colour as the group of those visual areas which are similar in colour to it and to each other, and not all similar in colour to anything outside the group.* In this definition, however, we have assumed that, if a given shade of colour exists in two visual areas, each visual area can be given a name; we have, in fact, assumed the distinction of *this* and *that*, apart from qualities, which we were intending to avoid. Let us, therefore, accept qualities as undefined terms for the present, and return later to the question of distinguishing between two qualities so similar that they cannot be distinguished in immediate perception.

Common sense regards a 'thing' as having qualities, but not as defined by them; it is defined by spatio-temporal position. I wish to suggest that, wherever there is, for common sense, a 'thing' having the quality C, we should say, instead, that C itself exists in that place, and that the 'thing' is to be replaced by the collection of qualities existing in the place in question. Thus 'C' becomes a name, not a predicate.

The main reason in favour of this view is that it gets rid of an unknowable. We experience qualities, but not the subject in which they are supposed to inhere. The introduction of an unknowable can generally, perhaps always, be avoided by suitable technical devices, and clearly it should be avoided whenever possible.

The main difficulty of the view that I am advocating is as regards the definition of 'place'. Let us see whether this difficulty can be overcome.

Suppose we see simultaneously two patches of a given shade of colour C; let the angular coordinates of the one patch in visual space be θ, ϕ, and those of the other θ', ϕ'. Then we are to say that C is at (θ, ϕ) and also at (θ', ϕ').

The angular coordinates of an object in the visual field may be regarded as qualities. Thus (C, θ, ϕ) is one bundle of qualities, and (C, θ', ϕ') is another. If we define a 'thing' as the bundle of qualities (C, θ, ϕ), then we may say that this 'thing' is at the place (θ, ϕ), and it is analytic that it is not at the place (θ', ϕ').

* Cf. Carnap's *Logischer Aufbau der Welt*.

Let us extend this process to the construction of physical space-time. If I start from Greenwich with a good chronometer, or with a receiving set on which I receive a daily message at noon G.M.T., I can determine my latitude and longitude by observation. Similarly I can measure altitude. Thus I can determine three co-ordinates which uniquely determine my position relative to Greenwich, and Greenwich itself can be defined by similar observations. We may, for simplicity, treat the coordinates of a place as qualities; in that case, the place may be defined as *being* its coordinates. It is therefore analytic that no two places have the same coordinates.

This is all very well, but it conceals the element of empirical fact upon which the utility of latitude and longitude depends. Suppose two ships ten miles apart, but able to see each other. We say that, if their instruments are sufficiently accurate, they will give different values for the latitude and longitude of the two ships. This is a question of empirical fact, not of definition; for when I say that the ships are ten miles apart, I am saying something which can be proved by observations quite independent of those that determine latitude and longitude. Geometry as an empirical science is concerned with such observed facts as the following: if the distance between the two ships is calculated from the difference of their latitude and longitude, we shall obtain the same result as if it is calculated by means of direct observations made of either ship from the other. All such observed facts are summed up by the statement that space is roughly Euclidean and that the surface of the earth is roughly spherical.

Thus the empirical element comes in when we explain the *utility* of latitude and longitude, but not in giving the *definition*. Latitude and longitude are connected by physical laws with other things with which they are not connected logically. It is empirical that if you can see that two places are a long way apart, they will not be found to have the same latitude and longitude; this is what we should naturally express by saying that a place on the earth's surface is uniquely defined by its latitude and longitude.

When I say that redness can be in two places at once, I mean that redness can have to itself one or more of those spatial relations which, according to common sense, no 'thing' can have to itself. Redness may be to the right of redness, or above redness, in the immediate visual field; redness may be in America and in Europe, in physical space. We need, for physics, something that cannot be in America and Europe at the same time; for physics, nothing can count as a 'thing' unless it occupies a continuous portion of space-time, which redness does not. Nay, more: whatever occupies more than a point of space-time must, for physics, be divisible into smaller 'things'. Our purpose is, if possible to construct out of qualities bundles having the spatio-temporal properties that physics requires of 'things'.

Latitude, longitude, and altitude are, of course, not directly observed qualities, but they are definable in terms of qualities, and it is therefore a harmless avoidance of circumlocution to call them qualities. They, unlike redness, have the necessary geometrical properties. If θ, ϕ, h are a latitude, a longitude, and an altitude, we shall find that the bundle (θ, ϕ, h) cannot be north or south or east or west or above or below itself, as redness can. If we define a 'place' by the coordinates (θ, ϕ, h), spatial relations will have the properties we expect of them; if we define it by such qualities as redness and hardness, it will not.

So much for space – let us now consider time.

In regard to time, we desire to find empirical objects such that, in regard to them, time shall be serial, that is to say, we desire to find a class definable in terms of observable objects, such that, if x, y, z are members of the class, we shall have:

(1) x does not precede x;
(2) if x precedes y and y precedes z, then x precedes z;
(3) if x and y are different, either x precedes y or y precedes x.

We may, to begin with, ignore the third of these conditions, which applies only to instants, not to events. The construction of instants as classes of events is a problem with which I have dealt elsewhere.

What we want is a class of events having a temporal uniqueness analogous to the spatial uniqueness of latitude, longitude, and altitude.

Artificially, we can take the date and time of day as determined by an observatory. But here mistakes are possible; we want, if possible, something less artificial.

Eddington uses for this purpose the second law of thermodynamics. The drawback to this is that the law only holds of the universe as a whole, and may be false as applied to any finite volume; but only finite volumes are observable. While, therefore, Eddington's method might be satisfactory for omniscience, it is more or less inadequate for us empirically.

Bergson's memory, if one could believe in it, would serve our purpose perfectly. According to him, nothing experienced is ever forgotten; therefore my memories at an earlier date are a subclass of my memories at a later date. My total memories at different times can, therefore, be serially ordered by the relation of class-inclusion, and the times can be serially ordered by correlation with the total memories. Perhaps memory could be used for our purpose without the assumption that nothing is ever forgotten, but I am inclined to doubt this. In any case, memory is useless in relation to geological and astronomical time, which includes periods during which no memory is supposed to have existed.

Before proceeding with the search for a class of events having the desired properties, let us consider a little more carefully what it is that we are supposing. We are supposing that there are only qualities, not also instances of qualities. Since a given shade of colour can exist at two different dates, it can precede itself; therefore 'preceding' is not in general asymmetrical, but will be so, at best, in regard to some special kind of qualities or bundles of qualities. It is not logically necessary that any such kind should exist; if it does, that is a fortunate empirical fact.

Many writers have imagined that history is cyclic, that the present state of the world, exactly as it is now, will sooner or later recur. How shall we state this hypothesis on our view? We shall have to say that the later state is numerically identical with the earlier state; and we cannot say that this state occurs twice, since that would imply a system of dating which the hypothesis makes impossible. The situation would be analogous to that of a man who travels round the world: he does not say that his starting-point and his point of arrival are two different but precisely similar places, he says they are the same place. The hypothesis that history is cyclic can be expressed as follows: form the group of all qualities contemporaneous with a given quality; in certain cases the whole of this group precedes itself. Or: in these cases, every group of simultaneous qualities, however large, precedes itself. Such an hypothesis cannot be regarded as logically impossible so long as we say that only qualities occur. To make it impossible, we should have to suppose a momentary subject of qualities, and to hold that this subject owes its identity, not to its character, but to its space-time position.

The identity of indiscernibles, which follows analytically from our theory, is rejected by Wittgenstein and others on the ground that, even if a and b agree in all their properties, they may still be two. This assumes that identity is indefinable. Moreover it makes enumeration theoretically impossible. Suppose you wish to count a collection of five objects A, B, C, D, E, and suppose that B and C are indistinguishable. It follows that, in the moment of counting B, you will also count C, and therefore you will conclude that there are four objects to be counted. To say that B and C are 'really' two, although they seem one, is to say something which, if B and C are totally indistinguishable, seems wholly devoid of meaning. Indeed, I should claim it as the principal merit of the theory I am advocating that it makes the identity of indiscernibles analytic.

Let us now return to the search for a set of qualities, or groups of qualities, which has the properties required for constructing the time-series. I do not think this can be done without taking account of empirical laws; it follows that it cannot be done with certainty. But so long as we are not in search of logical certainty, we can arrive at what is empirically sufficient by the means which we formerly rejected, e.g., memory and the second law of thermodynamics. Not all the causal laws with which we are acquainted are reversible, and those that are not afford means of dating. It is easy to construct a clock which, in addition to showing hours and minutes, will every day exhibit a number greater by one than that exhibited on the previous day. By such means we can make sure of having a complex of qualities which will not recur, at any rate while our civilization lasts. More than this we cannot *know*, though we may find reason to think a large-scale exact recurrence very improbable.

My conclusion is that qualities suffice, without our having to suppose that they have instances. Incidentally, we have reduced to the empirical level certain properties of spatio-temporal relations which threatened to be synthetic *a priori* general truths.

From the standpoint of theory of knowledge, there is still a question to be answered before our theory can be considered established. It is part of the larger question of the relation of conceptual precision to sensible vagueness. All science uses concepts which are in theory precise, but in practice more or less vague. 'One metre' was defined with all possible care by the French Revolutionary Government: it was the distance between two marks on a certain rod at a certain temperature. But there were two difficulties: the marks were not points, and temperature cannot be determined exactly. Or take time-determinations, say midnight G.M.T. at the end of 31 December 1900. (The English thought this was the end of the nineteenth century, but they ought to have substituted the meridian of Bethlehem for that of Greenwich.) Midnight can only be determined by observations, say of chronometers; but no observation is exact, i.e., there is a finite period of time during which any given chronometer will *seem* to point to midnight; and, moreover, no chronometer is exactly right. Therefore no one could know exactly when the nineteenth century ended. Two views may be taken of this situation: first, that there was an exact instant when the century ended; second, that exactness is illusory, and that precise dating is even conceptually impossible.

Let us apply similar considerations to the case of colours, which more directly concerns our present problem. I have supposed that a proper name should be given to each shade of colour, but a shade of colour has the same kind of precision as an exact date or an exact metre, and can never be determined in practice.

There is a formal procedure which is applicable to all the cases in which we seek to derive, from something given in sense, a concept having an exactness that is no part of the datum. This is a device for passing from *indistinguishability* to *identity*. Let 'S' stand for 'indistinguishability'. Then given two patches of colour, we may observe that the shade of one patch has the relation S to the shade of the other. We can, however, prove that S does not imply identity, for identity is transitive, but S is not. That is to say, given three shades of colour x, y, z, existing in three visible patches, we may have x S y and y S z but not x S z. Therefore x is not identical with z, and therefore y cannot be identical with both x and z, although it is indistinguishable from both. We can only say that x and y are identical if x S z always implies y S z, and vice versa. The precise shade of colour of x can now be defined as the colour common to all patches y which are such that whatever is indistinguishable in colour from x is also indistinguishable in colour from y, and vice versa, so that every patch is distinguishable from both x and y or from neither.

This reduces the determination of the precise shade of some given coloured patch to the collection of a number of data each one of which can, in principle, be obtained from observation. The difficulty, now, is not in relation to any one of the requisite data, but in relation to their multiplicity. Our definition supposes, in its second clause, that *every* patch of colour z can be compared with every y that is indistinguishable from x. This is, in practice, impossible, since it requires a complete survey of the visible universe, past, present, and future. We can never know that two patches x and y are of the same shade, for, though every z that we have observed may have the relation S either to both or to neither, a new z may always be found later for which this is not true. Consequently, if 'C' is the name of an exact shade of colour, no proposition of the form 'C exists here' can ever be known, unless 'C' is defined as 'the shade that exists here'.

It should be observed that difficulties of the same sort exist in regard to all empirical concepts. Take, e.g., the concept 'man'. If all the stages in the evolution of modern man were spread out before us, there would be some specimens of which we should say unhesitatingly 'that is a man', and others of which we should say unhesitatingly 'that is not a man'; but there would be intermediate specimens concerning which we should be doubtful. In theory, nothing that we can do to make our definition more precise will avoid this uncertainty. It may be that, in fact, at some stage in evolution there was such a great and sudden mutation as to justify us in giving the name 'man' to what came after but not to what went before, but if so this is a lucky accident, and intermediate forms could still be imagined. In short, every empirical concept has the sort of vagueness that is obvious in such examples as 'tall' or 'bald'. Some men are certainly tall, others are certainly not tall; but of intermediate men we should say: 'tall? Yes, I *think* so,' or 'no, I shouldn't be inclined to call him tall'. This state of affairs is to be found, in a greater or less degree, in regard to every empirical quality.

Science consists largely of devices for inventing concepts having a greater degree of precision than is found in the concepts of every-day life. The degree of precision possessed by a concept is capable of exact numerical definition. Let '$P(x)$' mean 'x has the predicate P'. Let us survey all the known instances of things of the sort that might be expected to have the predicate P; suppose the number of such things to be n. Suppose that in m of these instances we can definitely assert 'not-$P(x)$'. Then m/n is a measure of the precision of our concept P. Take for example measurement: the statement 'the length of this rod exceeds or falls short of one metre' can, by scientific methods, be shown to be true except in a very small percentage of cases, but rough-and-ready methods leave a much larger percentage of doubtful cases. But now take 'the length of this rod is one metre'. This can never be proved, but it cannot be *disproved* in the cases in which our previous proposition cannot be proved. Thus the more precision we give to a concept, the oftener it can be proved to be inapplicable, and the seldomer it can be proved to be applicable. When it is completely precise, it can *never* be proved to be applicable.

If 'metre' is intended to be a precise concept, we shall have to divide lengths into three classes: (1) those certainly less than a metre; (2) those certainly greater than a metre; (3) those belonging to neither of the first two classes. We may, however, think it preferable to make 'metre' an inexact concept; it will then mean 'any length which, by existing scientific methods, is not distinguishable from that of the standard metre'. In that case, we can sometimes say 'the length of this rod is one metre'. But the truth of what we say is now relative to existing technique; an improvement in the apparatus of measurement may make it false.

All that we have been saying about lengths applies, *mutatis mutandis*, to shades of colour. If colours are defined by wavelengths, the argument applies word for word. It is evident that, throughout, the fundamental empirical concept is indistinguishability. Technical devices can diminish but not wholly remove the inexactness essential to this concept.

We shall say: the colour of this given patch is to be called 'C'. Then the colours of all other patches are divided into two classes: (1) those that we know to be not C; (2) those that we do not know to be not C. The whole purpose of methods of precision is to make the second class as small as possible. But we can never reach the point where we know that a member of the second class must be identical with C; all that we can do is to make the second class consist of colours more and more like C.

We thus arrive at the following statement: I give the name 'C' to the shade of colour that I see at the visual place (θ, ϕ); I give the name 'C' to the colour at (θ', ϕ'). It may be that C and C' are distinguishable; then they are certainly different. It may be that they are indistinguishable, but that there is a colour C'' distinguishable from one, but not from the other; in that case also, C and C' are certainly different. Finally, it may be that every colour known to me is either distinguishable from both or indistinguishable from both; in that case, C and C' *may* be identical, i.e., 'C' and 'C'' may be two names for the same thing. But since I can never know that I have surveyed *all* colours, I can never be sure that C and C' are identical.

This answers the question concerning the relation of conceptual precision to sensible vagueness.

It remains, however, to examine possible objections to our theory derived from what I call 'egocentric particulars'. This will be done in the next chapter.

CHAPTER 7

EGOCENTRIC PARTICULARS

THE words with which I shall be concerned in this chapter are those of which the denotation is relative to the speaker. Such are *this, that, I, you, here, there, now, then, past, present, future*. Tense in verbs must also be included. Not only 'I am hot', but 'Jones is hot', has a significance which is only determinate when we know the time at which the statement is made. The same applies to 'Jones was hot', which signifies 'Jones's hotness precedes the present', and thus changes its significance as the present changes.

All egocentric words can be defined in terms of 'this'. Thus: 'I' means 'The biography to which this belongs'; 'here' means 'The place of this'; 'now' means 'The time of this'; and so on. We may therefore confine our inquiry to 'this'. It does not seem equally feasible to take some other egocentric word as fundamental, and define 'this' in terms of it. Perhaps, if we gave a name to 'I-now', as opposed to 'I-then', this name could replace 'this'; but no word of common speech seems capable of replacing it.

Before embarking upon more difficult questions, let us observe that no egocentric particulars occur in the language of physics. Physics views space-time impartially, as God might be supposed to view it; there is not, as in perception, a region which is specially warm and intimate and bright, surrounded in all directions by gradually growing darkness. A physicist will not say 'I saw a table', but like Neurath* or Julius Caesar, 'Otto saw a table'; he will not say 'A meteor is visible now', but 'A meteor was visible at 8h. 43m. G.M.T.', and in this statement 'was' is intended to be without tense. There can be no question that the non-mental world can be fully described without the use of egocentric words. Certainly a great deal of what psychology

* See Chapter 10.

wishes to say can also dispense with them. Is there, then, any need for these words at all? Or can *everything* be said without them? The question is not easy.

Before we can investigate this question, we must decide, if we can, what is meant by the word 'this', and why egocentric particulars have been found convenient.

The word 'this' appears to have the character of a proper name, in the sense that it merely designates an object without in any degree describing it. It might be thought to ascribe to an object the property of being present to attention, but this would be a mistake: many objects on many occasions are present to attention, but on each occasion only one is *this*. We may say: 'this' means 'the object of *this* act of attention'; but this obviously is no definition. 'This' is a name which we give to the object to which we are attending, but we cannot define 'this' as 'the object to which I now attend', because 'I' and 'now' involve 'this'.* The word 'this' does not mean: 'what is in common among all the objects successively called "this"'; for on each occasion when the word 'this' is used there is only one object to which the word applies. 'This' is apparently a proper name which is applied to different objects on every two occasions when it is used, and yet it is never ambiguous. It is not like the name 'Smith', which applies to many objects, but to each always; the name 'this' applies to only one object at a time, and when it begins to apply to a new object it ceases to be applicable to the old one.

We may state our problem as follows. The word 'this' is one word, which has, *in some sense*, a constant meaning. But if we treat it as a mere name, it cannot have in any sense a constant meaning, for a name means merely what it designates, and the designatum of 'this' is continually changing. If, on the other hand, we treat 'this' as a concealed description, e.g., 'the object of attention', it will then always apply to everything that is ever a 'this', whereas in fact it never applies to more than one thing at a time. Any attempt to avoid this undesired generality will involve a surreptitious reintroduction of 'this' into the *definiens*.

---

* Or, if we take 'I-now' as fundamental, exactly the same problems will arise concerning it as those that otherwise arise concerning 'this'.

(There is yet another problem about 'this', which is connected with the subject of proper names, and throws doubt, *prima facie*, on the conclusion of the preceding chapter. If we see simultaneously two patches of a given shade of colour, we shall say: 'this and that are precisely similar in colour'. We shall have no doubt that one of them is *this* and the other *that*; nothing will persuade us that the two are one. This, however, is a puzzle that is easily resolved. What we see is not *merely* a patch of colour, but a patch in a given visual direction. If 'this' means 'a patch in such a direction' and 'that' means 'a patch in such another direction', these two complexes are different, and there is no reason to infer that the bare colour is twofold.)

Is 'this' a name, or a description, or a general concept? To any answer there are objections.

If I say that 'this' is a name, I am left with the problem of explaining on what principle we decide what it names on different occasions. There are many men called 'Smith', but they do not share any property of Smithyness; in each case it is an arbitrary convention that the man has that name. (It is true that the name is usually inherited, but it can be adopted by deed-poll. A man's name is legally anything by which he publicly announces that he wishes to be called.) But it is not an arbitrary convention that leads us to call a thing 'this' when we do so call it, or to cease to call it 'this' on subsequent occasions when we have to mention it. In this respect, 'this' differs from ordinary proper names.

Equal difficulties arise if I say that 'this' is a description. It can of course mean 'what I-now am noticing', but that only transfers the problem to 'I-now'. We have agreed to take 'this' as our fundamental egocentric particular, and any other decision would have left us with precisely the same problem. No description not involving some egocentric particular can have the peculiar property of 'this', namely that it applies on each occasion of its use to only one thing, but to different things on different occasions.

Exactly the same kind of objection applies to the attempt to define 'this' as a general concept. If it is a general concept, it has instances, each of which is always an instance of it, and not only at one moment. There is obviously a general concept involved, namely 'object of attention', but something more than this general concept is required in order to secure the temporary uniqueness of 'this'.

It might be thought obvious that there would be no egocentric particulars in a purely physical world. This, however, is not an exact expression of what is true, partly because in a purely physical world there would be no words at all. What is true is that 'this' depends upon the relation of the user of a word to the object with which the word is concerned. I do not want to bring in 'mind'. A machine could be constructed which would use the word 'this' correctly: it could say 'this is red', 'this is blue', 'this is a policeman', on suitable occasions. In the case of such a machine, the words 'this is' are an otiose addition to the subsequent word or words; the machine might just as well be constructed to say 'abracadabra red', 'abracadabra blue', and so on. If our machine, later on, said '*that was* red', it would be getting nearer to the capacities of human speech.

Let us suppose that our machine has this further capacity. We will suppose that red light, falling upon it, sets in operation a mechanism which causes it first to say 'this is red', and then, after various internal processes have been completed, 'that was red'. We can describe the circumstances under which the machine says 'this' and those under which it says 'that'; it says 'this' when the external cause first operates upon it, and it says 'that' when the first effect has led to certain further occurrences in the machine. I have seen automatic machines that played golf in return for a coin; the coin started a process which continued for a certain length of time. It would obviously be possible for the process to begin by the machine saying 'this is a penny', and to end by its saying 'that was a penny'. I think the consideration of this ingenious toy may enable us to eliminate irrelevant problems.

What the machine does is to enable us to describe the circumstances under which people say 'this is' or 'that was'. A verbal reaction to a stimulus may be immediate or delayed. When it is immediate, the afferent current runs into the brain and continues along an efferent nerve until it affects the appropriate muscles and produces a sentence beginning 'this is'. When it is delayed, the afferent impulse goes into some kind of reservoir, and only produces an efferent impulse in response to some new stimulus. The efferent impulse, in this case, is not exactly what it was in the previous case, and produces a slightly different sentence, namely one beginning 'that was'.

We come back here to minimal and other causal chains. A minimal causal chain, in this connexion, is the shortest possible chain from a stimulus outside the brain to a verbal response. Other causal chains always involve some additional stimulus, causing the stored effect of the previous stimulus to be released and to produce a delayed verbal response. In the case of a minimal causal chain we say 'this is', and in the case of a longer one we say 'that was'. This, of course, is too schematic to count as actual physiology, but it seems sufficient to solve our difficulties of principle as regards egocentric particulars.

Let us enlarge this statement. Whenever I utter the word 'cat', I do so – broadly speaking – because a cat is or was perceived by me. (The limitations to this statement may be ignored.) If I do so because a cat *was* perceived, this past fact is obviously not the whole cause of my saying 'cat'; there must also be some present stimulus. Thus the perceptive and the reminiscent uses of the word 'cat' are not the results of precisely similar causes. In a person of suitably developed linguistic habits, the effects also are not precisely similar; the perceptive effect begins with the words 'this is', and the reminiscent effect with the words 'that was'.

Thus the difference between a sentence beginning 'this is' and one beginning 'that was' lies not in their meaning, but in their causation. The two sentences 'The Declaration of Independence was in 1776', uttered by us, and 'The Declaration of Independence is in 1776', which might have been uttered by Jefferson, have exactly the same meaning, but the former implies that the causation is indirect, and the latter that it is direct, or as direct as possible.

It might be objected that many statements about the present are quite as indirect as statements about the past. If I say 'Finland is being invaded', I do so because, first, I remember what I have read in the newspaper, and secondly, I infer that the invasion is not likely to have ceased in the last few hours. But this is a derivative and inferential use of 'is', involving causal laws by which knowledge of the present is obtained from knowledge of the past. The 'present' that is involved is not the 'present' in the *psychological* sense; it is not something 'presented'. It is the 'present' in the *physical* sense, i.e., something which, in physical time, is contemporaneous with the psychological 'present'. 'Present' and 'past' are *primarily* psychological terms, in the sense of involving different causal relations between the speaker and that of which he speaks; their other uses are all definable in terms of this primary use.

Does the above theory explain the use of the word 'I'? We said at the beginning of this chapter that 'I' could be defined in terms of 'this': 'I' is the biography to which 'this' belongs. But although we have explained the use of the word 'this', we have done so by depriving the word itself of all significance in isolation. We cannot therefore be sure that the above definition of 'I' can be maintained.

If our theory of 'this' is correct, it is a word which is not needed for a complete description of the world. We wish to prove that the same conclusion holds as regards 'I' and other egocentric words.

The word 'I', since it applies to something which persists throughout a certain period of time, is to be derived from 'I-now', as that series of events which is related to 'I-now' by certain causal relations. The phrase to be considered is 'I am', which may be replaced by 'I-now is', where the 'is' may be regarded as timeless.

The connexion between 'I-now' and 'this' is obviously very close. 'I-now' denotes a set of occurrences, namely all those that are happening to me at the moment. 'This' denotes some one of these occurrences. 'I', as opposed to 'I-now', can be defined by causal relations to 'this', just as well as to 'I-now'; for I can only denote by 'this' something that I am experiencing.

For reasons which will appear more fully in later chapters, I think that the phrase 'I am' can always be replaced by the phrase 'this is', or vice versa. Which of the two phrases we use depends upon accident or prejudice. We say 'I am hot' rather than 'this is hotness', if we are hot from exercise and not because of the surrounding temperature. But when we go into the engine-room of a ship, we say 'Ouf! it is hot here', which is equivalent (roughly) to 'this is hotness'. We say 'this is a cat', and *intend* to make a statement about something which is not merely a part of our own biography. But if the word 'this' is to apply as it should, to something that we directly experience, it cannot apply to the cat as an object in the outer world, but only to our own percept of a cat. Thus we must not say 'this is a cat', but 'this is a percept such as we associate with cats', or 'this is a cat-percept'. This phrase, in turn, can be replaced by 'I am cat-perceptive', which asserts a state of myself, and is true on exactly the same occasions as those on which I am tempted (rashly) to say 'this is a cat', and on which I am justified in saying 'this is a cat-percept'. What we directly know when we say 'this is a cat' is a state of ourselves, like being hot.

Thus in every statement containing 'this' we may substitute 'what I-now notice', and in every statement containing 'I-now' we may substitute 'what is compresent with this'.

It follows that what has been said of 'this' applies equally to 'I-now'; what distinguishes 'I-now' from a proper name is no part of what is stated by a sentence containing 'I-now', but is only an expression of the causal relation between what is stated and the stating of it.

The word 'you' involves difficulties other than those characteristic of egocentric particulars; these difficulties will be considered in later chapters. So far as our present problem is concerned, it is sufficient to notice that 'you' is always determined by relation to some present percept, which at the moment is 'this'. Consequently the explanation of 'this' also explains 'you', in so far as the difficulty is that of egocentric particulars.

This, so far as I can see, solves the problem of egocentric particulars, and shows that they are not needed in any part of the description of the world, whether physical or psychological.

Note. Professor Reichenbach has kindly allowed me to see an unpublished treatment by him of the question of 'egocentric particulars'. He approaches the problem in a somewhat different way, but I do not think there is any inconsistency between his theory and mine, which complete each other.

CHAPTER 8

PERCEPTION AND KNOWLEDGE

THE word 'perception' is one which philosophers, at an early stage, took over, somewhat uncritically, from common sense. Theaetetus, when Socrates asks him for a definition of 'knowledge', suggests that knowledge is perception. Socrates persuades him to abandon this definition, mainly on the ground that percepts are transient, whereas true knowledge must be of something eternal; but he does not question the occurrence of perception conceived as a relation between subject and object. To common sense it seems obvious that we perceive 'things', at any rate with the senses of sight and touch. Sight may, on occasion, be misleading, as in the case of Macbeth's dagger, but touch never. An 'object' is etymologically something thrown up in my way: if I run into a post in the dark, I am persuaded that I perceive an 'object', and do not merely have a self-centred experience. This is the view implied in Dr Johnson's refutation of Berkeley.

From various points of view, this common sense theory of perception has been called in question. The Cartesians denied interaction between mind and matter, and could not therefore admit that, when my body runs into a post, this event is the cause of the mental occurrence which we call 'perceiving the post'. From such a theory it was natural to pass either to psychophysical parallelism, or to Malebranche's doctrine that we see all things in God, or to Leibniz's monads which all suffer simultaneous similar but systematically differing illusions called 'mirroring the universe'. In all these systems, however, there was felt to be something fantastic, and only philosophers with a long training in absurdity could succeed in believing them.

A much more serious attack on the common sense theory of perception has come from science, through study of the causes of sensations. The first impact of this attack upon the opinions of philosophers led to Locke's doctrine that the secondary qualities are subjective. Berkeley's denial of matter is derived in part, though not mainly, from the scientific theories of light and sound. In the later British empiricists, the scientific transformation of common sense doctrines of perception becomes increasingly important. J. S. Mill's definition of 'matter' as 'a permanent possibility of sensation' results from a combination of science and Berkeley. So does the doctrine of the materialists, sanctified throughout the U.S.S.R. by the authority of Lenin, that 'matter' is 'the cause of sensations'.

In order to be clear as to what science has to say on this question, it is important to forget, to begin with, the Berkeleyan metaphysics to which, rightly or wrongly, it is hoped or feared that the argument may lead. It will be remembered that we distinguished at the outset two kinds of theory of knowledge, one inspired by Cartesian doubt and the search for certainty, the other merely a branch of science, in which, accepting whatever science seems to establish, we seek to define the events that can be called cognitions, and the relation to other events that makes them such. Let us, for the moment, adopt the second kind of theory of knowledge, and examine those events which common sense regards as 'perceivings', with a view to determining whether they are cognitions, and, if they are not, how they are related to our empirical knowledge of matters of fact. In this inquiry we assume that the world is such as it appears in science, without, for the present, asking ourselves whether this assumption is justified.

Let us begin with an astronomical object, say the sun. We have a number of experiences which we call 'seeing the sun'; there is also, according to astronomy, a large lump of hot matter which *is* the sun. What is the relation of this lump to one of the occurrences called 'seeing the sun'? The causal relation is as follows: at every moment a large number of atoms in the sun are emitting radiant energy in the form of light waves or light quanta, which travel across the space between the sun and my eye in the course of about eight minutes. When they reach my eye, their energy is transformed into new kinds: things happen in the rods and cones, then a disturbance travels along the optic nerve, and then something (no one knows what) happens in the appropriate part of the brain, and then I 'see the sun'. This is an account of the causal relation between the sun and 'seeing the sun'. But what we want to know is the *resemblance*, if any, between the sun and 'seeing the sun'; for it is only in so far as there is resemblance that the latter can be a source of knowledge concerning the former.

Adhering to our uncritical acceptance of science, we find that there are important resemblances between the sun and 'seeing the sun'. To begin with, the sun looks round and is round. This resemblance, it is true, is not so close as it sounds, for the sun *looks* round in my visual space and *is* round in physical space. Nevertheless, the resemblance can be clearly stated. The definition of roundness is the same in one space as in another, and certain relations – notably contiguity – are common to physical and visual space.

Again: if we see sun-spots, there are sun-spots. In the sense just explained, the spots in the astronomical sun have the same shape (roughly speaking) as the spots in the visual sun. Moreover the sun feels hot, and the astronomical sun has a corresponding property as contrasted with the surrounding regions of physical space.

There are, however, limitations to the similarities of the visual and astronomical sun. During a partial eclipse, the sun *looks* like the crescent moon, but *is* just as round as at other times. By squinting we can see two suns, but cannot create two 'real' suns. All such matters, however, can be dealt with in detail, and raise no difficulty of principle.

I began with astronomical objects, because of the simplicity derived from their being perceptible to only one sense. Let us now consider ordinary terrestrial objects. Berkeley considers a tree, and this will do as well as any other. So far as the sense of sight is concerned, everything that has just been said about the sun applies equally to the tree, except that the light by which we see it is reflected light, so that it is invisible except when it is exposed to light from the sun, or to lightning, or to some artificial illumination. But the tree can also be touched, heard, smelt, and tasted. When I 'touch' the tree, certain electrons in my finger are sufficiently near to certain electrons in the tree for violent forces of repulsion to be generated; these cause a disturbance to travel along the nerves from my finger to the brain, where they have an effect of unknown nature, which finally causes a sensation of touch. Here, again, we have to ask ourselves: what resemblances are there between my sensation of touch and the part of the tree with which I falsely imagine my finger to be in contact?

There are qualities of touch – hard and soft, rough and smooth – which correspond to qualities of the object touched. By feeling round an object, we can infer its shape, just as we can by seeing it; the 'real' shape inferred is the same for a man who sees the object and for a blind man who only feels it. And when I say 'the same', I mean strictly the same: there is *no* difference between the physical space inferred from touch and that from sight, except as regards degrees of nicety.

In addition to shape, there is location. An object touched but not seen may be above my head or at my feet or at any intermediate altitude; it may be at arm's length, or touching my face, or in any one of a multitude of positions relative to my body. In all these respects, there is a similarity between my sensations and the properties of the physical object.

It is unnecessary to consider hearing, smell, and taste, since exactly similar considerations apply.

The above account rests upon a dogmatic acceptance of physics and physiology. Before we relinquish this comfortable dogmatism, there are some points to be added. The sensations caused by external objects are events like any others, and have not the characteristics that we associate with the word 'cognition'. This fact has to be brought into relation with the common-sense view that there are occurrences called perceivings, in which we become aware of objects. Shall we completely abandon this common-sense view, or shall we retain it, by making the perceptual object something quite different (except for the above-noted resemblances) from the physical object? And before dealing with this question we must examine the psychological distinction between 'sensation' and 'perception' – 'perception', here, being still merely a certain kind of event resulting from a stimulus, and not being assumed to have any cognitive status.

In our reaction to a sensory stimulus there are two theoretically distinguishable elements, first, that due merely to the stimulus, second, that due to its habitual concomitants. A visual sensation is never pure: other senses are also stimulated in virtue of the law of habit. When we see a cat, we expect it to mew, to feel soft, and to move in a cat-like manner; if it barked, or felt like a stone, or moved like a bear, we should experience a violent shock of surprise. This sort of thing has to do with our belief that we see 'objects', and do not merely have visual sensations. If we are considering the psychology of animals, and not only of human beings, it is not safe to attribute this filling-out entirely to habit; some of it seems to be of the nature of innate reflex. This is shown, for example, in a chicken's power of pecking at grains, without first having to learn a 'beak-eye' coordination. The question of habit versus unconditioned reflex is, however, in this connexion, not very important; what is important is that sensations are rounded out by spontaneous images or expectations of their usual accompaniments.

When we have the experience which we call 'seeing a cat', there is an antecedent causal chain analogous to that which we considered in connexion with 'seeing the sun'. When the experience is veridical, this causal chain, at a certain point in its backward course, reaches a cat. (I am still dogmatically assuming the truth of physics.) But it is clear that if, at any point in this chain, the event (light-waves, agitation of rods and cones, or disturbance of optic nerve or brain) which usually has its origin in a cat, can be produced otherwise, we shall have exactly the experience called 'seeing a cat', without any cat being there. I must beg the reader to remember that I am talking science, not philosophy. I am thinking of such things as images in mirrors, the effect of a blow on the eyes in causing a man to see stars, or the cerebral disturbances (whatever they are) which may cause me to 'see a cat' in a dream.

We may put the matter schematically as follows. A certain experience E (e.g., that which is the visual core in what we call 'seeing a cat') has, in my previous history, been usually closely accompanied by certain other experiences. Hence, by virtue of the law of habit, the experience E is now accompanied by what Hume would call 'ideas', but what I should prefer to call 'expectations', which may be purely bodily states. In any case, these expectations deserve to be called 'beliefs', as we shall find later when we come to analyse belief. Thus while the sensory core is not cognitive, its associative accompaniments, being beliefs, must be classed as cognitions (including possibly erroneous beliefs under this head). If this view seems odd, that is because we tend to think of beliefs in an unduly intellectualist fashion.

I do not like to use the word 'perception' for the complete experience consisting of a sensory core supplemented by expectations, because the word 'perception' suggests too strongly that the beliefs involved are true. I will therefore use the phrase 'perceptive experience'. Thus whenever I think I see a cat, I have the perceptive experience of 'seeing a cat', even if, on this occasion, no physical cat is present.

Since the filling out of the sensation into a perceptive experience is an example of habit, it follows that, in my past, the collocations which the perceptive experience assumes have usually existed. Put briefly – and still assuming physics – hitherto, when I have 'seen a cat', there has usually been a cat to be seen, for if this had not been the case I should not have acquired the habits which I now have. We have therefore inductive grounds for holding (on a common sense basis) that when I 'see a cat' there probably is a cat. We cannot go beyond 'probably', since we know that people sometimes see cats that are not there, for instance in dreams. And the possibility of perceptive experiences as results of sensory stimuli depends entirely upon the fact that we live in a world in which objects have a certain stability and also fit into natural kinds. These things depend upon temperature. So, no doubt, does the possibility of life. Certainly 'experience' depends upon our having a more or less stable body. A 'spirit' in the etymological sense – i.e., a gas in motion – would not have the physical stability required for experience or the formation of habits.

To sum up this part of our discussion: in our environment it frequently happens that events occur together in bundles –

such bundles as distinguish a cat from another kind of object. Any one of our senses may be affected by a stimulus arising from some characteristic of the bundle in question. Let us suppose the stimulus to be visual. Then physics allows us to infer that light of certain frequencies is proceeding from the object to our eyes. Induction allows us to infer that this pattern of light, which, we will suppose, looks like a cat, probably proceeds from a region in which the other properties of cats are also present. Up to a point, we can test this hypothesis by experiment: we can touch the cat, and pick it up by the tail to see if it mews. Usually the experiment succeeds; when it does not, its failure is easily accounted for without modifying the laws of physics. (It is in this respect that physics is superior to ignorant common sense.) But all this elaborate work of induction, in so far as it belongs to common sense rather than science, is performed spontaneously by habit, which transforms the mere sensation into a perceptive experience. Broadly speaking, a perceptive experience is a dogmatic belief in what physics and induction show to be probable; it is wrong in its dogmatism, but *usually* right in its content.

It results from the above that, in any perceptive experience, the sensory core has higher inferential value than the rest. I may see a cat, or hear it mew, or feel its fur in the dark. In all these cases, I have a perceptive experience of a cat, but the first is a visual experience, the second auditory, the third tactile. In order to infer from my visual experience the light-frequencies at the surface of the cat, I need (if I am not dreaming and my eyesight is normal) only the laws of physics; but in order to infer the other characteristics of cats, I need, further, the experience that objects having such coloured shapes are more apt to mew than to bark. While, therefore, none of the inferences from the perceptive experience is certain, the inferences drawn from the sensory core have a higher probability than those drawn from the other parts of the perceptive experience. This can only be denied by those who are willing to deny physics or physiology.

I now pass to a slightly different topic, namely, the relation of perceptive experiences to our knowledge of matters of fact. That there is such a relation is evident from the difference between our knowledge of the experienced past and present on the one hand, and our knowledge of the future and the unexperienced past and present on the other hand. We know that Caesar was murdered, but until this event occurred it was not known. It was known to eye-witnesses because they perceived it; it is known to us because of statements that we perceive in history-books. We sometimes know future facts, for instance the dates of coming eclipses; but such knowledge is inferred inductively from knowledge based directly on percepts, and is less certain than the knowledge upon which it is based. All our knowledge of matters of fact – i.e., all knowledge in which there is a reference to temporal position – is causally dependent upon perceptive experiences, and involves at least one premiss referring to the present or the past. But while this is obvious, the logical relation of empirical knowledge to perceptive experience is by no means easy to state clearly.

There are some schools of philosophy – notably the Hegelians and the instrumentalists – which deny the distinction between data and inferences altogether. They maintain that in all our knowledge there is an inferential element, that knowledge is an organic whole, and that the test of truth is coherence rather than conformity with 'fact'. I do not deny an element of truth in this view, but I think that, if taken as the whole truth, it renders the part played by perception in knowledge inexplicable. It is surely obvious that every perceptive experience, if I choose to notice it, affords me either new knowledge which I could not previously have inferred, or, at least, as in the case of eclipses, greater certainty than I could have previously obtained by means of inference. To this the instrumentalist replies that any statement of the new knowledge obtained from perception is always an interpretation based upon accepted theories, and may need subsequent correction if these theories turn out to be unsuitable. If I say, for example, 'Look, there is an eclipse of the moon', I use my knowledge of astronomy to interpret what I see. No words exist, according to the instrumentalist, which do not embody theories or hypoetheses, and the crude fact of perception is therefore for ever ineffable.

I think that this view underestimates the powers of analysis. It is undeniable that our everyday interpretations of perceptive experiences, and even all our everyday words, embody theories. But it is not impossible to whittle away the element of interpretation, or to invent an artificial language involving a minimum of theory. By these methods we can approach asymptotically to the pure datum. That there must be a pure datum is, I think, a logically irrefutable consequence of the fact that perception gives rise to new knowledge. Suppose, for example, that I have hitherto entertained a certain group of theories, but I now perceive that somewhere among these theories there is a mistake. There is necessarily, in this case, something not deducible from previous theories, and this something is a new datum for my knowledge of matters of fact, for we mean by a 'datum' merely a piece of knowledge that is not deduced. To deny data in this sense is, it seems to me, only possible for a Hegelian panlogism.

The question of data has been, mistakenly I think, mixed up with the question of certainty. The essential characteristic of a datum is that it is not inferred. It may not be true, and we may not feel certain that it is true. The most obvious example is memory. We know that memory is fallible, but there are many things that we believe, though not with complete assurance, on the basis of memory alone. Another example is derived from faint perceptions. Suppose you are listening to a sound which is gradually growing more distant, for example, a receding aeroplane. At one time, you are sure that you hear it; at a later time, you are sure that you do not hear it. At certain intermediate times, you think that you still hear it, but cannot be sure; at these times you have an uncertain datum. I am prepared to concede that all data have *some* uncertainty, and should therefore, if possible, be confirmed by other data. But unless these other data had some degree of independent credibility, they would not confirm the original data.

There is here, however, a distinction to be made. While I hold that no actual statement in words is completely indubitable, it is possible to define classes of statements which are certainly all true; in this case, what is doubtful is whether a given statement belongs to one of these classes. For many purposes, it is convenient to define the class of premisses so that all are true;

but if we do so, we can never be sure that a given statement belongs to the class of premises.

I shall henceforth assume that there are data, in the sense of propositions for which the evidence is not wholly derived from their logical relation to other propositions. I shall not assume that the actual data which we can obtain are ever completely certain, nor yet that a proposition which is a datum cannot be also a consequence of other accepted propositions. This latter case occurs whenever we see a predicted eclipse. But when a proposition concerning a particular matter of fact is inferred, there must always be among the premises other matters of fact from which some general law is obtained by induction. It is therefore impossible that all our knowledge of matters of fact should be inferred.

The question of how to obtain from perceptual experiences propositions which are premises for empirical knowledge is difficult and complicated, but fundamental for any empirical theory of knowledge.

We must now examine a question of considerable importance, namely, that of the part played by egocentric particulars in perceptive judgements. We may first set out the nature of the problem, which is as follows. We saw in Chapter 7 that it is the ideal of science to dispense with egocentric particulars, and it seemed, from the discussion in that chapter, as if this ideal were attainable. If it is attainable, there can be empirical impersonal knowledge, and two men who both believe (say) that hydrogen is the lightest of elements *may* be both believing the same proposition. If, on the other hand, all empirical words are, strictly speaking, defined in terms of egocentric particulars, then, since two people cannot attach the same meaning to the same egocentric words, no two people can attach the same meaning to *any* empirical word, and there is no empirical proposition that two different people can both believe. This unpleasant conclusion has, however, much to be said in its support. Our empirical vocabulary is based upon words having ostensive definitions, and an ostensive definition consists of a series of percepts which generate a habit. When the vocabulary has been mastered, it is perception that gives us the primary knowledge of matters of fact upon which science is based; and perceptive knowledge, *prima facie*, demands egocentric words in its verbal expression. This argument must now be scrutinized.

Let us begin with 'meaning', and let us take the word 'hot' for purposes of illustration. I shall suppose a schematic simplicity in the experiences by means of which I learnt the meaning of the word in childhood: that there was an open fire in my nursery, and every time I went near it someone said 'hot'; that they used the same word when I perspired on a summer's day, and when, accidentally, I spilled scalding tea over myself. The result was that I uttered the word 'hot' whenever I noticed sensations of a certain kind. So far, we have nothing beyond a causal law: a certain kind of bodily state causes a certain kind of noise. It would be easy to construct a machine which would say 'hot' whenever it reached a certain temperature. This, however, is not, for us, the important point. What is important, for us, is that this primitive use of the word 'hot' has the distinctive characteristic of egocentric particulars, namely (to quote Chapter 7) that it 'depends upon the relation of the user of the word to the object with which the word is concerned'. We have held, throughout our discussion of object-words, that, in their most primitive use, they are perceptive judgements: what we express at first by the one word 'hot!' is what we afterwards express by 'this is hot' or 'I am hot'. That is to say, every object-word, in its primitive use, has an implicit egocentricity, which the subsequent development of speech renders explicit.

But when we have advanced to the point at which we can explicitly consider the meanings of words, we see that this egocentricity is no part of the meaning of the word 'hot' as it exists in a developed language. The word 'hot' means only that quality in occurrences which, *if* the occurrences are suitably related to me, will make them causes of my utterance of the word 'hot'. In passing from 'hot!' to 'this is hot', we effect an analysis: the quality 'hot' is freed from egocentricity, and the formerly implicit egocentric element is rendered explicit by the words 'this is'. Thus in a developed language object-words such as 'hot', 'red', 'smooth', etc., are not egocentric.

This, however, does not decide as to the egocentric element

in judgements of perception. The question is: can we express what we know when we make such judgements, without the use of 'this' or 'I-now'? If we cannot, the theory of proper names suggested in Chapter 6 will have to be abandoned.

Perceptive judgements, on the face of it, are of two kinds. In looking at a fire we may say 'this is hot' and 'this is bright'; these are of the first kind. But we may also say 'hotness and brightness are compresent'; this is of the second kind. Whenever we can say 'this is A, this is B, this is C, etc.', where 'A', 'B', 'C', ... are names of qualities, we can also say 'A, B, C, ... are compresent'. But in this latter judgement the spatio-temporal uniqueness of 'this' is lost; we are no longer speaking of *this* occasion, and, so far as our judgement shows, there may be many occasions on which A, B, C, ... are all compresent.

If we are to preserve the theory of Chapter 6, we shall have to say that 'this' is a name (with the limitations explained in Chapter 7) of a bundle of compresent qualities, and that, if our qualities are suitably chosen or sufficiently numerous, the whole bundle will not occur more than once, i.e., will not have to itself any of those spatial or temporal relations which we regard as implying diversity, such as before, above, to the right of, etc. If this theory can be maintained, the egocentricity in such a proposition as 'this is hot' lies, not in what is known, but in the causation of our knowledge and in the words by means of which we express it. The word 'this' may be replaced by something that is strictly a name, say 'W', denoting that whole complex of qualities which constitutes all that I am now experiencing. The impersonal truth asserted when I say 'this is hot' will then be translated into the words 'hotness is part of W'. In this form, what I have learnt from perception is ready for incorporation in impersonal science.

Whether we accept or reject this view, grave difficulties confront us. Let us examine first those involved in acceptance.

There are, to begin with, certain difficulties as to space-time. These were considered in Chapter 6, and I shall assume that they were there satisfactorily disposed of.

More serious is the apparent consequence that all judgements of perception are analytic. If 'W' is the name of a whole consisting of a bundle of qualities, and 'this is hot' only says that hotness is one of the qualities composing W, then, as soon as 'W' is defined, the proposition 'this is hot' becomes analogous to such propositions as 'rational animals are animals' or 'hexagons are polygons'. But this is absurd: it does away with the distinction between empirical and logical knowledge, and makes the part played by experience in empirical knowledge inexplicable.

The only answer is to say that, although 'W' is, in fact, the name of a certain bundle of qualities, we do not know, when we give the name, *what* qualities constitute W. That is to say, we must suppose that we can perceive, name, and recognize a whole without knowing what are its constituents. In that case, the datum which appears as subject in a judgement of perception is a complex whole, of which we do not necessarily perceive the complexity. A judgement of perception is always a judgement of analysis, but not an analytic judgement. It says 'the whole W, and the quality Q, are related as whole-and-part', where W and Q are independently given. The fact that they are 'given' enters into the causation of what we know, and into its verbal expression if we use the word 'this', but not into its verbal expression in the form 'Q is part of W'.

The above theory has the consequence that we cannot express our knowledge without names for complex wholes, and that we can be acquainted with complex wholes without knowing of what constituents they consist. I shall revert to this question in Chapter 14, where grounds will be given for accepting the view as to wholes that our present theory requires.

I conclude, provisionally, that the difficulties of accepting our present theory are not insuperable.

Let us now examine the difficulties which result from rejecting it.

If we reject our theory, we accept either 'this' or 'I-now' as a necessary constituent of judgements of perception. I shall assume that we adhere to 'this'. The argument is exactly the same whichever alternative we choose.

The difficulty that arises here is not as to egocentric particulars, but as to 'substance'. If I admit propositions of the form 'this is hot', where 'this' does not designate a bundle of qualities, then 'this' becomes the name of something which is *merely* a subject of predicates, and which serves no purpose except that predicates 'inhere' in it. All propositions of the form 'this is hot' are supposed to be synthetic, so that 'this' is not defined when all its predicates are enumerated. If it were, it would be superfluous, and we could revert to the theory that 'this' denotes a bundle of qualities (which now are no longer syntactically predicates). We must therefore hold it possible that this and that should have exactly the same predicates. The identity of indiscernibles, if true, will be a fortunate accident, and 'identity' will be an indefinable. Moreover it may happen that this and that are not identical, although no evidence of this is imaginable. Counting will be impossible, for, if a and b are indistinguishable, I shall give them the same name, and any act in which I count one of them will necessarily be also an act in which I count the other. It is clear therefore that, if there be a concept of identity which allows indiscernibles to be not identical, such a concept can never be applied, and can have no relation to our knowledge. We should, therefore, prefer a theory which does not require it.

I conclude, therefore, that the theory of proper names developed in Chapter 6 is to be maintained, and that all knowledge stated by means of egocentric particulars can be stated without employing them.

CHAPTER 9

EPISTEMOLOGICAL PREMISSES

THEORY of knowledge is rendered difficult by the fact that it involves psychology, logic, and the physical sciences, with the result that confusions between different points of view are a constant danger. This danger is particularly acute in connexion with the problem of our present chapter, which is that of determining the premisses of our knowledge from an epistemological point of view. And there is a further source of confusion in the fact that, as already noted, theory of knowledge itself may be conceived in two different ways. On the one hand, accepting as knowledge whatever science recognizes as such, we may ask: how have we acquired this knowledge, and how best can we analyse it into premisses and inferences? On the other hand, we may adopt the Cartesian standpoint, and seek to divide what passes for knowledge into more certain and less certain portions. These two inquiries are not so distinct as they might seem, for, since the forms of inference involved are not demonstrative, our premisses will have more certainty than our conclusions. But this fact only makes it the more difficult to avoid confusion between the two inquiries.

An epistemological premiss, which we shall now seek to define, must have three characteristics. It must be (a) a logical premiss, (b) a psychological premiss, and (c) true so far as we can ascertain. Concerning each of these something must be said.

(a) Given any systematic body of propositions, such as is contained in some science in which there are general laws, it is possible, usually in an indefinite number of ways, to pick out certain of the propositions as premisses, and deduce the remainder. In the Newtonian theory of the solar system, for example, we can take as premisses the law of gravitation together with the positions and velocities of the planets at a given moment. Any moment will do, and for the law of gravitation we can substitute Kepler's three laws. In conducting such analyses, the logician, as such, is indifferent to the truth or falsehood of the body of propositions concerned, provided they are mutually consistent (if they are not, he will have nothing to do with them). He will, for example, just as willingly consider an imaginary planetary system and a gravitational law other than that of the inverse square. Nor does he pretend that his premisses give the grounds for believing in their consequences, even when both are true. When we are considering grounds of belief, the law of gravitation is an inference, not a premiss.

The logician, in his search for premisses, has one purpose which is emphatically not shared by the epistemologist, namely, that he seeks a *minimum* set of premisses. A set of premisses is a minimum set, in relation to a given body of propositions, if from the whole set, but not from any part of the set, all the given body of propositions can be deduced. Usually many minimum sets exist; the logician prefers those that are shortest, and, among two equally short, the one that is simplest. But these preferences are merely aesthetic.

(*b*) A psychological premiss may be defined as a belief which is not caused by any other belief or beliefs. Psychologically, any belief may be considered to be inferred when it is caused by other beliefs, however invalid the inference may be for logic. The most obvious class of beliefs not caused by other beliefs are those that result directly from perception. These, however, are not the only beliefs that are psychological premisses. Others are required to produce our faith in deductive arguments. Perhaps induction also is based, psychologically, upon primitive beliefs. What others there may be I shall not at the moment inquire.

(*c*) Since we are concerned with theory of *knowledge*, not merely of *belief*, we cannot accept all psychological premisses as epistemological premisses, for two psychological premisses may contradict each other, and therefore not all are true. For example I may think 'there is a man coming downstairs', and the next moment I may realize that it is a reflection of myself in a mirror. For such reasons, psychological premisses must be subjected to analysis before being accepted as premisses for theory of knowledge. In this analysis we are as little sceptical as possible.

We assume that perception *can* cause knowledge, although it *may* cause error if we are logically careless. Without this fundamental assumption, we should be reduced to complete scepticism as regards the empirical world. No arguments are logically possible either for or against complete scepticism, which must be admitted to be one among possible philosophies. It is, however, too short and simple to be interesting. I shall, therefore, without more ado, develop the opposite hypothesis, according to which beliefs caused by perception are to be accepted unless there are positive grounds for rejecting them.

Since we can never be completely certain that any given proposition is true, we can never be completely certain that it is an epistemological premiss, even when it possesses the other two defining properties and seems to us to be true. We shall attach different 'weights' (to use a term employed by Professor Reichenbach) to different propositions which we believe and which, if true, are epistemological premisses: the greatest weight will be given to those of which we are most certain, and the least to those of which we are least certain. Where there is a logical conflict we shall sacrifice the less certain, unless a large number of these are opposed to a very small number of the more certain.

Owing to the absence of certainty, we shall not seek, like the logician, to reduce our premises to a minimum. On the contrary, we shall be glad when a number of propositions which support one another can all be accepted as epistemological premises, since this increases the probability of all of them. (I am not thinking of logical deducibility, but of inductive compatibility.)

Epistemological premisses are different according as they are momentary, individual, or social. Let us illustrate. I believe that $16^2 = 256$; at the moment, I believe this on grounds of memory, but probably at some time I did the sum, and I have convinced myself that the received rules of multiplication follow from the premises of logic. Therefore taking my life as a whole, $16^2 = 256$ is inferred, not from memory, but from logic. In this case, if my logic is correct, there is no difference between the individual and the social premises.

But now let us take the existence of the Straits of Magellan. Again, my momentary epistemological premiss is memory. But I have had, at various times, better reasons: maps, books of travel, etc. *My* reasons have been the assertions of others, whom I believed to be well-informed and honest. *Their* reasons, traced back, lead to percepts: Magellan, and others who have been in the region concerned when it was not foggy, saw what they took to be land and sea, and by dint of systematized inferences made maps. Treating the knowledge of mankind as one whole, it is the percepts of Magellan and other travellers that provide the epistemological premisses for belief in the Straits of Magellan. Writers who are interested in knowledge as a social phenomenon are apt to concentrate upon social epistemological premisses. For certain purposes this is legitimate, for others not. Social epistemological premisses are relevant in deciding whether to spend public money on a new telescope or an investigation of the Trobriand Islanders. Laboratory experiments aim at establishing new factual premisses which can be incorporated in the accepted system of human knowledge. But for the philosopher there are two prior questions: what reason (if any) have I for believing in the existence of other people? And what reason (if any) have I now for believing that I existed at certain past times, or, more generally, that my present beliefs concerning past times are more or less correct? For me now, only my momentary epistemological premisses are really premisses; the rest must be in some sense inferred. For me as opposed to others, my individual premisses are premisses, but the percepts of others are not. Only those who regard mankind as in some mystical sense a single entity possessed of a single persistent mind have a right to confine their epistemology to the consideration of *social* epistemological premisses.

In the light of these distinctions, let us consider possible definitions of empiricism. I think that the great majority of empiricists are *social* empiricists, a few are *individual* empiricists, and hardly any are *momentary* empiricists. What all empiricists have in common is emphasis upon *perceptive premisses*. We shall seek a definition of this term presently; for the moment I shall say only a few preliminary words.

Speaking psychologically, a 'perceptive premiss' may be defined as a belief caused, as immediately as possible, by a percept. If I believe there *will be* an eclipse because the astronomers say so, my belief is not a perceptive premiss; if I believe there *is* an eclipse because I see it, that is a perceptive premiss. But immediately difficulties arise. What astronomers call an eclipse is a public event, whereas what I am seeing may be due to a defect in my eye or my telescope. While, therefore, the belief 'there is an eclipse' may arise in me without conscious inference, this belief goes beyond the mere expression of what I see. Thus we are driven, in epistemology, to define 'perceptive premiss' more narrowly than would be necessary in psychology. We are driven to this because we want a 'perceptive premiss' to be something which there is never good reason to think false, or, what comes to the same thing, something so defined that two perceptive premisses cannot contradict each other.

Assuming 'perceptive premisses' to have been adequately defined, let us return to the definition of 'empiricism'. My momentary knowledge consists largely of memory, and my individual knowledge consists largely of testimony. But memory, when it is veridical, is related to a previous perceptive premiss, and testimony, when it is veridical, is related to some one else's perceptive premiss. Social empiricism takes these perceptive premisses of other times or other persons as *the* empirical premisses for what is now accepted, and thus evades the problems connected with memory and testimony. This is plainly illegitimate, since there is reason to believe that both memory and testimony sometimes deceive. I, now, can only arrive at the perceptive premisses of other times and other persons by an inference from memory and testimony. If I, now, am to have any reason to believe what I read yesterday in the Encyclopaedia, I must, now, find reason to trust my memory, and to believe, in suitable circumstances, what comes to me in the form of testimony. I must, that is to say, start from *momentary* epistemological premisses. To do anything else is to evade problems which it is part of the business of epistemology to consider.

It follows from the above considerations that epistemology cannot say: 'knowledge is wholly derivable from perceptive premisses together with the principles of demonstrative and probable inference'. Memory premisses, at least, must be added to perceptive premisses. What premisses, if any, must be added in order to make testimony admissible (with common sense limitations), is a difficult question, which must be borne in mind, but need not be discussed at the moment. The paramount importance of perception, in any tenable form of empiricism, is causal. Memory, when veridical, is causally dependent upon a previous perception; testimony, when veridical, is causally dependent upon some one else's perception. We may say, therefore: 'all human knowledge of matters of fact is in part *caused* by perception'. But a principle of this sort is clearly one which can only be known by inference, if at all; it cannot be a premiss in epistemology. It is fairly clear that part of the *cause* of my believing in the Straits of Magellan is that certain people have seen them, but this is not the *ground* of my belief, since it has to be proved to me (or rather made probable) that such people have had such percepts. To me, their percepts are inferences, not premisses.

CHAPTER 10

BASIC PROPOSITIONS

'BASIC Propositions', as I wish to use the term, are a sub-class of epistemological premisses, namely those which are caused, as immediately as possible, by perceptive experiences. This excludes the premisses required for inference, whether demonstrative or probable. It excludes also any extra-logical premisses used for inference, if there be such – e.g., 'what is red is not blue', 'if A is earlier than B, B is not earlier than A'. Such propositions demand careful discussion, but whether premisses or not, they are in any case not 'basic' in the above sense.

I have borrowed the term 'basic proposition' from Mr A. J. Ayer, who uses it as the equivalent of the German *Protokollsatz* employed by the logical positivists. I shall use it, perhaps, not in exactly the same sense in which it is used by Mr Ayer, but I shall use it in connexion with the same problems as those which have led him and the logical positivists to require such a term.

Many writers on theory of knowledge hold that from a single occurrence nothing is to be learnt. They think of all empirical knowledge as consisting of inductions from a number of more or less similar experiences. For my part, I think that such a view makes history impossible and memory unintelligible. I hold that, from any occurrence that a man notices, he can obtain knowledge, which, if his linguistic habits are adequate, he can express in sentences. His linguistic habits, of course, have been generated by past experiences, but these only determine the words he uses. The truth of what he says, given the meanings of his words, can, given adequate care, be wholly dependent upon the character of one occurrence that he is noticing. When this is the case, what he is asserting is what I call a 'basic proposition'.

The discussion of basic propositions has two parts. First, it is necessary to argue, as against opposing opinions, that there are basic propositions. Secondly, it is necessary to determine just what sort of thing they can affirm, and to show that this is usually much less than common sense asserts on the occasions on which the basic propositions in question are epistemologically justifiable.

A basic proposition is intended to have several characteristics. It must be known independently of inference from other propositions, but not independently of evidence, since there must be a perceptive occurrence which gives the cause and is considered to give the reason for believing the basic proposition. Then again, from a logical point of view, it should be possible so to analyse our empirical knowledge that its primitive propositions (apart from logic and generalities) should all have been, at the moment when they were first believed, basic propositions. This requires that basic propositions should not contradict each other, and makes it desirable, if possible, to give them a logical form which makes mutual contradiction impossible. These conditions demand, therefore, that a basic proposition should have two properties:

(1) It must be caused by some sensible occurrence;
(2) It must be of such a form that no other basic proposition can contradict it.

As to (1): I do not wish to insist upon the word 'caused', but the belief must arise on the occasion of some sensible occurrence, and must be such that, if questioned, it will be defended by the argument 'why, I see it' or something similar. The belief refers to a certain time, and the reasons for believing it did not exist before that time. If the event in question had been previously inferred or expected, the evidence beforehand was different from that afforded by perception, and would generally be considered less decisive. Perception affords for the belief evidence which is considered the strongest possible, but which is not verbal.

As to (2): the judgements that common sense bases upon perception, such as 'there is a dog', usually go beyond the present datum, and may therefore be refuted by subsequent evidence. We cannot know, from perception alone, anything about other times or about the perceptions of others or about bodies understood in an impersonal sense. That is why, in the search for data, we are driven to analysis: we are seeking a core which is logically independent of other occurrences. When you think you see a dog, what is really given in perception may be expressed in the words 'there is a canoid patch of colour'. No previous or subsequent occurrence, and no experience of others, can prove the falsehood of this proposition. It is true that, in the sense in which we infer eclipses, there can be evidence against a present judgement of perception, but this evidence is inductive and merely probable, and cannot stand against 'the evidence of the senses'. When we have analysed a judgement of perception in this way, we are left with something which cannot be *proved* to be false.

We may then define a 'basic proposition' as follows: it is a proposition which arises on occasion of a perception, which is the evidence for its truth, and it has a form such that no two propositions having this form can be mutually inconsistent if derived from different percepts.

Examples would be: 'I am hot', 'that is red', 'what a foul smell'. All basic propositions in the above sense are personal, since no one else can share my percepts, and transitory, for after a moment they are replaced by memories.

In place of the above definition, we *can* adopt a logical definition. We can consider the whole body of empirical knowledge, and define 'basic propositions' as those of its logically indemonstrable propositions which are themselves empirical, i.e., assert some temporal occurrence. This definition, I think, is extensionally equivalent to the above epistemological definition.

Some among logical positivists, notably Neurath and Hempel, deny that any set of propositions can be singled out as 'basic', or as in any important epistemological sense premisses for the remainder. Their view is that 'truth' is a *syntactical*, not a *semantic* concept: a proposition is 'true' within a given system if it is consistent with the rest of the system, but there may be other systems, inconsistent with the first, in which the proposition in question will be 'false'. There is no such process, according to them, as deriving the truth of a proposition from some non-verbal occurrence: the world of words is a closed self-contained world, and the philosopher need not concern himself with anything outside it.

In logic and mathematics, the view that 'truth' is a syntactical concept is correct, since it is syntax that guarantees the truth of tautologies. Truth, in this sphere, is discoverable by studying the *form* of the proposition concerned; there is no need to go outside to something that the proposition 'means' or 'asserts'. The authors in question assimilate empirical to logical truth, thus reverting unconsciously to the tradition of Spinoza, Leibniz, and Hegel. In rejecting their view, as I shall contend that we must, we are committing ourselves to the opinion that 'truth' in empirical material has a meaning different from that which it bears in logic and mathematics.

The coherence theory of truth, as I have just said, is that of Hegel. It is worked out, from a Hegelian point of view, in Joachim's book *The Nature of Truth*, which I criticized, from the standpoint of the correspondence theory, in *Philosophical Essays* (1910). The Hegelian theory, however, differs from that of Neurath, since it holds that only one body of mutually coherent propositions is possible, so that every proposition remains definitely true or false. Neurath, on the contrary, takes the view of Pirandello: 'so it is, if you think so'.

The theory of Neurath and Hempel is set forth in articles in *Erkenntnis* and *Analysis*. The following are quotations or paraphrases of their words.

An assertion is called right when we can fit it in (*eingliedern*).

Assertions are compared with assertions, not with 'experiences' (*Erlebnissen*).

There are no primary *Protokollsätze* or propositions needing no confirmation.

All *Protokollsätze* should be put into the following form: 'Otto's protocol at 3.17: {Otto's word-thought at 3.16 (In the room at 3.15 was a table perceived by Otto)}.'

Here the repeated use of the word 'Otto' instead of 'I' is essential.

Although, according to the above, it would seem as if we were debarred from knowing anything about the physical world except that physicists make certain assertions about it, Neurath nevertheless commits himself to the statement that sentences are mounds of ink or systems of air-waves (*Erkenntnis* I v, 209). He does not tell us how he discovered this fact; presumably he only means that physicists assert it.

Neurath in 'Radikaler Physikalismus und Wirkliche Welt' (*Erkenntnis* IV, 5, 1934), maintains the following theses:

1. All *Realsätze* of science including *Protokollsätze*, are chosen as the result of *Entschlüsse* (decisions), and can be altered.

2. We call a *Realsatz false* when it cannot fit into the edifice of science.

3. The control of certain *Realsätze* is compatibility with certain *Protokollsätze*: instead of *die Wirklichkeit* we have a number of mutually incompatible but internally coherent bodies of propositions, choice between which is '*nicht logisch ausgezeichnet*'.

The practice of life, Neurath says, quickly reduces ambiguity; moreover the opinions of neighbours influence us.

Carl G. Hempel 'On the logical positivist's theory of truth' (*Analysis* II, 4 January 1935) sets forth the history of the views of logical positivists as to *Protokollsätze*. He says the theory developed step by step from a correspondence theory into a restrained coherence theory. He says that Neurath denies that we can ever compare reality with propositions, and that Carnap agrees.

We started, he says, from Wittgenstein's atomic propositions; these were replaced by *Protokollsätze*, at first thought to express the results of observation. But then *Protokollsätze* were no longer the result of observation, and then no class of statements was admitted as basic.

Carnap (Hempel continues) says there are *no* absolutely first statements for science; even for *Protokollsätze* further justification may be demanded. Nevertheless:

'Carnap and Neurath do by no means intend to say: "There are no facts, there are only propositions"; on the contrary, the occurrence of certain statements in the protocol of an observer or in a scientific book is regarded as an empirical fact, and the propositions occurring as empirical objects. What the authors do intend to say, may be expressed more precisely thanks to Carnap's distinction between the material and the formal mode of speech. ...

'The concept of truth may be characterized in this formal mode of speech, namely, in a crude formulation, as a sufficient agreement between the system of acknowledged *Protokollsätze* and the logical consequences which may be deduced from the statement and other statements which are already adopted. ...

'Saying that empirical statements "express facts" and consequently that truth consists in a certain correspondence between statements and the "facts" expressed by them, is a typical form of the material mode of speech.' (p. 54) [i.e., 'truth' is syntactic, not semantic.]

'In order to have a relatively high degree of certainty, one will go back to the *Protokollsätze* of reliable observers.' [Two questions arise: A. How do we know who are reliable? B. How do we know what they say?]

'The system of *Protokollsätze* we call true ... may only be characterized by the historical fact, that it is the system which is actually adopted by mankind, and especially by the scientists of our culture circle.

'A *Protokollsätz*, like every other statement, is at the end adopted or rejected by a decision.'

Protokollsätze are now superfluous. It is implied that there is no definite world with definite properties.

I think Neurath and Hempel may be more or less right as regards *their* problem, which is the construction of an encyclopaedia. They want public impersonal propositions, incorporated in public science. But *public* knowledge is a construction, containing less than the sum of *private* knowledges.

The man who is constructing an encyclopaedia is not expected himself to conduct experiments; he is expected to compare the opinions of the best authorities, and arrive, so far as he can, at the standard scientific opinion of his time. Thus in dealing with a scientific question his data are opinions, not direct observations of the subject-matter. The individual men of science, however, whose opinions are the encyclopaedist's premisses, have not themselves merely compared other investigators' opinions; they have made observations and conducted experiments, on the basis of which they have been prepared, if necessary, to reject previously unanimous opinions. The purpose of an observation or experiment is to give rise to a perceptive experience, as a result of which the percipient has new knowledge, at first purely personal and private. Others may repeat the experiment, and in the end the result becomes part of *public* knowledge; but this public knowledge is merely an abstract or epitome of private knowledges.

All theory of knowledge must start from 'what do *I* know?' not from 'what does mankind know?' For how can I tell what mankind knows? Only by (*a*) personal observation of what it says in the books it has written, and (*b*) weighing the evidence in favour of the view that what is said in the books is true. If I am Copernicus, I shall decide against the books; if I am a student of cuneiform, I may decide that Darius did not say what he is supposed to have said about his campaigns.

There is a tendency – not confined to Neurath and Hempel, but prevalent in much modern philosophy – to forget the arguments of Descartes and Berkeley. It may be that these arguments can be refuted, though, as regards our present question, I do not believe that they can be. But in any case they are too weighty to be merely ignored. In the present connexion, the point is that *my* knowledge as to matters of fact must be based upon *my* perceptive experiences, through which alone I can ascertain what is received as public knowledge.

This applies, in particular, to what is to be found in books. That Carnap's books say whatever they do say is the sort of thing that would be generally accepted as public knowledge. But what do I know?

(1) What I see when I look at them
(2) What I hear when others read them aloud
(3) What I see when others quote them in print
(4) What I see when I compare two copies of the same book.

Hence, I pass, by elaborate and doubtful inferences, to *public* knowledge.

On Neurath's view, language has no relation to non-linguistic occurrences, but this makes many every-day experiences inexplicable. For instance: I arrived in Messina from a sea voyage in 1901 and found flags at half-mast; on inquiry I learnt that McKinley had been murdered. If language has no relation to the non-linguistic, this whole procedure was frivolous.

As we saw, Neurath says the proper form of a protocol sentence is: 'Otto's protocol at 3.17: {Otto's word-thought at 3.16 was: (In the room at 3.15 there was a table perceived by Otto)}.'

It seems to me that, in giving this form to protocol sentences, Neurath shows himself far more credulous than the man who says 'there's a dog'. In the inside bracket he perceived a table, which is just as bad as perceiving a dog. In the outside bracket he finds words for what he has perceived, viz.: 'in the room at 3.15 there was a table perceived by Otto'. And a minute later he writes down the words at which he has arrived. This last stage involves memory and the continuity of the ego. The second stage involves memory also, and in addition involves introspection.

Let us take the matter in detail.

To begin with the inner bracket: 'in the room at 3.15 there was a table perceived by Otto'. We may take the words 'in the room' as merely meaning that the table had a perceptual background, and in that sense they may be allowed to pass. The words 'at 3.15' imply that Otto was looking at his watch as well as at the table, and that his watch was right. These are grave matters, if taken seriously. Let us suppose that, instead of 'at 3.15' we say 'once upon a time', and instead of '3.16' we say 'a little later', and instead of '3.17' we say 'a little later still'. This eliminates the difficulties of time-measurement, which surely Neurath cannot have intended to introduce. We come now to the words 'there was a table'. These are objectionable on the same grounds as 'there's a dog'. It may not have been a table, but a reflection in a mirror. Or perhaps it was like Macbeth's dagger, a phantasm called up by the intention of committing a murder on a table. Or perhaps a very unusual collocation of quantum phenomena caused a momentary appearance of a table, which was going to disappear in another moment. It may be conceded that this last hypothesis is improbable, that Dr Neurath is not the sort of person who would think of murdering anybody, and that his room probably contains no mirror large enough for the reflection of a table that is elsewhere. But such considerations ought not to be necessary where protocol-sentences are concerned.

I come now to a still more serious matter. We are told, not only that there was a table, but that there was a table 'perceived by Otto'. This last is a social statement, derived from experience of social life, and by no means primitive; in so far as there is reason to believe it, it is based upon argument. Otto perceives the table, or rather a tabular appearance – well and good – but he does not perceive that Otto perceives it. What is 'Otto'? So far as he can be known, either to himself or others, he is a series of occurrences. One of them is the visual appearance which he rashly calls a table. By the help of conversation, he is led to the conclusion that the occurrences people mention form bundles, each of which is one person, and that the appearance of the table belongs to the same bundle as the subsequent word-thought and the still more subsequent act of writing. But all this elaboration is no part of the visual datum. If he always lived alone, he would never be led to distinguish between 'there's a table' and 'I see a table'; in fact, he would always use the former phrase, if one could suppose him using phrases at all. The word 'I' is a word of limitation, meaning 'I, not you'; it is by no means part of any primitive datum. And this is still more evident when, instead of 'I', Neurath says 'Otto'.

So far we have only been concerned with what happened at 3.15. It is now time to consider what happened at 3.16.

At 3.16, Otto put into words what had happened at 3.15. Now I am willing to admit that the words he used are such as well might be employed by a man who was not on the lookout for pitfalls. There is, therefore, less to criticize at this stage. What he thought may well not have been true, but I am quite willing to concede that he thought it, if he says so.

At 3.17, Otto carried out an act of introspection, and decided that, a minute ago, a certain phrase had been in his thoughts, not just as a phrase, but as an assertion concerning an earlier perception which, at 3.16, he still remembered. It is only what happens at 3.17 that is actually asserted. Thus according to Neurath the data of empirical science are all of the following form:

'A certain person (who happens to be myself, but this, we are told, is irrelevant) is aware at a certain time that a little while ago he believed a phrase which asserted that a little while before that he had seen a table.'

That is to say, all empirical knowledge is based upon recollections of words used on former occasions. Why recollections should be preferred to perceptions, and why no recollections should be admitted except of thought-words, is not explained. Neurath is making an attempt to secure publicity in data, but by mistake has arrived at one of the most subjective forms of knowledge, namely recollection of past thoughts. This result is not encouraging to those who believe that data can be public.

The particular form given to protocol-sentences by Neurath is, perhaps, not an essential part of his doctrine. Let us therefore examine it more generally.

Let us repeat some quotations.* 'Statements are compared with statements, not with experiences' (N.) 'A protocol-statement, like every other statement, is at the end adopted or rejected by a decision' (N). 'The system of *Protokollsätze* we call true . . . may only be characterized by the historical fact, that it is the system which is actually adopted by mankind, and especially by the scientists of our culture circle' (H). 'Instead of *reality* we have a number of mutually incompatible but internally coherent bodies of propositions, choice between which is not logically determined (*logisch ausgezeichnet*)' (N).

This attempt to make the linguistic world self-sufficient is open to many objections. Take first the necessity of empirical statements about words, e.g., 'Neurath says so-and-so'. How do I know this? By seeing certain black marks on a white ground. But this experience must not, according to Neurath and Hempel, be made a ground for my assertion that Neurath says so-and-so. Before I can assert this, I must ascertain the opinion of mankind,

* In what follows, 'N' stands for 'Neurath' and 'H' for 'Hempel'.

and especially of my culture circle, as to what Neurath says. But how am I to ascertain it? I go round to all the scientists of my culture circle, and say: 'what does Neurath say on p. 364?' In reply I hear certain sounds, but this is an experience, and therefore does not give any ground for an opinion as to what they said. When A answers, I must go round to B, C, D, and the rest of my culture circle, to ascertain what they think A said. And so on throughout an endless regress. If eyes and ears do not enable me to know what Neurath said, no assemblage of scientists, however distinguished, can enable me to know. If Neurath is right, his opinions are not known to me through his writings, but through my decisions and those of my culture circle. If we choose to attribute to him opinions completely different from those which he in fact holds, it will be useless for him to contradict, or to point to pages in his writings; for by such behaviour he will only cause us to have experiences, which are never a ground for statements.

Hempel, it is true, denies such consequences of his doctrine. He says: 'Carnap and Neurath do by no means intend to say: "there are no facts, there are only propositions"; on the contrary, the occurrence of certain statements in the protocol of an observer or in a scientific book is regarded as an empirical fact, and the propositions occurring as empirical objects.' But this makes nonsense of the whole theory. For what is an 'empirical fact'? To say: 'A is an empirical fact' is, according to Neurath and Hempel, to say: 'the proposition "A occurs" is consistent with a certain body of already accepted propositions'. In a different culture circle another body of propositions may be accepted; owing to this fact, Neurath is an exile. He remarks himself that practical life soon reduces the ambiguity, and that we are influenced by the opinions of neighbours. In other words, empirical truth can be determined by the police. This doctrine, it is evident, is a complete abandonment of empiricism, of which the very essence is that only experiences can determine the truth or falsehood of non-tautologous propositions.

Neurath's doctrine, if taken seriously, deprives empirical propositions of all meaning. When I say 'the sun is shining', I do not mean that this is one of a number of sentences among which there is no contradiction; I mean something which is not verbal, and for the sake of which such words as 'sun' and 'shining' were invented. The purpose of words, though philosophers seem to forget this simple fact, is to deal with matters other than words. If I go into a restaurant and order my dinner, I do not want my words to fit into a system with other words, but to bring about the presence of food. I could have managed without words, by taking what I want, but this would have been less convenient. The verbalist theories of some modern philosophers forget the homely practical purposes of every-day words, and lose themselves in a neo-neo-Platonic mysticism. I seem to hear them saying 'in the beginning was the Word', not 'in the beginning was what the word means'. It is remarkable that this reversion to ancient metaphysics should have occurred in the attempt to be ultra-empirical.

CHAPTER II

FACTUAL PREMISSES

ASSUMING, as I shall do henceforth, that there are basic propositions, it seems to me that, for theory of knowledge, 'basic propositions' may be alternatively defined as 'those propositions about particular occurrences which, after a critical scrutiny, we still believe independently of any extraneous evidence in their favour'.

Let us consider the clauses of this definition, and let us begin at the end. There may be evidence in favour of a basic proposition, but it is not this evidence *alone* that causes our belief. You may wake up in the morning and see that it is daylight, and you may see from your watch that it must be daylight. But even if your watch pointed to midnight, you would not doubt that it is daylight. In any scientific system, a number of propositions based on observations support each other, but each is capable of commanding belief on its own account. Moreover mutual support among basic propositions is only possible on the basis of some theory.

There are cases, however – chiefly where memory is concerned – in which our belief, though not inferential, is more or less uncertain. In such cases, a system composed of such beliefs wins more acceptance than any one of them singly. I think Mr Z. invited me to dinner on Thursday; I look in my diary, and find an entry to that effect. Both my memory and my diary are fallible, but when they agree I think it unlikely that they are both wrong. I will return to this kind of case later; for the present, I wish to exclude it. It is to be observed, meantime, that a non-inferential belief need not be either certain or indubitable.

Now comes the question of critical scrutiny, and a very awkward question it is. You say 'there's a dog', and feel quite satisfied of the truth of your statement. I shall not suppose your faith attacked by Bishop Berkeley, but by one of his allies in modern business. The producer comes to you and says: 'ah, I hoped you would think it was a dog, but in fact it was recorded by the new system of Technicolor, which is revolutionizing the cinema'. Perhaps the physiologist in future will be able to stimulate the optic nerve in the way necessary for seeing a dog; I have gathered from the works of Bulldog Drummond that contact of a fist with the eye enables people to see the starry heavens as well as the moral law. And we all know what hypnotists can do; we know also how emotional excitement can produce phenomena like Macbeth's dagger. On these grounds, which are all derived from common sense, not from philosophy, a man possessed of intellectual prudence will avoid such rash credulity as is involved in saying 'there's a dog'.

But what, then, will such a man say on such an occasion? Having been badly brought up, he will have an *impulse* to say 'dog', which he will have to restrain. He will say: 'there is a canoid patch of colour'. Suppose, now, having been impressed by the method of Cartesian doubt, he tries to make himself disbelieve even this. What reason can he find for disbelieving it? It cannot be disproved by anything else that he may see or hear; and he can have no better reason for believing in other sights or sounds than in this one; if he carries doubt to this length, he cannot even know that he said 'dog', if he did say so.

We should note that basic propositions must be just as true when applied to dreams as when applied to waking life; for, after all, dreams do really occur. This is a criterion for discriminating between what is basic and what is interpretative.

We thus arrive at the momentary object of perception as the least questionable thing in our experience, and as therefore the criterion and touchstone of all other certainties and pseudo-certainties.

But for theory of knowledge it is not sufficient that we should perceive something; it is necessary that we should express what we perceive in words. Now most object-words are condensed inductions; this is true of the word 'dog', as we have already had occasion to notice. We must avoid such words, if we wish to be merely recording what we perceive. To do this is very difficult, and requires a special vocabulary. We have seen that this vocabulary includes predicate-words such as 'red', and relation-words such as 'precedes', but not names of persons or physical objects or classes of such terms.

We have considered the subject of 'basic propositions' or *Protokollsätze*, and tried to show that empirical knowledge is impossible without them. It will be remembered that we defined a 'basic proposition' by two characteristics:

(1) It arises on occasion of a perception, which is the evidence for its truth;

(2) It has a form such that no two propositions having this form can be mutually inconsistent if derived from different percepts.

A proposition having these two characteristics cannot be disproved, but it would be rash to say that it *must be* true.

Perhaps no actual proposition quite rigidly fulfils the definition. But pure perceptive propositions remain a limit to which we can approach asymptotically, and the nearer we approach the smaller is the risk of error.

Empirical knowledge requires, however, other premisses asserting matters of fact, in addition to pure perceptive propositions. I shall give the name 'factual premiss' to any uninferred proposition which asserts something having a date, and which I believe after a critical scrutiny. I do not mean that the date is part of the assertion, but merely that some kind of temporal occurrence is what is involved in the truth of the assertion.

Factual premisses are not alone sufficient for empirical knowledge, since most of it is inferred. We require, in addition, the premisses necessary for deduction, and those other premisses, whatever they may be, that are necessary for the non-demonstrative inferences upon which science depends. Perhaps there are also some general propositions such as 'if A precedes B, and B precedes C, then A precedes C' and 'yellow is more like green than like blue'. Such propositions, however, as already mentioned, call for a lengthy discussion. For the present, I am only concerned with those premisses of our empirical knowledge which have to do with particular occurrences, i.e., with those that I am calling 'factual premisses'. These, it seems to me, are of four kinds:

I. Perceptual propositions.

II. Memory propositions.

III. Negative basic propositions.

IV. Basic propositions concerning present propositional attitudes, i.e. concerning what I am believing, doubting, desiring, etc.

I. *Perceptual Propositions*. Suppose, as in an earlier chapter, that we see a red square inscribed in a blue circle. We may say 'there is a square in a circle', 'there is a red figure in a blue one', 'there is a red square in a blue circle'. All these are judgements of perception. The perceptual datum always allows many propositions, all expressing some aspect of it. The propositions are more abstract than the datum, of necessity, since words classify. But there is no theoretical limit to the accuracy of specification that is possible, and there is nothing in the perceptual datum that is essentially incapable of being expressed in words.

The correspondence theory of truth, as applied to judgements of perception, may be interpreted in a way which would be false. It would be a mistake to think that, corresponding to every true judgement of perception, there is a separate fact. Thus in the above case of the circle and the square, there is a circle of a certain colour and of certain angular dimensions, and inside it there is a square of a certain other colour and of certain other angular dimensions. All this is only one datum, from which a variety of judgements of perception can be derived. There is not, outside language, a fact 'that there is a square in a circle', and another fact 'that there is a red figure in a blue figure'. There are no facts 'that so-and-so'. There are percepts, from which, by analysis, we derive propositions 'that so-and-so'. But so long as this is realized, it will do no harm if percepts are called 'facts'.

II. *Memory Propositions*. There are considerable difficulties about basic propositions of this class. For, first, memory is fallible, so that in any given case it is difficult to feel the same degree of certainty as in a judgement of perception; secondly, no memory proposition is, strictly speaking, verifiable, since nothing in the present or the future makes any proposition about the past necessary; but thirdly, it is impossible to doubt that there have been events in the past, or to believe that the world has only just begun. This third consideration shows that there must be factual premisses about the past, while the first and second make it difficult to say what they are.

I think, to begin with, that we must exclude from the category of memories what we know about the *immediate* past. For instance, when we see a quick movement, we know that the object concerned was in one place and is in another; but this is all to be included in perception, and cannot be counted as a case of memory. This is shown by the fact that seeing a movement is different from seeing a thing first in one place and then in another.*

It is by no means easy to distinguish between memory and habit; in ordinary speech, the distinction is ignored where verbal habits are concerned. A child is said to 'remember' the multiplication table if he has the correct verbal habits, although the multiplication table never happened and he may not remember any of the occasions on which he learnt it. Our memory of past events is sometimes of the same sort: we have a verbal habit of narrative, but nothing more. This happens especially with incidents that one relates frequently. But how about past incidents that one has never recalled till now, or at any rate not for a long time? Even then, the memory may be recalled by association, which is a form of habit. Turgenev's *Smoke* opens with the smell of heliotrope recalling a long-past love affair. Here the memory is involuntary; there is, however, also deliberate recollection, for example in writing an autobiography. I think that association is still the main agent here. We start from some prominent incident that we remember easily, and gradually associations lead us on to things that we had not thought of for a long time. The prominent incident itself has remained prominent, usually, because it has many associative links with the present. It is obvious that we are not always remembering

---

* Ah, yet doth beauty, like a dial-hand,
Steal from his figure, and no pace perceived.
                [Shakespeare, Sonnet CIV]

everything that we can remember, and that what causes us to remember a given occurrence at a given moment is some association with something in the present. Thus association is certainly a vital factor in the occurrence of a recollection. But this leaves us still in doubt as to the epistemological status of memory.

Take, first, the fact that we know what is meant by the past. Would this be possible without memory? It may be said that we know what is meant by the future, although we have no memory of it. But I think the future is defined by relation to the past: it is 'a time when what is now the present is past'. Lapse of time, up to a point, can be understood from the specious present: when a person utters a short sentence, say 'dinner is served', we know there is a lapse of time between the first word and the last, though the whole sentence comes within the specious present. But in true memory there is a pastness of an altogether different kind, and this is something with which association has nothing to do. Say you meet a man whom you have not seen for twenty years: association will account for any words or images connected with the previous meeting that may come into your mind, but will not account for the reference of these words or images to the past. You may find it impossible to refer them to the present, but why not treat them as mere imaginative fantasies? You do not do this, but treat them as referring to something that really happened. It would seem, therefore, that the mere fact that we can understand the word 'past' implies knowledge that *something* happened in the past. Since it is hardly possible that our most primitive knowledge of the past should refer to a vague 'something', there must be more definite memories which are to be accepted as basic propositions.

Let us take some recollection that it is very difficult to doubt. Suppose you receive a telegram to say that your uncle in Australia has left you a million pounds, and you go upstairs to tell your wife. By the time you reach her, your first reading of the telegram has become a memory, but you can hardly doubt that it occurred. Or take more ordinary events: at the end of the day, you can recall many things that you have done since you got up, and concerning some, at least, you feel a high degree of certainty.

Suppose you set to work to remember as many as you can. There are things that you know because they always happen: that you dressed, breakfasted, and so on. But in regard even to them, there is a very clear difference between knowing that they must have occurred and remembering them. It seems to me that, in true memory, we have images to which we say 'yes' or 'no'. In some cases, we say 'yes' emphatically and without hesitation; in others, we depend partly upon context. For our purpose, the emphatic cases are the important ones. Images come, it seems to me, in three ways: as merely imaginary, or with a yes-feeling, or with a no-feeling. When they come with a yes-feeling, but do not fit into the present, they are referred to the past. (I do not mean that this is a complete account of what happens in memory.) Thus all memory involves propositional attitudes, meaning, and external references; in this it differs from judgements of perception.

No memory is indubitable. I have had memories in dreams, just as definite as the best memories of waking life, but wholly untrue. I once, in a dream, remembered that Whitehead and I had murdered Lloyd George a month ago. Judgements of perception are just as true when applied to dreams as when applied to waking life; this, indeed, is a criterion for the correct interpretation of judgements of perception. But memory judgements in dreams, except when they consist in remembering an earlier part of the dream or a real event of waking life, are erroneous.

Since memories are not indubitable, we seek various ways of reinforcing them. We make contemporary records, or we seek confirmation from other witnesses, or we look for reasons tending to show that what we recollect was what was to be expected. In such ways we can increase the likelihood of any given recollection being correct, but we cannot free ourselves from dependence on memory in general. This is obvious as regards the testimony of other witnesses. As regards contemporary records, they are seldom *strictly* contemporary, and if they are, it cannot be subsequently known except through the memory of the person making the record. Suppose you remember on November 8th that last night you saw a very bright meteor, and you find on your desk a note in your handwriting saying: 'at 20h. 32m. G.M.T. on November 7th, I saw a bright meteor in the constellation Hercules. Note made at 20h. 33m. G.M.T.' You may remember making the note; if so, the memory of the meteor and the note confirm each other. But if you are discarding memory as a source of knowledge, you will not know how the note got there. It may have been made by a forger, or by yourself as a practical joke. As a matter of logic, it is quite clear that there can be no demonstrative inference from a set of shapes now seen on paper to a bright light seen in the sky last night. It would seem, therefore, that, where the past is concerned, we rely partly on coherence, and partly on the strength of our conviction as regards the particular memory which is in question; but that our confidence as regards memory in general is such that we cannot entertain the hypothesis of the past being wholly an illusion.

It will be remembered that, in an earlier chapter, we decided that memory propositions often require the word 'some'. We say 'I know I saw that book somewhere', or 'I know he said something very witty'. Perhaps we can remember even more vaguely, for instance 'I know something happened yesterday'. We *might* even remember 'there have been past events', which we rejected as a factual premiss a little while ago. I think that to accept this as a factual premiss would be going too far, but there certainly are uninferred memory propositions (at any given moment) which involve 'some'. These are logically deducible from propositions not involving 'some' which were, at some previous time, expressions of present perception. You say to yourself one day 'oh there is that letter I had lost', and next day 'I know I saw that letter *somewhere* yesterday'. This is an important logical difference between memory and perception, for perception is never general or vague. When we say it is vague, that only means that it does not allow so many inferences as some other perception would allow. But images, in their representative capacity, may be vague, and the knowledge based upon them may involve the word 'some'. It is worthy of note that this word may occur in a factual premiss.

In admitting memory propositions among factual premisses, we are conceding that our premisses may be doubtful and sometimes false. We are all willing, on occasion, to admit evidence against what we think we remember. Memories come to us with different grades of subjective certainty; in some, there is hardly more doubt than as regards a present percept, whereas in others the hesitation may be very great. Memories, in practice, are reinforced by inferences as casual as is possible, but such inferences are never demonstrative. It would be a great simplification if we could dispense with memory premisses, or if, failing that, we could distinguish two kinds of memory, of which one is infallible. Let us examine these possibilities.

In an attempt to dispense with memory, we shall still allow knowledge of whatever falls within the specious present; thus we shall be still aware of temporal sequence. We shall know what is mean by 'A is earlier than B'. We can therefore define 'the past' as 'what is earlier than the specious present'. We shall construct our knowledge of the past by means of causal laws, as we do in geology, where memory does not come in. We shall observe that we have a habit of making a record of an event that for any reason is important to us, either in writing or by creating in ourselves a verbal habit. We do the latter, for example, if, when we are introduced to a man, we repeat his name over and over to ourselves. We may do this so often that, when we next see him, we think of his name at once. We are then said, in popular language, to 'remember' his name, but we do not necessarily recall any past event. Is it possible to build up our knowledge of the past in this way, by means of records and verbal habits alone? In this view, if I see a man and know that his name is Jones, I shall infer that I must have met him on some former occasion, just as I do if his face is vaguely familiar. When I see a record, I can know that it is in my handwriting without having to invoke recollection, because I can copy the record now and make comparisons; I can then go on to infer that the record tells of something that once happened to me. In theory, the small but finite stretch of time comprised within the specious present should suffice for the discovery of causal laws, by means of which we could infer the past without having to appeal to memory.

I am not prepared to maintain that the above theory is logically untenable. There is no doubt that we could, without the help of memory, know *something* of the past. But I think it is clear that, in fact, we know more of the past than can be accounted for in this way. And while we must admit that we are sometimes mistaken as to what we think we remember, some recollections are so nearly indubitable that they would still command credence, even if much contrary evidence were produced. I do not see, therefore, on what ground we could reject memory as one of the sources of our knowledge concerning the course of events.

It remains to inquire whether there are two kinds of memory, one fallible and one infallible. We might maintain this without maintaining that we could know infallibly to which kind a given recollection belonged; we should then still have reason for some degree of uncertainty in every particular case. But we should at least have reason to think that *some* memories are correct. The theory, therefore, is worth examining.

I should not have considered seriously the possibility of there being two kinds of memory of which one is infallible, but for the fact that I heard this theory advocated in discussion by G. E. Moore. He did not then elaborate it, and I do not know how tenaciously he held it. I shall, therefore, independently attempt to give it as much plausibility as I can.

It must be held, on logical grounds, that no occurrence gives *demonstrative* grounds in favour of belief in any other occurrence. But the grounds are often such as we cannot fail to accept as giving *practical* certainty. We saw that there can be no reason for disbelieving the proposition 'that is red' when made in the presence of a red percept; it must, however, be admitted that belief in this proposition is logically possible in the absence of a red percept. Such grounds as exist for supposing that this does not occur are derived from causal laws as to the occurrence of language. We can, however, in theory, distinguish two cases in relation to a judgement such as 'that is red': one, when it is caused by what it asserts, and the other when words or images enter into its causation. In the former case it must be true, in the latter not.

This, however, is a statement which needs elaborating. What can be meant when we say that a percept 'causes' a word or a sentence? On the face of it, we have to suppose a considerable process in the brain, connecting visual centres with motor centres; the causation, therefore, is by no means direct. Perhaps we may state the matter as follows: in the course of learning to speak, certain causal routes (language-habits) are established in the brain, which lead from percepts to utterances. These are the shortest possible routes from percepts to utterances; all others involve some further association or habit. When an utterance is associated with a percept by a minimal causal route, the percept is said to be the 'meaning' of the utterance, and the utterance is 'true' because what it means occurs. Thus wherever this state of affairs exists, the truth of a judgement of perception is logically guaranteed.

We have to inquire whether anything similar is possible in the case of memory.

The stimulus to a judgement of recollection is obviously never the event recollected, since that is in the not immediate past. The stimulus may be a percept, or may be a 'thought'. Let us take the former case as the simpler. You find yourself, let us suppose, in some place where an interesting conversation occurred, and you remember the conversation. The cerebral mechanism involved is as yet hypothetical, but we may suppose it very similar to that involved in the passage from a percept to a word which 'means' it. When two percepts A and B occur together, the occurrence of a percept closely similar to A on a future occasion may cause an image closely similar to B. It may be argued that a certain type of association between a percept like A and an image like B can only occur if, on a previous occasion, A and B, as percepts, have occurred together, and that, therefore, the recollection resulting from the percept resembling A must be correct. Where fallacious memories occur, it may be said, the associative causal chains involved must be longer than in the case of correct memories. Perhaps, in this way, the case of memory can be assimilated to that of perception.

The above type of argument, however, while it may be correct at its own level, can have no direct relevance to the question of factual premisses, since it presupposes elaborate knowledge concerning the brain, which, obviously, can only be built up by means of factual premisses some of which are recollections.

It must be admitted that a factual premiss need not be indubitable, even subjectively; it need only command a certain degree of credence. It can therefore always be reinforced if it is found to harmonize with other factual premisses. What characterizes a factual premiss is not indubitability, but the fact that it commands a greater or less degree of belief on its own account, independently of its relations to other propositions. We are thus led to a combination of self-evidence with coherence: sometimes one factor is very much more important than the other, but in theory coherence always plays some part. The coherence required, however, is not strict logical coherence, for factual premisses can and should be so stated as to be deductively independent of each other. The kind of coherence involved is a matter which I shall consider at a later stage.

III. *Negative Basic Propositions*. We have already had occasion to consider negative empirical propositions, but I want now to consider afresh whether they are ever themselves factual premisses, or are always derived from incompatibility propositions.

The question to be considered is: how do we know negative empirical propositions, such as 'there is no cheese in the larder' or 'there are no snakes in Ireland'? We entertained the hypothesis, when we considered this question in an earlier chapter, that such propositions are inferred from premisses among which there are propositions such as 'where there is red there is not yellow', or 'what feels hard does not feel soft'. I want now to examine afresh the whole question of negative empirical knowledge.

It is plain, to begin with, that sensible qualities fall into genera. There are colours, there are sounds, there are smells and tastes, there are various sorts of sensations of touch, there are sensations of temperature. As to these, certain things are to be noted. We can see two colours at once, but not in the same place. We can hear two sounds at once, and there need be no discoverable difference in their direction of origin. Smells have no location except in the nose, and two smells are not essentially incompatible. A sensation of touch has qualities of which we may note two kinds: a local quality, according to the part of the body touched, and a quality of greater or less pressure; in each kind, different qualities have the sort of incompatibility that colours have, i.e. they can be experienced simultaneously, but not in the same place on the surface of the body. The same applies to temperature.

It thus appears that, as regards incompatibility, there are differences between qualities belonging to different senses. But as regards negative judgements there are no such differences. If someone brings you, in the dark, into the neighbourhood of a ripe Gorgonzola, and says 'can't you smell roses?' you will say no. When you hear a foghorn, you know it is not the song of the lark. And when you smell nothing or hear nothing, you can be aware of the fact. It seems that we must conclude that pure negative propositions can be empirically known without being inferred. 'Listen. Do you hear anything?' 'No.' There is nothing recondite about this conversation. When you say 'no' in such a case, are you giving the result of an inference, or are you uttering a basic proposition? I do not think this kind of knowledge has received the attention that it deserves. If your 'no' gives utterance to a basic proposition (which must obviously be empirical), such propositions may not only be negative, but apparently general, for your 'no' may, if logic is to be believed, be expressed in the form: 'all sounds are unheard by me now'.* Thus the logical difficulties of general empirical knowledge will be greatly lessened. If, on the other hand, your 'no' expresses an inference, it must use some general premiss, for otherwise no general conclusion could be inferred; and thus we shall still have to admit that some basic propositions not belonging to logic are general.

When a person says 'listen', and then you hear no sound, you are in a condition to notice a noise if there were one. But this does not always apply. 'Didn't you hear the dinner-bell?' 'No, I was working.' Here you have a negative memory judgement, and a cause (not a ground) assigned for its truth; and in this case you are sure of the negative although you were *not* listening at the time.

---

* I shall argue later that theory of knowledge need not accept this logical interpretation.

The conclusion seems irresistible that a percept or a memory may give rise to a negative factual premiss as well as to a positive one. There is an important difference: in the case of a positive basic proposition, the percept may cause the words, whereas in the case of a negation the words, or corresponding images, must exist independently of the percept. A negative basic proposition thus requires a propositional attitude, in which the proposition concerned is the one which, on the basis of perception, is denied. We may therefore say that, while a positive basic proposition is caused only by a percept (given our verbal habits), a negative one is caused by the percept plus a previous propositional attitude. There is still an incompatibility, but it is between imagination and perception. The simplest way of expressing this state of affairs is to say that, in consequence of perception, you know that a certain proposition is false. In a word: it is possible, in a certain sense, to notice what is not there as well as what is there. This conclusion, if true, is important.

IV. *Factual Premisses concerning present propositional attitudes.* These propositions, just as much as 'this is red', report a present occurrence, but they differ from basic propositions of Class I by their logical form, which involves mention of a proposition. They are propositions asserting that something is believed, doubted, desired, and so on, in so far as such propositions are known independently of inference. The something believed or doubted or desired can only be expressed by means of a sub- ordinate proposition. It is clear that we can be aware of believing or desiring something, in just as immediate a way as we can be aware of a red patch that we see. Someone says, let us suppose, 'is today Wednesday?' and you reply 'I think so'. Your state- ment 'I think so' expresses, in part at least, a factual premiss as to your opinion. The analysis of the proposition offers diffi- culties, but I do not see how to deny that it contains at least a kernel which expresses a datum.

It will be observed that propositions of this class are usually, if not always, psychological. I am not sure that we could not use this fact to define 'psychology'. It might be said that dreams belong to psychology, and that basic propositions concerning percepts in dreams are exactly on a level with other basic propositions concerning percepts. But to this it may be replied that the scientific study of dreams is only possible when we are awake, and that, therefore, all the data for any possible science of dreams are memories. Similar answers could be made as regards the psychology of perception.

However that may be, there is certainly an important department of knowledge which is characterized by the fact that, among its basic propositions, some contain subordinate propositions.

The factual premisses considered in the above discussions all have in common a certain characteristic, namely that they each refer to a short period of time, which is that at which they (or other propositions from which they are deducible) first became premisses. In the case of recollections, if they are veridical, they are either identical with or logically inferrible from judgements of perception made at the times to which the recollections refer. Our knowledge of the present and the past consists partly of basic propositions, whereas our knowledge of the future consists wholly of inferences – apart, possibly, from certain immediate expectations.

An 'empirical datum' might be defined as a proposition referring to a particular time, and beginning to be known at the time to which it refers; this definition, however, would be inadequate, since we may infer what is now happening before we perceive it. It is essential to the conception of an empirical datum that the knowledge should be (in some sense) caused by what is known. I do not wish, however, to introduce the conception of cause by a back door, and I shall therefore, at present, ignore this aspect of empirical knowledge.

Among the premisses of our knowledge there must be propositions not referring to particular events. Logical premisses, both deductive and inductive, are generally admitted, but it seems possible that there are others. The impossibility of two different colours in the same part of the visual field is perhaps one. The question of propositions of this sort is difficult, and I will say nothing dogmatic about them.

I will observe, however, that empiricism, as a theory of

knowledge, is self-refuting. For, however it may be formulated, it must involve *some* general proposition about the dependence of knowledge upon experience; and any such proposition, if true, must have as a consequence that itself cannot be known. While, therefore, empiricism may be true, it cannot, if true, be known to be so. This, however, is a large problem.

CHAPTER 12

AN ANALYSIS OF PROBLEMS
CONCERNING PROPOSITIONS

THE purpose of the present chapter is to state problems, not to solve them. Attempts at solution will be given in subsequent chapters.

The first question is: does logic or theory of knowledge need 'propositions' as well as 'sentences'? Here we may define a 'proposition', heuristically, as 'what a sentence signifies'. Some sentences are significant, others are not; it is natural, though perhaps mistaken, to suppose that, when a sentence is significant, there is something that is its significance. If there is such a something, it is what I mean by the word 'proposition'. Since 'having the same significance' is a relation which can certainly hold between two sentences – e.g. 'Brutus killed Caesar' and 'Caesar was killed by Brutus' – we can make sure of *some* meaning for the word 'proposition' by saying that, if we find no other meaning for it, it shall mean 'the class of all sentences having the same significance as a given sentence'.

Whether or not there is a substantive 'significance', there is certainly an adjective 'significant'. I apply this adjective to any sentence that is not nonsense. 'Significant' and 'significance' are words that I apply to sentences, whereas 'meaning' is a word that I apply to single words. This distinction has no basis in usage, but it is convenient. When a sentence is not significant, I call it 'nonsensical'.

No ordinary language contains syntactical rules forbidding the construction of nonsensical sentences; e.g. the sentence 'quadruplicity drinks procrastination' is not one that grammarians can condemn. Yet it seems clear that it must be possible to construct a language having the following two properties:

(1) Every sentence composed according to the rules of syntax out of words having meaning is significant;

(2) Every significant sentence consists of words having meaning and put together according to the rules of syntax.

It should be observed that meaning of words and significance of sentences are intertwined except as regards object-words. Other words are defined by means of the significance of the simplest sentences in which they can occur.

But although it should be possible, in a good language, to give syntactical rules determining when a sentence is significant, it must not be supposed that 'significance' is a syntactical concept. On the contrary, a non-tautologous sentence is significant in virtue of some relation that it has to certain states of the person using the sentence. These states are 'believings' and are instances of the same belief which is 'expressed' by the sentence. In defining the relation of the sentence to the belief (which latter is in general non-verbal), we have to remember that false sentences are significant as well as true ones. And when the relation has been defined, we have to show that our syntactical rules of significance are such as it justifies.

The analysis of belief as a state of the believer does not involve the concepts 'true' and 'false'; while we are concerned with belief on the subjective side, we need only consider sentences as 'expressing' states of those who use them. But it is part of the purpose of a sentence in the indicative to 'indicate' one or more facts which, in general, are not states of the person pronouncing the sentence. As soon as we consider this aspect of sentences, we become concerned with truth and falsehood, since only true sentences succeed in indicating. What sentences 'indicate' is considered in Chapter 15, and from this point onwards we are concerned with problems involving 'truth' and 'falsehood'.

In the analysis of what I call 'propositional attitudes', i.e. occurrences such as believing, doubting, desiring, etc., which are naturally described by sentences containing subordinate sentences, e.g. 'I think it will rain', we have a complicated mixture of empirical and syntactical questions. On the face of it, the syntactical form of 'A believes p' is peculiar in the fact that it contains a subordinate sentence 'p'. The occurrence which makes 'A believes p' true seems to be a complex containing a subordinate complex, and we have to inquire whether there is any way of avoiding such an account of belief.

Propositional attitudes, *prima facie*, throw doubt on two principles that are assumed by many mathematical logicians, namely the principles of extensionality and atomicity.

The principle of extensionality has two parts:

I. The truth-value of any function of a proposition depends only upon the truth-value of the argument, i.e. if p and q are both true or both false, then any sentence containing p remains true or false, as the case may be, if q is substituted for p.

II. The truth-value of any function of a function depends only on the extension of the function, i.e. if whenever ϕx is true, ψx is true, and vice versa, then any sentence about the function ϕ remains true or false as the case may be, if ψ is substituted for ϕ.

Neither of these *appears* to be true of propositional attitudes. A man may believe one true proposition without believing another; he may believe that some featherless bipeds are not men without believing that some men are not men. Thus we become involved in an analysis of belief and other propositional attitudes in our attempt to decide what looks like a purely logical question.

The principle of atomicity is stated by Wittgenstein as follows (*Tractatus*, 2.0201): 'Every statement about complexes can be analysed into a statement about their constituent parts, and into those propositions which completely describe the complexes.' This, if true, implies that in 'A believes p', p does not occur as a unit, but only its constituents occur.

In the above form, the meaning of the principle of atomicity is not very clear. But there is a technical form of the principle, not perhaps strictly equivalent to Wittgenstein's form, but easier to discuss, more definite, and therefore (I think) more important. In this form, it states that everything we wish to say can be said in sentences belonging to the 'atomistic hierarchy' which will be defined in section C of Chapter 13. For logic it is important to know whether, in this technical form, the principle is true. What is meant by saying that the principle is 'true' is that it is possible to construct a language such that (*a*) every sentence in the language is constructed in accordance with the principle, and (b) every significant sentence in any language can be translated into our constructed language.

We have thus to discuss the following questions in the following order:

I. What is meant by the 'significance' of a sentence, and what syntactical rules can we give to determine when a sentence is significant?

II. Have we any need of 'propositions' as opposed to 'sentences'?

III. What is the correct analysis of 'A believes p', and in what sense, if any, does 'p' occur in 'A believes p'? (What is said about belief may be extended to other propositional attitudes.)

IV. Can we construct an adequate language in which the principle of extensionality holds? I mean by an 'adequate' language one into which we can translate any significant sentence of any language.

V. Can we construct an adequate language in which the principle of atomicity holds?

CHAPTER 13

THE SIGNIFICANCE OF SENTENCES

A. GENERAL

THE question as to what makes a sentence significant is forced upon us by various problems.

There are, in the first place, the recognized rules of syntax in ordinary languages. 'Socrates is a man' is constructed in accordance with these rules, and is significant; but 'is a man', considered as a complete sentence, violates the rules and is nonsensical. (I use 'nonsensical' as the contradictory of 'significant'.) The rules of syntax in ordinary languages are obviously intended to prevent nonsense, but they fail to achieve their purpose completely. As we have already noted, 'quadruplicity drinks procrastination' is nonsense, but violates no rules of English syntax. It must clearly be part of our present problem to construct better rules of syntax, which shall automatically prevent nonsense. In the early stages of our discussion, we are guided by the mere *feeling* as to what is significant, but we hope in the end to arrive at something better.

There is one sense of the word 'possibility' which is connected with our present problem. We may say that whatever is asserted by a significant sentence has a certain kind of possibility. I will define this as 'syntactic' possibility. It is perhaps narrower than logical possibility, but certainly wider than physical possibility. 'The moon is made of green cheese' is syntactically possible, but not physically. It is difficult to give any indisputable instance of a logical possibility which is not syntactically possible; perhaps 'this is both red and blue' is an instance, and perhaps 'the sound of a trombone is blue' is an instance.

I shall not ask, at this stage, *what* it is that is possible in the case of a sentence which is significant and false. It cannot be the sentence, for that is actual, nor can it be 'that the sentence is true', for that is merely another false sentence. There is thus a problem, but for the present I shall not pursue it.

The question of 'significance' is difficult and somewhat intricate. It will perhaps help to clarify the discussion to state, in outline, the conclusion at which I shall arrive, which is as follows.

An assertion has two sides, subjective and objective. Subjectively, it 'expresses' a state of the speaker, which may be called a 'belief', which may exist without words, and even in animals and infants who do not possess language. Objectively, the assertion, if true, 'indicates' a fact; if false, it intends to 'indicate' a fact, but fails to do so. There are some assertions, namely those which assert present states of the speaker which he notices, in which what is 'expressed' and what is 'indicated' are identical; but in general these two are different. The 'significance' of a sentence is what it 'expresses'. Thus true and false sentences are equally significant, but a string of words which cannot express any state of the speaker is nonsensical.

In the following discussion the above theory will gradually emerge as, in my opinion, the only one which gives a clear solution of the problems that present themselves.

The question of significance may be brought into connexion with sentences heard rather than spoken. The hearing of a significant statement has effects dependent upon the nature of the statement but not upon its truth or falsehood; the hearing what is recognized as nonsense has no such effects. It is true that what is in fact nonsense, may have effects such as only a significant statement should have, but in that case the hearer usually imagines a signification of which the words are not strictly susceptible. Broadly speaking, we may say that a heard statement, interpreted by the hearer as significant, is capable of effects of which *obvious* nonsense is incapable. This is one of the points to be borne in mind in seeking a definition of 'significance'.

The subject of significance has been shown to be more difficult than it seemed by the paradoxes. It is clear that all the paradoxes arise from the attribution of significance to sentences that are in fact nonsensical. The paradoxes must be taken account of in formulating syntactical rules for the exclusion of nonsense.

The problem of the law of excluded middle is also connected with our present question. It is customary to say that every *proposition* is true or false, but we cannot say that every *sentence* is true or false, since nonsensical sentences are neither. If we are to apply the law of excluded middle to sentences, we must first know what sentences are significant, since it is only to them that the law can apply. Whether it applies to all of them is a question which I shall consider after the discussion of propositional attitudes is concluded.

I shall first consider the adjective 'significant', and then examine the question whether, when a sentence is significant, there is something that it 'signifies'. The word 'Caesar' means Caesar; is there anything analogous in regard to sentences? Technically, if '*p*' is a sentence, can we distinguish between '*p*' and *p*, as we distinguish between 'Caesar' and Caesar?

With these preliminaries, let us proceed to detailed discussion.

Sentences are of three sorts: true, false, and nonsensical. It follows that 'false', when applied to sentences, is not synonymous with 'not true', for a nonsensical sentence is not true, but is also not false. We must therefore, if '*p*' is a nonsensical sentence, distinguish between '*p* is false' and '"*p* is true" is false'. The latter will be true, but not the former. Assuming that 'not-*p*' means '*p* is false', we shall have, if *p* is nonsensical, 'not-(*p* is true)', but we shall not have 'not-*p*'. We shall say that, when '*p*' is meaningless, so is 'not-*p*'.

Thus if '*p*' is a phrase concerning which we have not yet decided whether it has significance or not, the situation is as follows:

From '*p* is true' we can infer '*p*', and vice versa;

From '*p* is false' we can infer '*p* is not true', but *not* vice versa;

From '"*p* is false" is true' we can infer '"*p* is true" is false', but not vice versa;

From '"*p* is false" is false' we can only infer '*p* is true or nonsense', but from '"*p* is not true" is not true' we can infer '*p* is true'.

Let us illustrate by an example. We will start with the sentence 'this is red', where 'this' is a proper name. Let us call this sentence '*p*'. Now consider the sentence '*p* is red'. This seems obviously nonsense; but if we meant by 'p' a written or printed sentential shape, it would not be, for this might be red. This is easy to understand if we accept the distinction between 'p' and p, where 'p' is a sentence, and p is the proposition that it signifies; for 'p' may be red, but 'p is red' is nonsense. For the moment, we may take p to be a thought, and 'p' the phrase in which the thought is expressed. In that case, 'p is red' is meaningless. If we can distinguish between 'p' and p, the whole matter becomes clear. Let us give the proper name 'P' to the sentential utterance 'this is red'. Then we say that P signifies p, that p is true, and that P signifies a truth. Let us give the name 'Q' to the sentential utterance 'p is red'. In that case, no statement of the form 'Q signifies q' is true, and Q signifies neither a truth nor a falsehood. Assuming still that there is a distinction between 'p' and p, I prefer to say that 'p' *signifies* p rather than that 'p' *means* p, because 'meaning' is better kept for single words. In that case, we shall say that a 'proposition' (if there is such a thing) is something 'signified' by some phrase, and that nonsensical phrases signify nothing. The problem that remains, in that case, is to decide what phrases signify something, and what this something is.

But all this assumes that we can refute whatever reasons exist for denying the distinction between 'p' and p, or at least arrive at some relevant distinction not affected by those reasons. I shall return to this question presently.

The distinction between strings of words that signify something and strings of words that signify nothing is, in many cases, perfectly clear. 'Socrates is a man' signifies something, but 'is a man' does not. 'Socrates, having drunk the hemlock, bade farewell to his friends' signifies something, but 'having drunk the hemlock, bade farewell to' signifies nothing. In these instances, there are too few words to make sense, but there may be too many. For example, '"Socrates is a man" is a man' signifies nothing. 'The law of contradiction is yellow' is a similar kind of nonsense. Sometimes there may be doubt, for instance in such a case as 'the sound of a trombone is blue'. The paradoxes arise from sentences that seem to signify something, but do not. Of these the simplest is 'I am lying'. This is capable of an infinite number of significations, but none of them is quite what we should have thought we meant. If we mean 'I utter a false proposition in the primary language', we are lying, since this is a proposition in the secondary language; the argument that, if we are lying, we are speaking the truth, fails, since our false statement is of the second order and we said we were uttering a false statement of the first order. Similarly if we mean 'I utter a false proposition of order n'. If I try to say 'I utter a false proposition of the first order, likewise one of the second, of the third, fourth . . . *ad infinitum*', I shall be asserting simultaneously (if it were possible) an infinite number of propositions, of which the 1st, 3rd, 5th . . . would be false, the 2nd, 4th, 6th . . . true.

The question whether a form of words signifies anything is thus not always easy, but there can be no doubt that some forms of words signify something, while others do not, and that among those that signify something some signify what is true, while others signify what is false. We must therefore find some way of defining the difference between strings of words that are nonsense and strings of words that signify something; and in the case of a sentence that signifies something, we have to inquire whether the something must be different from the sentence, or whether significance can be merely adjectival.

If a form of words signifies a proposition, I shall call the proposition the 'significance' of the form of words. For the moment I assume that there is a proposition which a significant sentence signifies.

Two questions arise: (1) what is meant by the 'significance' of a form of words? (2) what syntactical rules can be given as to when a form of words is significant?

What is meant by the 'significance' of a form of words? I use the word 'significance', here, in a restricted sense; the significance in question must be propositional. E.g. 'the King of England' is a phrase which has meaning in one sense, but does not have 'significance' in the sense with which I am concerned. For our present purpose, what the phrase signifies must be something true or false. What I am calling 'significance' might be called 'propositional significance', to distinguish it from other kinds, but for brevity I shall omit the word 'propositional'.

A sufficient but not necessary criterion of significance is that perceptual experiences can be imagined, or actually occur, which make us use the phrase (or its contradictory) as an assertion. In certain circumstances, we may say, as expressing what we perceive, 'snow is white'; therefore the phrase 'snow is white' is significant. In certain perceptive circumstances we may say 'snow is not black'; therefore the phrase 'snow is not black' is significant. Perhaps this will give us a hint as to what, in general, is 'signified' by a phrase which has significance.

When I say 'snow is white', what makes my statement true is one thing and what I express is another. What makes my statement true is a fact of physics, concerned with snow, but I am expressing a state of mind, namely a certain belief – or, to allow for lying, a desire that others should have a certain belief. We may omit this complication, and assume that, in asserting the words, I express a belief. But I am not asserting that I have a belief; I am asserting the object of the belief. Is there an object of the belief, which is what is asserted by the phrase 'snow is white'? Certain experiences cause us to believe that snow is white; if this belief has an object, we may say that I express the fact that I believe something (namely, that snow is white) by asserting this object. I do not assert that I believe the object; that would be a different assertion, which might be true even if snow were black. Our problem is: is there something, and if so what, that I believe when I believe that snow is white?

Again: what are you asking if you say 'is snow white'? Let us suppose that you grew up in Ethiopia, but that, as a result of an air raid, you were captured, blindfolded, and transported to the Arctic Circle, where you became acquainted with the touch and taste and smell of snow, and learnt that 'snow' was the name of the substance thus manifested to three of your senses. You might then ask 'is snow white?' You would not be asking about the *word* 'snow' and the *word* 'white', but about percepts. You might mean: do those who are not blindfolded, when they have the sensations of touch and smell that I have learnt to associate with the word 'snow', see whiteness? But even this is still too verbal. If you are, at the moment, touching and smelling snow, you may mean 'is *this* usually associated with whiteness?'

And if you are imagining whiteness, the thought in your mind may be 'is *this* usually associated with *that*?' where *this* is the tactual and olfactory percept, and *that* is the image of whiteness. But 'that' must not be interpreted as the image itself; it must rather mean a percept like the image. At this point, however, it becomes very difficult to be clear; for the image seems to 'mean' a percept in the same sort of way in which a word does.

It is obvious that, if beliefs have objects, what I believe when I believe that snow is white is the same as what I doubt when I ask 'is snow white?' This, whatever it is, is, on this hypothesis, the significance of the sentence 'snow is white'. If the significance of the sentence is true, that is in virtue of occurrences which are neither words nor images; if it is *known* to be true, these occurrences must be or have been percepts. The same holds, *mutatis mutandis*, if it is false. Truth and falsehood depend upon a relation between the significance of the sentence and something which is neither words nor images (except when the sentence is about words or images).

If we can decide what is meant by the 'significance' of a sentence, we shall say that it is this significance that is to be called a 'proposition', and that is either true or false. A sentence may signify a truth, or signify a falsehood, or signify nothing; but if a sentence signifies anything, then what it signifies must be true or false.

To try to discover what is meant by the 'significance' of a sentence, let us contrast a significant sentence with one that is not significant. Take 'Socrates drinks the hemlock' and 'quadruplicity drinks procrastination'. Of these the former logically can be, and once was, a judgement of perception; when it is not a judgement of perception, it is capable of calling up a complex image which has the same significance as, or, perhaps, *is* the significance of, the phrase. But we cannot form an image of quadruplicity drinking. When we try to do so, we merely imagine some man whom, for fun, we call 'Quadruplicity'. Let us ask ourselves: how can such a word as 'quadruplicity' refer to anything experienced? Suppose you are being subjected to military drill, and constantly hearing the order 'form fours'. You may, if you are fond of abstract words, reflect 'quadruplicity is prominent in drill'. This means: 'in drill, there are many occurrences in the verbal description of which it is natural to use the word "four"'. We may define 'quadruplicity' as 'that property of a propositional function which consists in being true for exactly four values of the variable'. Thus we have to ask: how do we know that it is nonsense to suppose that a property of a propositional function can drink? It is difficult, but not very difficult, to construct rules of syntax which, given the meanings of the separate words, shall insure that every combination of words which obeys the rules shall be significant, and every significant combination of words shall obey the rules. This work has, in fact, been done by the logicians, not perhaps completely, but with a fair degree of adequacy. The trouble is that, in this work, they have, at least in part, been guided by feeling, like the plain man. We cannot rest satisfied with our rules of significance unless we can see some reason for them, and this requires that we should decide what a form of words signifies when it is significant.

We may put the question in the form: 'what do we believe when we believe something?' Let us take an illustration. In some quarries, there is a big blasting operation every day at twelve o'clock. The signal to clear out of the way is given by a horn; there may also be men with red flags on the neighbouring roads and paths. If you ask them why they are there, they will say 'because there is going to be an explosion'. The operatives who understand the horn, the neighbours who understand the red flag, and the passing stranger who needs words, all, in the end, believe the same proposition, namely that expressed by the words 'there is going to be an explosion'. But probably only the passing stranger and his informant put this belief into words; for the others, the horn and the red flag serve the purposes of language, and produce the appropriate actions without the need of any verbal intermediary.

The horn and the flag may count as language, since their purpose is to convey information. But an approaching shell would convey very similar information without being language, since its purpose would not be to instruct. The shell, the horn, and the flag may all alike cause belief without causing words.

When a number of people all believe that there is going to be an explosion, what have they in common? A certain state of tension, which will be discharged when the explosion occurs, but, if their belief was false, will continue for some time, and then give place to surprise. The state of tension may be called 'expectation'; but the difficulty arises as regards the connexion of this (a) with the explosion or its absence, (b) with something which, in order to be vague, we will call the 'idea' of the explosion. It is obvious that to expect an explosion is one thing, and to expect (say) the arrival of a train is another. They have in common the feeling of expectation, but they differ as to the event which will change this feeling into acquiescence or surprise. This feeling, therefore, cannot be the only thing that constitutes the state of the person who is expecting something, since, if it were, any event would satisfy his expectation, whereas, in fact, only an event of a certain kind will do so. Perhaps, however, the whole thing could be explained physiologically? Everybody who is expecting a flash-light has sensations in the eyes, and the expectation of a loud noise involves something similar in connexion with the ears. It might be said, therefore, that expectation of a sensible phenom-enon consists in a state of receptivity of the appropriate sense-organs. But there are feelings connected with such a state of receptivity, and these feelings may be taken as constituting the mental part of an expectation.

It would seem, therefore, that what is in common among a number of people who all believe what is expressed by the words 'there is about to be a bang' is a state of tension connected with the appropriate sense-organs, a physiological condition of those organs, and the feelings which accompany such a condition. We can say the same of 'there is about to be a flash' or 'there is about to be the smell of a room full of ferrets'. But these are very emphatic occurrences, and are all in the immediate future. When I believe something less exciting – that tomorrow's *Times* will contain a weather forecast, or that Caesar crossed the Rubicon – I cannot observe any such occurrences in myself. If you were to tell me 'you will be murdered in a minute', perhaps my hair would stand on end; but when you tell me that Caesar was murdered on the Ides of March, my hair remains no more untidy than before, in spite of the fact that I quite believe what you say.

This difference, however, is probably only one of degree, unless the belief involved is merely verbal. When I speak of a belief being 'merely verbal', I do not mean only that it is expressed in words, but that what the words signify is not in the mind of the believer, who is merely thinking that the words are correct. We know that 'William the Conqueror 1066' is correct, but we do not often stop to think what this phrase signifies. In such a case we are not believing 'p', but believing '"p" signifies a truth'. The beliefs of educated people are largely of this kind. But the beliefs that primarily concern us are those that are not purely verbal. For until we have dealt with them we cannot explain what is meant by 'signifying a truth'.

When you are expecting an explosion, your body is in a certain state, and your mind in a corresponding state. This may bring the word 'explosion' into your mind, and the word 'explosion', at any rate with a small verbal addition, may cause the state of expectation. If you are told 'there has just been an explosion', and you vividly believe what you are told, your state of body and mind will become to some extent like what it would have been if you had heard the explosion, though less intense. Imagination, if sufficiently powerful, can have physical effects analogous to those of perception; this is especially the case when what is imagined is believed to have taken place. Words, without images, may, through association, have these effects. And wherever there are such physical effects there are concomitant mental effects.

Perhaps we can now explain the 'significance' of a sentence as follows. First: some sentences signify observed facts; how this happens, we have already considered. Second: some observed facts are beliefs. A belief need not involve any words at all in the believer, but it is always possible (given a suitable vocabulary) to find a sentence signifying the perceived fact that I have such-and-such a belief. If this sentence begins 'I believe that', what follows the word 'that' is a sentence signifying a proposition, and the proposition is said to be what I am believing. Exactly similar remarks apply to doubt, desire, etc.

According to this view, if p is a proposition, 'I believe p', 'I doubt p', 'I desire p', etc., may signify observed facts; also it *may* happen that 'p' signifies an observed fact. In this last case, 'p' can stand alone and be significant of a percept, but otherwise 'p' alone signifies nothing perceived. Perhaps, 'p' alone does signify *something*; perhaps, as we suggested earlier, it signifies a subordinate complex which is a constituent of a propositional attitude. In that case, however, we shall have to explain why such complexes never occur except as constituents of propositional attitudes.

The above theory has difficulties. One difficulty is to explain the relation of p to the fact when p is true. Suppose, for example, I see the letters 'A B' in that order, and I judge 'A is to the left of B'. I am, in that case, believing a proposition p which has a certain relation to a fact. We are supposing that p is not verbal, but is something non-verbal, which is signified by the words 'A is to the left of B', but is not the fact in virtue of which these words express a truth. It might be urged that we have to assign to words two different uses, one when we assert p, and another when we assert that we believe p. For when we assert p (assuming p to be a judgement of perception), the words of 'p', it may be said, denote objects, whereas, when we assert that we believe p, the words have to have some mental meaning. According to this view, when I say 'Socrates is Greek', Socrates is involved, but when I say 'I believe that Socrates is Greek', only my idea of Socrates is involved. This seems hardly credible.

I think this objection is invalid. Suppose I see a red circle and say 'this is red'. In using words, I have passed away from the percept; if, instead of words, I use images, they, like the words, *mean* the percept, but are something different from it. When I say 'this is red', or when I have a red image with a yes-feeling, I have a belief; if I afterwards say 'I believe that was red', the words and images involved may be just the same as they were when I made a judgement of perception. Seeing is *not* believing, and a judgement of perception is not a perception.

Our present suggestion is that a sentence 'p' is significant if 'I believe that p' or 'I doubt that p' or etc., can describe a perceived fact in which words need not occur. There are difficulties:

'*can* describe' is vague; 'words *need* not occur' needs eluci-
dation. Nevertheless, perhaps something could be made of our
suggestion.

In the first place, we must elucidate the statement that words
need not occur. Sometimes they occur, sometimes they do not;
in propositions which are complicated, they are *practically* indispensable, though with greater mental powers we might be able
to do without them. The other question, as to what is meant by
'*can* describe a perceived fact', is more difficult. We obviously do
not wish to exclude all sentences which have not in fact entered
into propositional attitudes. We want to find a characteristic of
sentences which makes us feel that it is *possible* to believe or doubt
them, and until this is found our problem is not solved.

We might try to define significance in a more linguistic fashion. We first divide words into categories, having affinities with
the parts of speech. We then say: given any judgement of perception (which *may* be of the form 'I believe p'), any word may
be replaced by another word belonging to the same category
without making the sentence lose significance. And we allow the
formation of molecular and generalized propositions by the
methods already considered. We shall then say that the assemblage of sentences so obtained is the class of significant sentences.
But why? I do not doubt that some linguistic definition of the
class of significant sentences – either the above or another – is
possible; but we cannot rest content until we have found some
reason for our linguistic rules.

If a reason for our linguistic rules is to be found, it must consist of properties of complexes which are in some way related to
the rules. In such a proposition as 'A is to the left of B', when this
is a judgement of perception, we are analysing a complex percept.
It seems that, in any phrase expressing such an analysis, there
must be at least one relation-word. I do not believe that this is
only a property of language; I believe that the complex has a
corresponding constituent which is a relation. I think that when
we say that a phrase is significant, we mean that a complex
described by the phrase is 'possible'; and when we say that a
complex described by a phrase is 'possible', we mean that there
is a complex described by a phrase obtained from the given

phrase by substituting for one or more of its words other words belonging to the same categories. Thus if 'A' and 'B' are names of men, 'A killed B' is possible because Brutus killed Caesar; and if 'R' is the name of a relation of the same category as killing, 'A has the relation R to B' is possible for the same reason.

At this point we touch on the relations between linguistics and metaphysics. I shall deal with this matter in a later chapter.

Reverting now to what is meant by the 'significance' of a sentence, we shall say that, in the case of a sentence of atomic form, the significance is a state of the believer, or rather a set of such states having certain similarities. A possible form of such a state is a complex image, or rather a whole set of similar complex images. Images form a language, but the language differs from that of words in the fact that it does not contain any nonsense. To extend the definition of 'significance' beyond atomic sentences is obviously only a question of logic.

So far, I have been assuming that, when a sentence is significant, there is something that it signifies. Since a significant sentence *may* be false, it is clear that the signification of a sentence cannot be the fact that makes it true (or false). It must therefore be something in the person who believes the sentence, not in the object to which the sentence refers. Images are naturally suggested. Images 'mean' in much the same way as words do, but they have the advantage that there are no complex images corresponding to nonsensical sentences. Actual pictures have the same merit. I can make a picture of Brutus killing Caesar, or, if I choose, of Caesar killing Brutus, but I cannot make a picture, either real or imagined, of quadruplicity killing procrastination. The syntactical rules for obtaining other significant sentences from judgements of perception are really, according to this theory, psychological laws as to what can be imagined.

The above theory is, I think, a possible one. It is, however, in certain respects repellent. The use of images is to be avoided whenever possible; and Occam's razor makes us wish, if we can, to avoid propositions as something distinct from sentences. Let us, therefore, attempt to frame a theory in which significance is merely an adjective of sentences.

The most hopeful suggestion is to distinguish significant from nonsensical sentences by their causal properties. We can distinguish true from false sentences (where judgements of perception are concerned) by the causes of their being uttered; but since we are now dealing with a problem in which true and false sentences are on a level, we shall have to consider rather the effects in the hearer than the causes in the speaker.

Many heard sentences have no observable effect upon the hearer's actions, but they are always capable of having an effect in suitable circumstances. 'Caesar is dead' has very little effect upon us now, but had great effects at the time. Nonsensical sentences, recognized as such, do not promote any action relative to what their constituent words mean; the most they can produce is a request to the speaker to hold his tongue. They are therefore, it would seem, causally distinguishable from significant sentences.

There are, however, some difficulties. Lamb, in an altercation with a Billingsgate fish-wife, called her a she-parallelogram, and produced a greater effect than he could have done by any more significant abuse; this was because she did not know his sentence to be nonsense. Many religious people are much affected by such sentences as 'God is one', which are syntactically faulty, and must be regarded by the logician as strictly meaningless. (The correct phrase would be 'There is only one God'.) Thus the hearer in relation to whom significance is to be defined must be a logically trained listener. This removes us from the sphere of psychological observation, since it sets up a standard by which one hearer is logically preferable to another. What makes him preferable must be something in logic, not something definable in terms of behaviour.

In *Mind* for October 1939 there is an interesting article by Kaplan and Copilowish, on 'Must there be propositions?' They reply in the negative. I propose to restate and then examine their argument.

They introduce the term 'implicit behaviour' in a very wide sense, as whatever happens to or 'in' an organism when it uses signs. They leave open the question whether implicit behaviour is to be described behaviouristically or in images. Implicit

behaviour occasioned by a sign-vehicle is called an 'interpretation'. Associated with each sign-vehicle there is a law of *interpretation*, stating the kind of implicit behaviour that it occasions.
A *sign* is a class of sign-vehicles all having one and the same law
of interpretation; this law is called the *interpretant* of the sign. An
interpretation of a sign-vehicle is *correct* if the law describing
the interpretation has been previously set up as standard for such
sign-vehicles. We say O *understands* a sign when O correctly
interprets a member of it under certain conditions. O *believes*
a sign-vehicle when O has a correct interpretation of it together
with an 'attitude of affirmation' (provisionally undefined). Believing a *sign* is a disposition. We are told: 'an organism may be
said to have a belief even where signs are not involved. This is
the case where the organism has an implicit behaviour of such a
kind that, had it been occasioned by a sign-vehicle, it would have
constituted a belief of that sign-vehicle'.

We now come to the definition of 'appropriate': the implicit
behaviour of an organism O is *appropriate* to a situation S if it is
caused by S and O recognizes S. (The word 'recognize', which
occurs here, is not defined in the article, and has not been discussed previously.) Interpretation being a kind of implicit behaviour, we say that an interpretation of a sign is appropriate
to S if it would be appropriate to S if S were present and recognized. Hence follows a definition of 'true':

'A sentential sign is *true* if and only if there exists a situation
of such a kind that a correct interpretation of any sign-vehicle
of the sign is appropriate to the situation.'

Before we can successfully examine the adequacy of this
theory, there are some necessary preliminaries. First: the word
'sign', or rather 'sign-vehicle', is not defined. In order to define
it, I should say, we must begin near the end of the above set of
definitions. One event only becomes a sign-vehicle of another in
virtue of similarity in its effects. I should say: 'a class of events
S is, for an organism O, a *sign* of another class of events E, when,
as a result of acquired habit, the effects of a member of S on O
are (in certain respects and with certain limitations) those which
a member of E had before the habit in question was acquired'.
This definition is incomplete so long as the above-mentioned

respects and limitations are not specified; but this is not an objection of principle. Further: I am not sure that it is right to limit signs to *acquired* habits; perhaps unconditioned reflexes should also be admitted. Since, however, our principal concern is with language, it is convenient to exclude them.

The difficulty of this subject comes largely from the inter-mingling of scientific and normative terms. Thus in Kaplan and Copilowish's series of definitions we find the words 'correct' and 'appropriate'. Each of these is defined in a way which is not normative, at least in intention. Let us look at the definitions more closely.

'An interpretation of a sign-vehicle is *correct* if the law which describes that interpretation has previously been taken as stan-dard for sign-vehicles of that kind (i.e. of that sound or shape)'. The word 'standard' is vague. Let us make it precise: let us say that the 'correct' interpretation is that given by the *Oxford Dictionary*, supplemented (under the influence of Semiotics) by an eminent physiologist's description of his reactions to such words as have only an ostensive definition. The physiologist having been selected and his work completed, our definition of 'correct' is now freed from all ethical taint. But the results will be odd. Suppose a man who thinks that 'cat' means the kind of animal that other people call 'dog'. If he sees a Great Dane and says 'there is a cat', he is believing a true proposition, but uttering an incorrect one. It would seem, therefore, that 'correct' cannot be used in defining 'true', since 'correct' is a social concept, but 'true' is not.

Perhaps this difficulty could be overcome. When our man says 'there is a cat', what would ordinarily be called his 'thought' is true, but the 'thought' that he causes in his hearer is untrue. His implicit behaviour will be appropriate, in the sense that he will (for example) expect the animal to bark and not mew, but the hearer's implicit behaviour will, in the same sense, be in-appropriate. The speaker and the hearer use different languages (at least so far as the words 'cat' and 'dog' are concerned). I think that, in fundamental discussions of language, its social aspect should be ignored, and a man should always be supposed to be speaking to himself – or, what comes to the same thing, to a man whose language is precisely identical with his own. This eliminates the concept of 'correctness'. What remains – if a man is to be able to interpret notes written by himself on previous occasions – is constancy in his own use of words: we must suppose that he uses the same language today as he used yesterday. In fact, the whole residuum of what was to have been done by the concept of 'correctness' is this: speaker and hearer (or writer and reader) must use the same language, i.e. have the same interpretative habits.

I come now to the term 'appropriate'. Here I find less occasion for criticism, except that, in my opinion, the definition of 'appropriate' can be absorbed into the definition of 'sign-vehicle'. If s is, for O, a sign-vehicle of a class of events E, that means that O's reactions to s are 'appropriate' to E, i.e. are (with suitable limitations) identical with the reactions which O makes to a member of E on occasions when such a member is present. Let us now try to restate the above definition of 'true' without using the concept of 'correct'. We might say: 'a sentential sign present to an organism O is *true* when, *as sign*, it promotes behaviour which would have been promoted by a situation that exists, if this situation had been present to the organism'.

I say 'as sign', because we have to exclude behaviour which the sign promotes on its own account – e.g. it may be so loud as to cause the hearer to stop his ears. Such behaviour is irrelevant. I say 'if this situation had been present to the organism', meaning not to state that it is *not* present, but only to allow for the possibility of its not being present. If it is present, we cannot distinguish behaviour caused by the sign from behaviour caused by what it signifies.

There is a more or less formal emendation which is required in the above definition of 'true'. This has to do with the phrase 'behaviour which *would have been* promoted by a situation, if this situation had been present to the organism'. This definition will not have the intended significance in the case of a situation which has never, in fact, been present to the organism. Formally, since a false proposition implies every other proposition, the condition is satisfied, in this case, by any sentential sign. We must therefore amend our definition by saying that, on various occasions, situations sufficiently similar to the given situation have, in fact, promoted behaviour sufficiently similar to the behaviour now promoted by the sign. The degree of similarity required cannot be defined in general terms, and is essentially subject to a certain degree of vagueness. Moreover the 'situation' and the 'behaviour' involved must both be generic, not particular, since it is involved in the emended definition that each can occur more than once.

There is one grave objection to the above definition, and that is that it considers sentences exclusively from the standpoint of the hearer to the exclusion of that of the speaker. The most obvious example of truth is an exclamation caused by some feature of environment, such as 'fire!' or 'murder!' And it is by means of such exclamations on the part of elders that children's language habits are acquired.

Another objection is that, whenever the situation verifying a sentence is not present to the hearer, the truth of the sentence must be known only by subsequent inference. The premisses of such inference must be known by the simultaneous presence of the sentence and what it signifies; this knowledge must therefore exemplify the most primitive kind of truth, from which other kinds are derivative.

But as to the main question, namely 'must there be propositions?' I should say that the 'implicit behaviour' assumed by Kaplan and Copilowish is exactly what I mean by 'proposition'. If you say to an Englishman 'there's a cat', to a Frenchman 'voilà un chat', to a German 'da ist eine Katze', and to an Italian 'ecco un gatto', their implicit behaviours will be the same; this is what I mean by saying that they are all believing the same proposition, though they are believing quite different sentences. Moreover they can believe the proposition without using words; I should say that a dog is believing it when he is excited by the smell of a cat. It is the capacity of sentences to promote this kind of 'implicit behaviour' that makes them important. A sentence is significant to the hearer when it promotes this kind of implicit behaviour, and to the speaker when it is promoted by it. Precise syntactical rules as to what sentences are significant are not psychologically true; they are analogous to rules of etiquette. When

Lamb called the fish-wife a she-parallelogram, the sentence was to her significant, and meant 'you are an abominable female monster'. What can be said, apart from etiquette, in favour of such syntactical rules as the logician naturally suggests, is this: a language obeying these rules has, for those who understand it, the merit that every sentence expresses a proposition, and every proposition can be expressed by a sentence (provided the vocabulary is adequate). It has also the merit of a more precise and intimate relation between sentences and what they signify than exists in ordinary spoken languages.

I conclude, from this long discussion, that it is necessary to distinguish propositions from sentences, but that propositions need not be indefinable. They are to be defined as psychological occurrences of certain sorts – complex images, expectations, etc. Such occurrences are 'expressed' by sentences, but the sentences 'assert' something else. When two sentences have the same meaning, that is because they express the same proposition. Words are not essential to propositions. The exact psychological definition of propositions is irrelevant to logic and theory of knowledge; the only thing essential to our inquiries is that sentences signify something other than themselves, which can be the same when the sentences differ. That this something must be psychological (or physiological) is made evident by the fact that propositions can be false.

B. PSYCHOLOGICAL ANALYSIS OF SIGNIFICANCE

We have considered already the psychological character of the meanings of single words, when they are object-words. The meaning of a single word is defined by the situations that cause it to be used and the effects that result from hearing it. The significance of a sentence can be similarly defined; in fact, an object-word *is* a sentence when used in an exclamatory manner. So long as we confine ourselves to these generalities there is no problem as to the significance of sentences. The problems arise when we attempt to explain in psychological terms the relation between the significance of a sentence and the meanings of its constituent words. To the logician, the significance is definable in terms of the meanings of the words and the rules of syntax.

But psychologically the sentence is a causal unit, and its effect does not *seem* to be compounded of separate effects of separate words. Can we say that the effect of 'that is not cheese' is compounded of the effect of 'not' and the effect of 'cheese'? If we are to say this, we shall need a much more psychological theory of logical words than is customary, but I do not consider this a decisive argument.

The syntactical theory of significance – especially when connected with an artificial logical language – is a branch of ethics: it says 'logically well-behaved people will attach significance to sentences of the following kinds'. But there is also a purely psychological theory of significance. In this theory a spoken sentence is 'significant' if its causes are of a certain kind, and a heard sentence is 'significant' if its effects are of a certain kind. The psychological theory of significance consists in defining these kinds.

'Belief', we decided, is a certain condition of mind and body, not essentially involving words. A person A may be in a condition which is described in the words 'A believes that there is about to be a loud bang'. When A is in this condition, it may cause him to use the words 'there is about to be a loud bang'. A sentence 'p' is significant when there can be a state of mind and body described in the words 'A believes p'. Hearing the sentence 'p' is one possible cause of the state that consists in believing 'p'. A heard sentence is significant when it can be such a cause.

In the above we have two different definitions of 'significance'. One is relative to the linguistic habits of a person who says 'A believes p', the other to those of a person who hears A uttering p.

A man who is in a state of belief may utter a sentence 'p' with the intention of expressing his belief, but a hearer, with other linguistic habits, may consider the expression inaccurate. A man A may say 'the moon looks as large as a soup-plate'; B may say, 'no, only as large as a dollar'; C may say 'both your sentences are incomplete; you must specify the distance of the soup-plate or dollar from the eye'. What does C mean by 'must'? He means that the sentences of A and B, though apparently inconsistent, are not so really, since neither describes a definite state of affairs.

Every object-word has two uses, corresponding to Hume's 'impression' and 'idea'. When directly caused by a sensible occurrence, the word, in the speaker, applies to an impression; when heard, or used in narrative, it does not apply to an impression, but it is still a word, not a mere noise; it still 'means' something, and what it 'means' may be called an 'idea'. The same distinction applies to sentences: a spoken sentence *may* describe an impression, but a heard sentence does not. 'Impression' and 'idea' must be very closely related, since otherwise it would be impossible to give information: in some sense, what the hearer understands is what the speaker expressed.*

I assume that there is a certain state of a person A which can be described in the words 'A believes that there is about to be a loud bang', and that this state need not involve words in A. But it must be possible to describe A's state quite differently, by means of certain tensions and auricular stimulations. I shall say 'A believes p' if A is in a condition which, if he shares my linguistic habits, and sees occasion to speak, will cause him to utter the sentence 'p'.

The matter *seems* simpler when A has the sentence 'p' in his mind. But this is a mistake. A may have the sentence 'p' in his mind, and proceed to say 'I believe p', or simply to assert p; but it does not follow that he believes p. What he must be believing is '"p" is true'. He may be quite unaware of what 'p' means. E.g. the devout but uneducated believer who hears the Apostles' Creed in Greek, or the school-child who, to please the teacher, says '*and* is a conjunction'.

Let us try to enumerate the various uses of 'p'. Take the sentence 'there is a red light', which we will call 'p'. You are, we will suppose, sitting beside a careless driver. You utter the sentence because you see a red light; this may be called the exclamatory use of 'p'. Here 'p' is directly caused by a sensible fact, which it 'indicates', and by which it is 'verified'. But how about the driver who hears your exclamation? He acts exactly as he would have done if he had seen the red light; there is in him a conditioned reflex which leads him to respond to the words 'red

---

* This is only roughly true. Its limitations are considered in Chapters 15, 16, and 17.

light' as he responds to the sight of a red light. This is what we mean when we say that he 'understands' the words.

So far, we have no need of 'ideas'. You react to a visual stimulus, and the driver to an auditory stimulus; his reaction, like yours, is to a present sensible fact.

But now suppose that when you see the red light you hold your tongue, and a moment later remark 'it is fortunate there was no policeman there, because you ran past a red light', to which the driver replies 'I don't believe you'. Now 'p' shall be 'there was a red light'. You assert p, and the driver says he does not believe p.

In this case, the need for 'ideas' seems fairly evident. Neither you not the driver is concerned with words: you are not saying 'the words "there was a red light" express a truth', nor is he denying this. Both are speaking about what the words 'mean'.

So far as you are concerned, we could perhaps be content with the analogy of the automatic machine which first says 'this is a penny' and later 'that was a penny'. The man who has just seen a red light which he no longer sees is, no doubt, in a different state from that of a man who has seen no red light; this state may cause the use of the words 'there was a red light'. As for the driver, we may suppose in him a state (involving motor impulses) induced by the heard words 'there was a red light', combined with inhibitory impulses such as are expressed by the word 'disbelief'. So long as we do not introduce 'ideas', this is not sufficiently specific. The motor impulses in the driver will be just the same if you say 'you nearly ran over a dog', but his state will not be the same. Your words cause in him the 'thought' of there having been a red light, and he meets this thought with disbelief. It is unnecessary for us to decide what the 'thought' consists of, and how it is to be apportioned between psychology and physiology, but it seems that we must admit it, since many obviously different beliefs may be indistinguishable in their motor effects.

Thus the psychological theory of significance to which we have been led is as follows. There are states which may be called states of 'believing'; these states do not essentially involve words. Two states of believing may be so related that we call them instances of the same belief. In a man with suitable language-habits, one of the states which is an instance of a given belief is that in which he utters a certain sentence. When the utterance of a certain sentence is an instance of a certain belief, the sentence is said to 'express' the belief. A spoken sentence is 'significant' when there is a possible belief that it 'expresses'. A heard sentence 'S' may be believed or rejected or doubted. If believed, the hearer's belief is 'expressed' by the same sentence 'S'. If rejected, the hearer's disbelief is 'expressed' by the sentence 'not-S'; if doubted, by 'perhaps S'. A heard sentence 'S' is significant if it can cause any of the three kinds of states 'expressed' by 'S', 'not-S' and 'perhaps S'. When we say simply that 'S' is significant, we mean that it has this latter kind of significance.

This whole theory is completely independent of any consideration of truth and falsehood.

There is one important respect in which the above theory is still incomplete; it has not decided what two states must have in common in order to be instances of the same belief. When verbal habits are sufficiently developed, we may say that two states are instances of the same belief if they can be expressed by the same sentence. Perhaps the only definition is causal: two states are instances of the same belief when they cause the same behaviour. (This will, in those who possess language, include the behaviour that consists in uttering a certain sentence.) I am not quite satisfied that this causal definition is adequate, but, having no better alternative to offer, I shall tentatively accept it.

C. SYNTAX AND SIGNIFICANCE*

In the present section, I propose to consider the possibility of constructing a logical language in which the psychological conditions of significance, considered in the previous section, are translated into precise syntactical rules.

Starting from a vocabulary derived from perception, and from sentences expressing judgements of perception, I shall give a definition of an assemblage of significant sentences defined by their syntactical relation to the initial vocabulary and to

* The reader may with advantage omit this section if he is not interested in mathematical logic.

judgements of perception. When this assemblage has been defined, we can consider whether, in an adequate language, it can contain *all* significant sentences and no others.

The initial object-vocabulary consists of names, predicates, and relations, all having ostensive definitions. In theory, relations may have any finite number of terms; we need not inquire what is the greatest number of terms in any sentence expressing a relational fact that we actually perceive. All the words needed in the object-vocabulary have ostensive definitions; words having dictionary definitions are theoretically superfluous. The object-vocabulary is liable to be extended at any moment as a result of new experience – e.g. the first time you eat sharks' fins you may give a name to the flavour.

Sentences describing experiences, such as we considered in Chapter 3, are frequently, though perhaps not always, composed of a single relation or predicate together with a suitable number of names. Such sentences express 'judgements of perception'. They form the basis from which our syntactical construction proceeds.

Let $R_n(a_1, a_2, a_3 \ldots a_n)$ be a sentence expressing a judgement of perception, containing one n-adic relation R_n and n names $a_1, a_2, a_3 \ldots a_n$. We then lay down the *principle of substitution*: the sentence remains significant if any or all of the names are replaced by any other names, and R_n is replaced by any other n-adic relation. We thus obtain from judgements of perception a certain collection of significant sentences, which we call *atomic sentences*.

It might be objected that this principle will allow the construction of nonsensical sentences such as 'the sound of a trombone is blue'. With my theory of names, this would assert the identity of two objects having different names. This, I should say, is not nonsense, but false. I should include among judgements of perception such sentences as 'red is different from blue'; similarly, if s is the name of the quality of the sound of a trombone, 's is different from blue' can be a judgement of perception.

It is of course possible, since we are dealing with an artificial language, to supply a conventional significance to a sentence which has no natural significance, provided we can avoid the risk of contradiction. Sentences which have no natural significance are obviously not naturally true; therefore we can supply a false significance, such as 'this buttercup is blue', for every sentence (not containing the word 'not') that we wish to include but that does not naturally have any significance. Where atomic sentences are concerned there is no risk of contradiction; therefore, if the principle of substitution were otherwise doubtful, its validity could be secured by a convention. There is accordingly no reason for rejecting it.

The second principle in the formation of sentences may be called *combination*. A given sentence can be negated; two given sentences can be combined by 'or', 'and', 'if-then', 'if-then not', and so on. Such sentences are called 'molecular' if they result from a combination of atomic sentences, either directly or by any number of finite operations. The truth or falsehood of a molecular sentence depends only upon that of its 'atoms'.

All molecular sentences can be defined in terms of one operation. If 'p' and 'q' are any two sentences '$p \mid q$' (read 'p-stroke-q') is to mean 'p and q are not both true', or 'p and q are incompatible'. We can then define 'not-p' as '$p \mid p$', i.e. 'p is incompatible with p'; 'p or q' as '$(p \mid p) \mid (q \mid q)$', i.e. 'not-$p$ is incompatible with not-q'; 'p and q' as '$(p \mid q) \mid (p \mid q)$', i.e. '$p$ and q are not incompatible'. Starting from atomic propositions, and using the principle that any two sentences can be combined by the 'stroke' to form a new sentence, we obtain the assemblage of 'molecular propositions'. All this is familiar to logicians as the logic of truth-functions.

The next operation is *generalization*. Given any sentence containing either a name 'a' or a word 'R' denoting a relation or predicate, we can construct a new sentence in two ways. In the case of a name 'a', we may say that all sentences which result from the substitution of another name in place of 'a' are true, or we may say that at least one such sentence is true. (I must repeat that I am not concerned with inferring true sentences, but only with constructing sentences syntactically, without regard to their truth or falsehood.) For example, from 'Socrates is a man' we derive, by this operation, the two sentences 'everything is a man' and 'something is a man', or, as it may be phrased, '"x is a man" is always true' and '"x is a man" is sometimes true'. The variable 'x' here is to be allowed to take all values for which the sentence 'x is a man' is significant, i.e., in this case, all values that are proper names.

When we generalize a relation R – say a dyadic relation – the process is the same, except that, when we substitute a variable 'S', the possible values of 'S' are confined to dyadic relations by the conditions of significance. Take, for example, the advice to be all things to all men. If I succeed in obeying this precept, that means that, if x is any man and R any dyadic relation, I have the relation R to x; in other words, every sentence of the form 'if x is a man, I have the relation R to x' is true. Or take the statement 'no two men are wholly unrelated'. This means that, if x and y are men, some sentence of the form 'x has the relation R to y' is true. That is to say, every sentence of the form 'if x and y are men, some sentence of the form "x has the relation R to y" is true' is true.

It should be observed that the relations that occur in the above development, whether they are constants or variables, are relations in intension, not in extension.

Sentences involving generalization of predicates occur frequently in common speech. Examples are 'Napoleon had all the qualities of a great general' and 'Elizabeth had the virtues of both her father and her grandfather, but the vices of neither'. (I do not commit myself to the historical accuracy of this illustration.)

For reasons which will appear in Chapter 19, I shall call the assemblage of sentences obtained from atomic judgements of perception by the three operations of substitution, combination, and generalization, the *atomistic* hierarchy of sentences.

It is an important question whether this hierarchy can constitute an 'adequate' language, i.e., one into which any statement in any language can be translated. This question has two parts: first, can we be content with atomic sentences as the basis of the structure? second, can we be content with names, predicates, dyadic relations, etc., as our only variables, or do we need variables of other kinds? The first of these questions will be discussed in Chapters 19 and 24. The second, which is concerned with generalization and is relevant in solving the paradoxes, must be discussed now.

Generalization raises much more difficult problems than are raised by substitution or combination. The main question to be discussed in this chapter is: does generalization as above defined suffice for mathematical logic? or do we need variables of kinds not definable by means of the above kinds?

First let us observe that, if 'every sentence of the form $f(x)$ is true' or 'some such sentence is true' is to have any definite significance, the range of values of which 'x' is to be capable must be definite. If we have any extrinsic range of values, such as *men* or *natural numbers*, this will have to be stated. Thus 'all men are mortal' cannot be interpreted as 'all sentences of the form "x is mortal" are true, where the possible values of x are men', for this is not derived *merely* from the function 'x is mortal'.* The only way in which 'all sentences of the form "$f(x)$" are true' can be derived merely from the function is to allow x to take all values for which '$f(x)$' is significant. So long as we confine ourselves to names and relations as variables, the principle of substitution secures what is wanted in this respect.

We need, however, at the very beginning of mathematical logic, another sort of variable, namely variable propositions. We want to be able to enunciate the law of contradiction and the law of excluded middle, i.e. 'no proposition is both true and false' and 'every proposition is either true or false'. That is to say, 'every sentence of the form "it is false that p is both true and false" is true', and 'every sentence of the form "p is either true or false" is true'. Here the conditions of significance require that 'p' should be a sentence (or proposition), but do not, *prima facie*, place any other restriction on 'p'. The trouble is that we have apparently framed sentences which refer to all sentences, and therefore also to themselves.

More generally, if $f(p)$ is a propositional function of a propositional variable p, then 'every proposition of the form $f(p)$ is true', if admissible, is also a proposition. Is it a possible value of

---

* In Chapter 18 we shall develop a theory of general beliefs which might seem inconsistent with what is said above. But the inconsistency is only apparent, since here, but not there, our problem is purely syntactic.

p in '$f(p)$'? If it is, there is included in the totality of values of p a value defined in terms of that totality. This has the consequence that whatever collection of propositions we assign as the totality of values of p, we must be wrong, since there is another value of p defined in terms of that totality, and changing as the totality changes. The situation is analogous to that of Jourdain's Chinese Emperor and the nests of boxes. This Emperor attempted to enclose all nests of boxes in one room. At last he thought he had succeeded, but his Prime Minister pointed out that the room constituted another nest of boxes. Though the Emperor cut off the Prime Minister's head, he never smiled again.

Variable propositions thus involve difficulties, which come to a head in the contradiction of the liar.* I suggest that variable propositions are only legitimate when they are an abbreviation for name-variables and relation variables. Let 'p' be a variable which can stand for any sentence constructed by means of our three principles of substitution, combination, and generalization. Then we may say that 'every sentence of the form $f(p)$ is true' is not a single new sentence, but a conjunction of an infinite number of sentences, in which the variables are not sentences.

For this purpose, we proceed as follows. We first interpret the statement that, if 'p' is an atomic sentence, then '$f(p)$' is true. This is obviously equivalent to: whatever possible values R_1 and x_1 may have, $f\{R_1(x_1)\}$ is true; whatever possible values R_2 and x_1 and x_2 may have, $f\{R_2(x_1, x_2)\}$ is true; and so on. Here the variables are only xs and Rs.

We now proceed to the case in which 'p' is a molecular sentence. We shall assert that, for all possible values of the xs and ys and of R and S

$$f\{R(x_1, x_2 \ldots x_m) \mid S(y_1, y_2 \ldots y_n)\}$$

is true; and we shall proceed to similar assertions when the argument to f contains not only one stroke, but any finite number. Thus we shall now have interpreted the assertion that '$f(p)$' is true when 'p' is any molecular proposition.

Finally, we allow 'p' to be any sentence obtained from any one of our previous values of 'p' by generalization.

* See the opening of Chapter 4.

We thus obtain an interpretation of ' "$f(p)$" is always true if p is a sentence in the atomistic hierarchy'. The interpretation, however, makes this into many sentences, not one. If '$f(p)$' is such that, when 'p' belongs to the atomistic hierarchy, so does '$f(p)$', then all these many sentences belong to the atomistic hierarchy, and no sentence of a new sort has been generated.

We shall treat 'some sentence of the form "$f(p)$" is true' in an exactly similar way, treating it as an infinite *disjunction* consisting of the same terms as those in the above infinite *conjunction*.

Of course, technically, we can still use the variable 'p'. The only use of the above analysis, technically, is to prevent us from regarding '$f(p)$ is always true' as a possible value of 'p' in '$f(p)$'. That is to say, '$f(p)$ is always true' does not permit us to infer '$f\{f(p)$ is always true$\}$'. This is important, since, if assertions referring to the totality of possible values of 'p' (or of any other variable) are to have any definite significance, they must not themselves be among the values that 'p' can take.

We have next to consider variable functions. Let us denote by 'ϕa' a variable proposition, in the atomistic hierarchy, in which the name 'a' occurs, and let '$f(p)$' be some definite function of propositions belonging to the fundamental hierarchy. We can then form the function

$$f(\phi a)$$

in which the variable is ϕ, and we can consider '$f(\phi a)$ is true for every ϕ' and '$f(\phi a)$ is true for some ϕ'.

Quite common sentences may be of this form; e.g. 'Napoleon I I I had all the vices of his uncle and none of his virtues', or what the drunken man said to the expostulating parson: 'there must be some of all sorts, and I am of that sort'.

Exactly the same sort of difficulty arises here as in relation to '$f(p)$ is true for every p'. It would seem that '$f(\phi a)$ is true for every ϕ' is itself a function of a, and that therefore '$f(\phi a)$ is true for every ϕ' ought to imply '$f\{f(\phi a)$ is true for every $\phi\}$'.

But in that case there are values of ϕ defined in terms of the totality of values of ϕ, and every conceivable definition of the totality of values of ϕ can be shown to be inadequate.

Let us attempt to clarify the matter by some illustrations. What, for example, is meant by 'Napoleon I I I had all the vices of Napoleon I'? First, what is a 'vice'? Perhaps we may define it as 'a habit of which every instance is a sin'. But I do not want so serious an analysis, since my purpose is merely to illustrate a point in syntax. For my purpose, we may treat a 'vice' as a predicate of a certain kind. Thus if 'R_1' stands for a variable predicate, 'R_1 is a vice' is of the form '$F(R_1)$'. Now let us put 'a' for 'Napoleon I I I' and 'b' for 'Napoleon I'. Then 'Napoleon I I I had all the vices of Napoleon I' becomes: 'every sentence of the form: "$F(R_1)$ and $R_1(b)$ together imply $R_1(a)$" is true', where 'R_1' is the variable. This, however, is not yet quite satisfactory, because '$F(R_1)$' *prima facie*, treats 'R_1' as if it were a proper name and not a predicate. If '$F(R_1)$' is to be of a form admitted by the restriction to the atomistic hierarchy, this must be remedied. We may take 'vicious' as a predicate applicable to individuals, and a 'vice' as a predicate implying viciousness. Thus if '$V(x)$' means 'x is vicious', 'R_1 is a vice' means: 'sentences of the form "$R_1(x)$ implies $V(x)$ for all possible values of x" are true for all possible values of R_1'. This must now replace '$F(R_1)$' in the above analysis of our example. The result may seem somewhat complicated, but even so it is still made artificially simple for purposes of illustration.

Let us take another illustration, which will, incidentally, show the necessity of distinguishing between properties which involve a variable predicate and those that do not. Let our illustration be 'Pitt was a typical Englishman'. We may define a member of a class as 'typical' if it possesses all predicates possessed by a majority of the class. Thus we are saying that Pitt had every predicate R_1 which is such that the number of xs for which '$R_1(x)$ and x is English' is true exceeds the number for which 'not-$R_1(x)$ and x is English' is true. This is all very well, but if instead of 'predicate' we had used the general word 'property', we should have found that there could be no typical Englishman, because most Englishmen possess *some* property which most Englishmen do not possess, e.g., that of being between 5 ft 10 in. and 5 ft 11 in. in height or some analogous determination. That is to say, it is untypical to be typical. This shows that we run risks if we attempt to speak about 'all possible statements about a'.

We shall avoid the trouble if the variable ϕ, like the variable p, is merely a convenient abbreviation for other variables. Propositions in which a occurs will be

(1) $R_1(a)$, $R_2(a, b)$, $R_3(a, b, c)$, etc.

(2) Combinations of the above with one or more propositions in the atomistic hierarchy.

(3) Generalizations of propositions in (2), provided a is not replaced by a variable.

Thus '$f(\phi a)$ is true for every ϕ' will assert that

(a) $R_1(a)$, $R_1(a, b)$, etc., are true for all possible values of R_1, b, etc.

(b) Similar statements as regards $R_1(a) \mid R_1(b)$, etc.

(c) Generalizations of (b), which will be found to be merely a repetition of (b).

In this way the variable ϕ, like the variable p, can be reduced to name-variables and relation-variables, at the cost of making '$f(\phi a)$ is true for every ϕ' an infinite number of sentences instead of one.

In a language of the second order, '$f(p)$ is true for every p', '$f(\phi a)$ is true for every ϕ', can be admitted as single sentences. This is familiar, and I need not dwell upon it. In the language of the second order, variables denote symbols, not what is symbolized.

There is therefore no reason to admit as fundamental any variables except name-variables and relation-variables (in intension). Given the assemblage of propositions that are neither molecular nor general, we can – so I conclude – construct, from this assemblage, an adequate language, so far as mathematical logic is concerned, employing only the principles of combination and generalization.

The question of the principle of atomicity remains. This is a question concerning the propositions that are neither molecular nor general. It is the question whether all of these are of one or other of the forms

$$R_1(a), R_2(a, b), R_3(a, b, c), \ldots$$

Such propositions as 'I believe Socrates was Greek' are, *prima facie*, not of any of these forms. Still more difficult is 'I believe that all men are mortal', where the generality is applicable only to a subordinate proposition. My belief is not equivalent to: 'if x is a man, I believe that x is mortal', for I may have never heard of x, and then I cannot believe him to be mortal. Propositions of the form 'A is part of B' also raise difficulties. I shall discuss the principle of atomicity in later chapters.

There remains one question concerning generalization, and that is the relation of the range of the variable to our knowledge. Suppose we consider some proposition '$f(x)$ is true for every x', e.g. 'for all possible values of x, if x is human, x is mortal'. We say that if 'a' is a name, '$f(x)$ is true for every x' implies '$f(a)$'. We cannot actually make the inference to '$f(a)$' unless 'a' is a name in our actual vocabulary. But we do not *intend* this limitation. We want to say that everything has the property f, not only the things that we have named. There is thus a hypothetical element in any general proposition; '$f(x)$ is true of every x' does not merely assert the conjunction

$$f(a) . f(b) . f(c) \ldots$$

where $a, b, c \ldots$ are the names (necessarily finite in number) that constitute our actual vocabulary. We mean to include whatever will be named, and even whatever *could* be named. This shows that an extensional account of general propositions is impossible except for a Being that has a name for everything; and even He would need the general proposition: 'everything is mentioned in the following list: $a, b, c, \ldots$', which is not a purely extensional proposition.

CHAPTER 14

LANGUAGE AS EXPRESSION

LANGUAGE serves three purposes: (1) to *indicate facts*, (2) to *express* the state of the speaker, (3) to *alter* the state of the hearer. These three purposes are not always all present. If, when alone, I prick my finger and say 'ouch', only (2) is present. Imperative, interrogative, and optative sentences involve (2) and (3), but not (1). Lies involve (3), and, in a sense, (1), but not (2). Exclamatory statements made in solitude, or without regard to a hearer, involve (1) and (2), but not (3). Single words may involve all three, for instance if I find a corpse in the street and shout 'murder!'

Language may fail in (1) and (3): the corpse may have died a natural death, or my hearers may be sceptical. In what sense can language fail as regards (2)? Lies, mentioned above, do not *fail* in this respect, since it is not their purpose to express the state of the speaker. But lies belong to the reflective use of language; when language is spontaneous it cannot lie, and cannot fail to express the state of the speaker. It may fail to communicate what it expresses, owing to differences between speaker and hearer in the use of language, but from the speaker's point of view spontaneous speech must express his state.

I call language 'spontaneous' when there is no verbal intermediary between the external stimulus and the word or words – at least this is a first approximation to what I mean by 'spontaneous'. It is not an adequate definition, for two reasons: first, that the intermediary to be excluded need not be verbal, though it must have something in common with what is verbal; second, that the stimulus need not be, in any ordinary sense, 'external'. The second point being the simpler, let us consider it first.

Suppose I say 'I am hot', and suppose that I say so because I am hot. The stimulus here is a sensation. Suppose I say 'there is a red flower', because (in ordinary parlance) I see a red flower.

The immediate stimulus is again a sensation, though I believe the sensation to have outside causes, and, if it has not, my statement is false. When I say 'I am hot', I may not expect others to be hot, for instance if I have been running on a frosty day. But when I say 'there is a red flower' I expect others to see it too. If they do not, I am surprised, which shows that what I think they will see was part of what I was asserting. The statement 'I see a red patch of a certain shape' is therefore logically simpler than 'I see a red flower'. But 'I see a red patch' is on a level with 'I am hot'. It is, however, less spontaneous than 'I see a red flower' or 'there is a red flower'.

Thus instead of saying that a stimulus is 'external' we shall say that, in 'spontaneous' speech, the stimulus is a sensation.

We must now consider what sort of intermediaries between stimulus and words are to be excluded in defining 'spontaneous' speech. Take the case of a ready lie. The schoolboy, asked angrily 'who made the world?' replied without a moment's hesitation 'please, sir, it wasn't me'. Ethically, though not theologically, this was a lie. In such a case, the stimulus to the words is not what the words mean, nor even something having a close causal connexion with what the words mean; the stimulus is solely the desire to produce a certain effect upon the hearer. This requires a more advanced knowledge of language than is involved in its merely exclamatory use. I think that, in defining 'spontaneous' speech, we must give a subordinate place to the desire to affect the hearer. In certain situations, certain words occur to us, even if we do not utter them. The use of words is 'spontaneous' when the situation causing it can be defined without reference to the hearer. Spontaneous speech is such as might occur in solitude.

Let us confine ourselves for the present to speech that is spontaneous and indicative. I want to consider, in relation to such speech, the relation between (1) indicating facts and (2) expressing the state of the speaker.

In some cases, the distinction between (1) and (2) seems to be non-existent. If I exclaim 'I am hot!', the fact indicated is a state of myself, and is the very state that I express. The word 'hot' means a certain kind of organic condition, and this kind of condition can cause the exclamatory use of the word 'hot'. In such cases, the cause of the instance of the word is also an instance of the meaning of the word. This is still the case with 'I see a red patch', apart from certain reservations as to the words 'I see'. Where, as in such cases, there is no distinction between (1) and (2), the problem of truth or falsehood does not arise, for this problem is essentially connected with the distinction between (1) and (2).

Suppose I say 'you are hot', and suppose I believe what I say. In that case, I am 'expressing' my state and 'indicating' yours. Here truth and falsehood come in, since you may be cold, or you may even not exist. The sentence 'you are hot' is, in one sense, 'significant' if it can express a state of me; in what is perhaps another sense, it is 'significant' if it is true or false. Whether these are or are not different senses of 'significant' cannot be decided until we have defined 'true' and 'false'. For the moment, I shall confine myself to the first definition: I shall consider a sentence 'significant' primarily if it actually expresses a state of myself, and from this starting-point I shall endeavour gradually to reach a wider definition.

What is happening in me when my state is expressed by the words 'you are hot'? To this question there is no definite answer. I may be 'imagining' a sensation of heat combined with the sensation of touching you. I may be expecting you to say 'I am hot'. I may see beads of sweat on your face, and make an inference. All that can be said definitely is that certain possible occurrences would surprise me, while certain others would give me a feeling of confirmation.

The statement 'I believe you are hot' expresses a different state from that expressed by 'you are hot'; the fact that it *indicates* is the fact *expressed* by 'you are hot'. The question arises: can the statement 'I believe you are hot' be replaced by an equivalent statement referring only to myself, and not mentioning you?

Such a statement, I incline to think, would be possible, but very lengthy and complicated. It is customary to describe 'states of mind' by words having an external reference: we say we are thinking *of* this or that, wishing *for* this or that, and so on.

We have no vocabulary for describing what actually takes place in us when we think or desire, except the somewhat elementary device of putting words in inverted commas. It may be said that, when I think of a cat, I think 'cat'; but this is both inadequate and not necessarily true. To think 'of' a cat is to be in a state in some way related to the percept of a cat, but the possible relations are numerous. The same applies in a stronger degree to belief. We have thus a twofold difficulty: on the one hand that the occurrences which can be correctly described as believing a given proposition are very various, and on the other hand that we need a new vocabulary if we are to describe these occurrences otherwise than by reference to objects.

What must be occurring when I am believing the proposition 'Mr A is hot'? Mr A need not be occurring: he may be a purely imaginary person, whom in a dream I see in hell. No words need be occurring. I have seen water steaming when it was at freezing point; I might (if I had had less knowledge) have plunged my hands into it in the belief that it was hot, and have received a shock of surprise from the perception of its coldness, and in this case the belief could have been quite wordless. On the other hand, there must be in me something corresponding to the word 'hot', and something which, perhaps mistakenly, is *felt* as a sign of a person called 'Mr A'. It is almost impossible to make such statements sufficiently vague, but I am doing my best.

The one word 'belief' should, I think, be replaced by several. First: perception, memory, expectation. Next come habit-inferences, of the kind that Hume considers in connexion with causation. Last come deliberate inferences such as logicians sanction or condemn. It is necessary to distinguish these in our present discussion, because they produce different states of the believer. Suppose I am a Dictator, and at 5 p.m. on 22 October someone attempts to stab me with a dagger. As a result of reports by the secret police, I believe that this is going to happen; this is (or at least may be) a logically inferential belief; it may also be a belief produced by habit-inference. At 4.59 I see a known enemy taking a dagger from its sheath; at this moment I *expect* the assault. The inference to the immediate future now is not logical, but habitual. A moment later, the assassin rushes forward, the blade pierces my coat, but is stopped by the shirt of chain armour that I wear next the skin. At this instant, my belief is a matter of perception. Subsequently, the villain having been beheaded, I have the experience of 'emotion recollected in tranquillity', and my belief has become one of memory .It is obvious that my bodily and mental state is different on these four occasions, though what I am believing is the same throughout, in the sense that it can be indicated in the same words, viz. 'I believe that at 5 p.m. on 22 October an attempt is made to stab me with a dagger'. (The 'is' here is timeless, not the present tense; it is like the 'is' in '4 is twice 2'.)

It is perhaps convenient to exclude perception from the forms of belief. I have included it above, for the sake of the serial development. But in general I have excluded it.

Our problem may be stated as follows. There are a number of states of my mind and body, any one of which, when it exists, makes it true to say 'I believe you are hot'. We may assume that any one of these states can be described with sufficient accuracy by psychologists and physiologists. Assuming this has been done for all such states, will the psycho-physicist be able to know, concerning any one of them, that it is a case of believing you to be hot? And further, will he be able to discover anything in common among the states except their relation to you and hotness?

I think that in theory the answer to both questions should be in the affirmative. Essentially the problem is the same as that of discovering that 'hot' means hot, which most children solve in about 18 months. If I am in any state that can be described as believing that you are hot, and you say 'do you believe I am hot?' I shall answer that I do. This is an experimental causal property of the belief, quite as satisfactory as those that are used in chemical tests. There are of course complications – mendacity, difference of language, etc. – but none of these afford any difficulty of principle.

We can now say: the states of two persons who speak the same language are instances of the same belief if there is a sentence S such that each, in reply to the question: 'do you believe

S?' replies 'I do'.* The person who, to himself or to anyone that he does not wish to deceive, says 'S!', believes S. Two sentences S and S' have the same significance if whoever believes the one believes the other. Experimentally, in this case, if you hear a man say 'S' and you ask him 'do you believe S'?', he will reply 'certainly, I have just said so'. This applies if, for example, 'S' is 'Brutus killed Caesar' and 'S'' is 'Caesar was killed by Brutus'. The same applies if S and S' are in different languages, provided both are known to the persons concerned.

One purpose of this discussion is to decide whether 'A believes p' is a function of p. Let us substitute for the proposition p a sentence s. In logic, we are accustomed to thinking of either a proposition or a sentence primarily as capable of truth or falsehood; we can, I think, at least for the time being, discard propositions and concentrate on sentences. The essential point, technically, is that we are concerned with the arguments to truth-functions. If 's' and 't' are two sentences, 's or t' is a third sentence, whose truth or falsehood depends only upon the truth or falsehood of s and t. In logic, sentences (or propositions) are treated technically as if they were 'things'. But a sentential utterance, in itself, is merely a series of noises, of no more interest than a series of sneezes and coughs. What makes a sentence interesting is its significance, or, to be more specific, its capacity for *expressing* a belief and for *indicating* a fact (or failing to do so). It acquires the latter through the former, and the former through the meanings of its words, which meanings are causal properties of noises acquired through the mechanism of conditioned reflexes.

From what has just been said it follows that the relation of a sentence to the fact that makes it true or false is indirect, and passes through the belief expressed by the sentence. It is primarily the belief that is true or false. (I am for the present abstaining from any attempt to define 'true' and 'false'.) When, therefore, we say that 's or t' is a sentence, we must give substance to our statement by investigating the belief expressed by 's or t'. It

---

* I do not suggest that this is the best definition of what constitutes the 'same' belief. The best definition would be one taking account of the causes and effects of the belief. But this definition would be elaborate and difficult, and the above definition by means of sentences seems to suffice for our present purposes.

seems to me that a person or animal may have a belief correctly expressed by '*s* or *t*', but describable by the psycho-physiologist without the use of the word 'or'. Let us investigate this matter, remembering that what is said about 'or' is likely to apply to other logical words.

I suggest that there is a difference between the word 'or' and such words as 'hot' or 'cat'. The latter words are needed in order to indicate as well as in order to express, whereas the word 'or' is needed only in order to express. It is needed to express *hesitation*. Hesitation may be observed in animals, but in them (one supposes) it does not find verbal expression. Human beings, seeking to express it, have invented the word 'or'.

The logician defines '*p* or *q*' by means of the conception of 'truth', and is thus able to short-circuit the route through the belief expressed by '*p* or *q*'. For our purposes, this short-circuit is not available. We wish to know what are the occurrences that make the word 'or' useful. These occurrences are not to be sought in the facts that verify or falsify beliefs, which have no disjunctive quality, but are what they are. The only occurrences that demand the word 'or' are subjective, and are in fact hesitations. In order to express a hesitation in words, we need 'or' or some equivalent word.

Hesitation is primarily a conflict of two motor impulses. It may be observed, for instance, in a bird timidly approaching crumbs on a window-sill, or in a man contemplating a dangerous leap across a chasm in order to escape from a wild animal. The intellectual form of hesitation, which is expressed by a disjunction, is a development from purely motor hesitation. Each of the two motor impulses, if it existed alone, would be a belief, and could be expressed in an assertion. So long as both exist, no assertion is possible, except a disjunction, 'this or that'. Suppose, for example, that you see an aeroplane. In ordinary circumstances, you will be content to note 'there is an aeroplane'. But if you are in charge of an anti-aircraft gun, the action called for will be different according to what sort of aeroplane it is. You will say, if you are in doubt, 'that aeroplane is British or German'. You will then suspend all action except observation until you have decided the alternative. The intellectual life is mainly concerned with suspended motor impulses. Consider a young person cramming for an examination. His activity is governed by a disjunction: 'I shall be asked A or B or C or . . .' He proceeds to acquire motor habits appropriate to each of these alternatives, and to hold them in suspense until the moment when he learns which of them to let loose. His situation is thus closely analogous to that of the man with the anti-aircraft gun. In either case the state of mind and body of the doubter can, theoretically, be specified by a description of the motor impulses and their conflict without the use of the word 'or'. The conflict, of course, is to be described in psycho-physical terms, not in terms of logic.

Similar considerations apply to the word 'not'. Imagine a mouse which has frequently observed other mice caught in traps baited with cheese. It sees such a trap and finds the smell of the cheese attractive, but memory of the tragic fate of its friends inhibits its motor impulses. It does not itself use words, but we can use words to express its state, and the words to use are: 'that cheese is NOT to be eaten'. At one time I kept pigeons, and found them to be models of conjugal virtue. But I once introduced among them a new hen pigeon very like one of the previous married hens. The husband mistook the new hen for his wife, and began cooing round her. Suddenly he discovered his mistake, and looked just as embarrassed as a man would look in similar circumstances. His state of mind could have been expressed in the words: 'that is NOT my wife'. The motor impulses associated with the belief that it was his wife were suddenly inhibited. Negation expresses a state of mind in which certain impulses exist but are inhibited.

Speaking generally, language of the sort that logicians would call 'assertion' has two functions: to indicate a fact, and to express a state of the speaker. If I exclaim 'fire!', I indicate a blaze and express a state of my perceptive apparatus. Both the fact indicated and the state expressed are in general non-verbal. Words are of two sorts: those that are necessary in order to indicate facts, and those that are only necessary in order to express states of the speaker. Logical words are of the latter sort.

The question of truth and falsehood has to do with what words and sentences indicate, not with what they express. This, at least, is what one might hope. But how about lies? It would seem that, when a man lies, the falsehood is in the expression. A lie is still a lie if it happens to be objectively true, provided the speaker believes it to be false. And how about sheer mistakes? Psychoanalysts tell us that our beliefs are not what we think they are, and certainly this is sometimes the case. Nevertheless there seems to be some sense in which there is less chance of error as regards the expression than as regards the indication.

The solution lies, I think, in the conception of 'spontaneous' speech, which we considered earlier in this chapter. When speech is spontaneous, it must, I think, express the speaker's state of mind. This statement, rightly interpreted, is tautological. A given belief, we agreed, may be shown by various states of the organism, and one of those states is that of spontaneously pronouncing certain words. This state, being easier to observe than those that involve no overt behaviour, has been taken as the definition of a given belief, whereas it is in fact merely a convenient experimental test. The result has been an unduly verbal theory of truth and falsehood and logical words generally. When I say 'unduly', I mean unduly from the standpoint of theory of knowledge; for logic, the traditional acceptance of 'propositions' and the definition of (e.g.) disjunction by means of truth-values are convenient and technically justified, except in relation to certain crucial problems such as extensionality and atomicity. These problems, since they arise in connexion with propositional attitudes (believing, etc.), can only be dealt with by means of theory of knowledge.

CHAPTER 15

WHAT SENTENCES 'INDICATE'

WHEN 'truth' and 'falsehood' are regarded as applicable to sentences, there are, from the standpoint of theory of knowledge, two kinds of sentences: (1) those whose truth or falsehood can be inferred from their syntactical relation to other sentences, (2) those whose truth or falsehood is only derivable from a relation to something that may be called 'fact'. Molecular and general sentences may, for the moment, be regarded as of the first kind; whether this is strictly true we shall consider at a later stage. The problems with which we are concerned in the present work arise only in regard to sentences of the second kind, for, if we have defined 'truth' and 'falsehood' for such sentences, the problems that remain belong to syntax or logic, which is not our subject.

Let us, then, confine ourselves, to begin with, to indicative sentences of atomic form, and ask ourselves whether, in regard to such sentences, we can frame a definition of the words 'true' and 'false'.

We agreed in the last chapter that an indicative sentence 'expresses' a state of the speaker, and 'indicates' a fact or fails to do so. The problem of truth and falsehood has to do with 'indication'. It appeared that truth and falsehood apply primarily to beliefs, and only derivatively to sentences as 'expressing' beliefs.

The distinction between what is expressed and what is indicated does not always exist – for instance, if I say 'I am hot', what is *expressed* is always a present state of the speaker; what is *indicated* may be such a state, but usually is not. What is expressed and what is indicated can only be identical when what is indicated is a present state of the speaker. In this case, if what is spoken is 'spontaneous' in the sense defined in the last chapter, the problem of falsehood does not arise. We can therefore make a beginning by saying: *a spontaneous sentence which indicates what it expresses is 'true' by definition.*

But now suppose that, pointing at a visible object, I say 'that is a dog'. A dog is not a state of myself; consequently there is a difference between what I indicate and what I express. (The phrase 'what I indicate' is open to objection, since, in the case of falsehood, it may be contended that I fail to indicate anything, but I shall employ it to avoid circumlocution.) What I express may be inferred from what would surprise me. If the shape that I see suddenly vanishes, without the possibility of eclipse by some other object, I shall be amazed. If you say to me: all the doors and windows are shut; there are no hiding-places in the room; and I am sure that a moment ago no dog was here; I shall conclude, if I have been reading *Faust*, that what I saw was not a dog but Mephistopheles. If the object that I am watching suddenly begins, like the pug in Heine's *Atta Troll*, to talk German with a Swabian accent, I shall conclude, as Heine did, that it is a Swabian poet transformed by a wicked witch. Such occurrences, no doubt, are unusual, but they are not logically impossible.

Thus when I say 'that is a dog', certain more or less hypothetical expectations are part of the state that I express. I expect that, if I watch, I shall continue to see something like the shape that led to my remark; I expect that, if I ask a bystander who had been looking in the same direction, he will say that he also saw a dog; I expect that if the shape begins to make a noise, it will bark and not talk German. Each of these expectations, being a present state of myself, can be both expressed and indicated by a single sentence. Suppose, to be definite, that I actually, not hypothetically, expect a bark; I am then in the state called 'listening', and I may very possibly have an auditory image of a bark, or the word 'bark', though both may be absent. We have here the smallest gulf between expression and indication; if I say 'in a moment I shall hear a bark', I express my present expectation and indicate my future sensation. In this case, there is a possibility of error: the future sensation may not occur. *Known* error is, I think, always of this kind; the sole method of discovering error is, I believe, the experience of surprise owing to a disappointed expectation.

There is, however, still a difficulty. I have at every moment a large number of more or less latent expectations, and any one of these, if disappointed, gives way to surprise. In order to know which expectation was false, I must be able to relate my surprise to the right expectation. While I am expecting the dog to bark, I may be surprised to see an elephant walking along the street; *this* surprise does not prove that I was wrong in expecting the dog to bark. We say we are surprised *at* something; that is to say, we experience not *merely* surprise, but surprise related to a present percept. This, however, is still not enough to make us know that our previous expectation was erroneous; we must be able to relate our present percept to our previous expectation, and, moreover, to relate it in a negative way. Expectation makes us say 'the dog will bark'; perception makes us say 'the dog is not barking'; memory makes us say 'I expected the dog to bark'. Or we may expect the dog not to bark, and be surprised when he does. But I do not see how this simplest case of known error can be dealt with except by the above combination of expectation, perception, and memory, in which either the expectation or the perception must be negative.

The emotion opposite to surprise may be called *confirmation*; this arises when what has been expected happens.

We may now say, as a definition: an expectation as to an experience of my own is *true* when it leads to confirmation, and *false* when it leads to surprise. The words 'leads to', here, are an abbreviation for the process just described.

But when I say 'there is a dog', I am not *merely* making an assertion as to my own experiences, past, present, or future; I am stating that there is a more or less permanent thing, which can be seen by others, exists when unseen, and has a sentient life of its own. (I am assuming that I am a plain man, not a solipsistic philosopher.) The question 'why should I believe all this?' is an interesting one, but is not the one I wish to discuss at the moment. What I wish to discuss at the moment is: what is there on the side of expression corresponding to this indication of something outside my experience? Or, in old-fashioned language, how do I think of things that I cannot experience?

I find in almost all philosophers a great unwillingness to face this question. Empiricists fail to realize that much of the knowledge they take for granted assumes events that are not experienced. Those who are not empiricists tend to maintain that we do not experience separate events, but always Reality as a whole; they fail, however, to explain how we distinguish between (say) reading poetry and having a tooth pulled out.

Let us take an example. Suppose on a fine Sunday I go out for the day with my whole family, leaving my house empty; when I return in the evening, I find it burnt down, and am informed by neighbours that the fire was first noticed too late for the fire-engines to be able to put it out. Whatever my philosophy, I shall believe that the fire began in a small way, as fires do, and therefore existed for some time before any human being perceived it. This, of course, is an inference, but it is one in which I feel great confidence. The question I wish to ask at the moment is not 'is this inference justifiable?', but rather: 'assuming the inference justifiable, how am I to interpret it?'

If I am determined to avoid anything not experienced, there are several things that I can say. I can say, like Berkeley, that God saw the beginning of the fire. I can say that my house, unfortunately, is full of ants, and they saw it. Or I can say that the fire, until it was seen, was merely a symbolic hypothesis. The first of these suggestions is to be rejected because such uses of God have become against the rules of the game. The second is to be rejected because the ants are accidental, and the fire could obviously have burnt just as well without them. There remains, then, the third suggestion, which we must try to make more precise.

We may state this theory as follows: let us first develop physics on the usual realistic hypothesis that physical phenomena do not depend for their existence upon being observed; let us further develop physiology to the point where we can say under what physical conditions physical phenomena are observed. Let us then say: the equations of physics are to be regarded as only connecting *observed* phenomena; the intermediate steps are to be regarded as dealing only with mathematical fictions. The process suggested is analogous to a calculation which begins and ends with real numbers, but uses complex numbers in the course of the argument.

This theory may be carried further: I may exclude, not only events which no one observes, but events which *I* do not observe. We might, to simplify the hypothesis, suppose that observable phenomena are those that happen in my brain. We shall then, after developing a realistic physics, define the space-time region occupied by my brain, and say that, of all the events symbolically assumed in our physics, only those whose space-time coordinates are among those of my brain are to be regarded as 'real'. This will give me a complete solipsistic physics, symbolically indistinguishable from ordinary realistic physics.

But what can I mean by the hypothesis that, of all the events symbolically occurring in my physics, only a certain sub-class are 'real'? There is only one thing that I can mean, namely this: that the mathematical account of a physical event is a description, and that such descriptions are to be considered empty except in certain cases. The reason for not considering them empty in these cases must be that, apart from physics, I have reason to know the events described in these cases.

Now the only events in which I have reason to believe apart from physics (taking physics in a wide sense) are those that I perceive or remember.

It is evident that two hypotheses which have exactly the same consequences as regards what I perceive and remember are, for me, pragmatically and empirically indistinguishable. The course of my life will be exactly the same whichever of them is true, and it is analytically impossible that my experience should ever give me a ground for preferring one to the other. It follows that, if knowledge is to be defined either pragmatically or in terms of experience, the two hypotheses are indistinguishable. *Convertando*, if it is logically possible to distinguish the two hypotheses, there must be something wrong with empiricism. The interesting point about this result, to me, is that it only requires us to be able to distinguish the two hypotheses, not to know which of them is true.

This brings me back to the question: how I think of things that I cannot experience?

Take (say) the statement: 'sound is due to waves in air'. What meaning can such a statement have? Does this necessarily only mean: 'if I suppose sound to be due to waves in air, I shall be able to develop a theory connecting the sounds that I hear with other experiences'? Or is it capable of meaning, as it seems to do, that there are events in air that I do not experience?

This question turns upon the interpretation of existential propositions. Logic assumes that, if I understand a statement 'ϕa', I can understand the statement 'there is an x such that ϕx'. If this is assumed, then, given two understandable statements ϕa, ψa I can understand 'there is an x such that ϕx and ψx'. But it may happen that, in my experience, ϕx and ψx are never conjoined. In that case, in understanding 'there is an x such that ϕx and ψx', I am *understanding* something outside experience; and if I have reason to believe this, I have reason to *believe* that there are things which I do not experience. The former is the case of unicorns, the latter that of events before my birth or after my death.

The question thus reduces to the following: if 'there is an x such that ϕx' is not an analytical consequence of one or more propositions expressing judgements of perception, is there any significance in the statement 'I believe that there is an x such that ϕx'?

Let us take some simple example, such as 'my study exists when no one is in it'. The naïve realist interprets this as: 'what I see when in my study exists when I do not see it'. To avoid the word exist, we can translate this into: 'there are events in my experience which are simultaneous with what I see when in my study, but not with my seeing it'. This involves a separation between seeing and what I see; it also involves the hypothesis that what I see is causally independent of my seeing. A very little knowledge of the physics of light and the physiology of vision suffices to disprove the second of these hypotheses, and for the first it is hard to find good grounds. The realist is thus driven to a *Ding-an-sich* as the *cause* of his visual percepts, and to the statement that this *Ding-an-sich* can exist at times when it is not causing visual percepts. But we must be able to say something about this cause, if our assertion is not to be quite empty. The question is: what is the minimum that will save our assertion from emptiness?

Suppose we say: the sensation of red has one sort of cause, and that of green has another. We are then, when we try to pass from sensation to physics, attributing hypothetical predicates to hypothetical subjects. Our inference from sensation depends upon a principle of the following form: 'there is a property ϕ such that, whenever I see red, there is something having the property ϕ'. But this is not nearly enough. To try to get more precision, let us proceed as follows. Let 'the property ϕ has the property f "mean" ϕ is a shade of colour'.

Then I say there is a correlator S between the members of f and the members of a certain other function F, such that, if, in my visual field, ϕ has the property f and a has the property ϕ, and if ψ is the argument to F which is correlated to ϕ, then there is an x such that ψ has the property F and x has the property ψ. It is to be understood that here F and S are apparent variables.

Let us state this matter somewhat differently. Let us define a shade of colour as all the visual places having colour-similarity to a given visual place and to each other. Thus a shade of colour is a class, and colours are a class of classes, κ say. We now assume that there is a correlator S between a kind of physical occurrence (light-waves of suitable frequency) and a colour. I see a patch of which the colour is α, and I take this as evidence of the existence of the class which S correlates with α, which I denote by '$S^{c}a$'. That is, I assume that whenever a member of α exists, a member of $S^{c}a$ exists at roughly the same time. Formally, this assumption is:

If κ is the class of shades of colour (each shade being defined as all the patches that are of this shade), then there is a one-one relation S, whose converse domain is κ, and which is such that, if a is a κ and a is an α, there is an x which is roughly simultaneous with a and is a member of the class that S correlates with α.

Or, to state the same assumption in other words:

There is a one-one relation S which correlates classes of physical events with shades of colour, and which is such that, if α is a shade of colour, whenever a patch whose colour is α exists, a physical event of the class correlated with α exists at roughly the same time. (2)

The above hypothesis is only a part of what we must assume if we are to believe that cats and dogs exist when we are not seeing them. Credible or not, the hypothesis is at least intelligible, since it involves only variables and empirically known terms. It gives *an* answer – not *the* answer – to the question from which this discussion started, namely: 'how do I think of things that I cannot experience?'

It will be remembered that we phrased this question, at first, somewhat differently, namely: 'what is there on the side of expression corresponding to the indication of something outside my experience?' We seem, however, to have answered a question somewhat different from this. It now appears that, if the statement 'there is a dog' is interpreted in the way of naïve realism, it is false, while if it is interpreted in a way that may be true the dog has been transformed into an apparent variable and is no longer any part of what is expressed by what I say.

Let us revert to (1) on p. 209. Here we may say that x is 'indicated' by α; α is a patch of colour that we see when we 'see a dog', while x may belong to the dog himself. Thus, put too schematically, we may say that when I say 'I see a dog', I *express* α and *indicate* x. But in what I believe, correctly stated, x is a mere variable, and is not expressed at all. The case is analogous to that in which we wish to use proper names but are compelled to use descriptions.

We may say, generally: when I am in a state of believing, that aspect of the believing which *seems* to refer to something else does not really do so, but operates by means of apparent variables. To take the simplest case: if I am expecting an explosion, the verbal expression of my belief is 'there will be a noise'. Here 'a noise' is an apparent variable. Similarly if I am recollecting an occurrence by means of a memory-image, the verbal expression of my memory-belief is 'there was something like this', where 'this' is the memory-image and 'something' is an apparent variable.

We thus arrive at the following results: when the verbal expression of my belief involves no apparent variable, what is expressed and what is indicated are identical. When the verbal expression of my belief involves an existence-statement, say 'there is an x such that ϕx', this, as it stands, is the expression of the belief, but the indication is the verifier of the proposition 'ϕa' in virtue of which 'there is an x such that ϕx' is true, or rather it is what would verify 'ϕa' if we could assert 'ϕa'. We cannot assert it, because a lies outside our experience, and 'a' is not one of the names in our vocabulary. All this involves the assumption that propositions of the form 'there is an x such that ϕx' can be known when no proposition of the form 'ϕa' is known – e.g. 'that dog stole the leg of mutton when I wasn't looking'.

To sum up: a sentence in the indicative 'expresses' a belief; it is merely one of an indefinite multitude of acts that can express a given belief. If the sentence contains no apparent variable, it must mention only things now present to the believer; in that case, it is capable of having a peculiar causal relation to these things which makes it what, in an earlier chapter, we called a 'sentence describing an experience'. If it has this peculiar relation, the sentence (and the belief which it expresses) is called 'true'; if not, 'false'. In this case, what the sentence 'expresses' and what it 'indicates' are identical, unless, being false, it 'indicates' nothing.

But when a sentence goes beyond present experience, it must involve at least one apparent variable. If, for the moment, we adhere as closely as logic will permit to the metaphysic of common sense, we shall say that, when I experience a percept a, there is a one-one relation S between some 'thing' and a, the 'thing' being what I should commonly be said to be perceiving. E.g. let a be a canoid patch of colour; then $S^c a$ is the dog that I say I am seeing when I experience a. When I say 'this dog is ten years old', I am making a statement about $S^c a$, which involves apparent variables. If my statement is true, there is a c such that

$c = S^c a$; in this case, what I *indicate* is 'c is ten years old', or rather, is what makes this true.

But this is, as yet, very unsatisfactory. In the first place, the sentence 'c is ten years old' can never be pronounced, because the proper name c does not occur in my vocabulary. In the second place, for the same reason, I can never have a belief expressible in this sentence. In the third place, we decided that sentences are nothing but expressions of beliefs. In the fourth place, I made, above, the hypothesis that the sentence 'this dog is ten years old' was 'true', and so far we have not defined the 'truth' of sentences which contain apparent variables, as this sentence does.

We cannot extricate ourselves from this tangle except by considering what is to be meant by the 'verifier' of a belief. A belief, when it is sufficiently simple, has one or other of various possible casual relations to a certain other occurrence; this occurrence is called the 'verifier' of the belief, or of any sentence expressing the belief. Certain causal relations, by definition, make the belief 'true'; certain others, 'false'. But when a belief, by means of apparent variables, refers to matters outside my experience, there are certain complications. Let us revert to the illustration 'you are hot', which avoids irrelevant difficulties. This may be taken to mean 'there is a hotness related to my percept of your body as, when I am hot, the hotness of me is related to my percept of my body'.* When I am hot I can give a proper name to my hotness; when you are hot, your hotness, to me, is an hypothetical value of an apparent variable. There are here two stages. Suppose I represent my percept of my body by a, my percept of your body by b, my hotness by h, the relation which I perceive between a and h by H, then 'you are hot' is 'there is an h', such that b H h''.

There is here an hypothetical sentence 'b H h'', which I cannot utter, because I have no name 'h'' in my language. But there is also, if you are hot, an actual occurrence, which is hypothetically named by the hypothetical name h', and this occurrence is actually so related to b, that its relation to b would be a verifier

---

* This is a simplification, but one which does no harm in relation to our present problem. I shall attempt a more accurate theory in the next chapter.

of the sentence '*b* H *h'*' if I could pronounce this sentence. This whole state of affairs constitutes the verifier of the sentence 'there is an *h'* such that *b* H *h'*'. How we come to know all this, if we know it, I am not inquiring; I am *assuming* that I can know that you are hot, and asking what is the simplest possible account of such knowledge, supposing it to exist.

We say now that, in the simpler class of cases, what is *indicated* by a sentence is its verifier, when the sentence is true, but is nothing when the sentence is false.

In the case of 'you are hot', I could, if my vocabulary were sufficient, frame a sentence containing no variable, which would be verified by the same occurrence that verifies my actual sentence; it is a merely empirical fact that I have not sufficient proper names for this purpose. In the case of 'all men are mortal' the matter is different; no conceivable vocabulary could express this without variables. The difference is that one occurrence is a complete verifier of 'you are hot', whereas many occurrences are necessary to verify a general statement. From any standpoint except that of theory of knowledge, 'you are hot' may be interpreted as '*b* H *h'*'; it is only theory of knowledge that requires the interpretation 'there is an *h'* such that *b* H *h'*'.

It will be seen that the relation of a belief or a sentence to what it indicates, i.e. to its verifier (if any), is often somewhat remote and causal. Also that, although to 'know' a verifier means to perceive it, we must, unless our knowledge is to be unbelievably depleted, know the truth of many sentences whose verifiers cannot be perceived. Such sentences, however, always contain a variable where the name of the verifier would occur if our perceptive faculties were sufficiently extensive.

CHAPTER 16

TRUTH AND FALSEHOOD: PRELIMINARY DISCUSSION

FROM what has been said so far, it would seem that, if our knowledge is to be roughly coextensive with what we all think we know, it must be derived from three sources:

(1) Beliefs (or sentences) having a certain kind of relation to some occurrence, which in general is non-linguistic.

(2) Principles of logical inference.

(3) Principles of extra-logical inference.

Of these three sources, we have so far been concerned only with the first. The second we may omit from our consideration, since it does not raise the problems as to empirical knowledge which we are attempting to solve. The third raises questions of very great difficulty, but it cannot be profitably discussed until the first is disposed of.

We may put the matter as follows: given any empirical sentence which we believe, our reason for believing it may be one or more other sentences which we already believe, or may be solely some non-linguistic occurrence having a certain relation to the sentence believed. In the latter case, the sentence is a 'basic factual sentence'. In the former case, in which the sentence is inferred, there must be among the premisses of the inference at least one basic factual sentence; the other premisses will belong to classes (2) and (3) above.

In the present chapter, I wish to discuss, not knowledge, but truth. What I know must be true, but truth is wider than knowledge in two respects. First, there are true sentences (if we accept the law of excluded middle) as to which we have no opinion whatever; second, there are true sentences which we believe and yet do not know, because we have arrived at them from faulty reasoning. I once met a Christadelphian who held, on grounds derived from the Book of Revelation, that there would shortly be trouble in Egypt. There was. His belief was true, but not knowledge.

'True' and 'false', we decided, are predicates, primarily, of beliefs, and derivatively of sentences. I suggest that 'true' is a wider concept than 'verifiable', and, in fact, cannot be defined in terms of verifiability.

When an empirical belief is true, it is true in virtue of a certain occurrence which I call its 'verifier'. I believe that Caesar was assassinated; the verifier of this belief is the actual event which happened in the Senate House long ago. My purpose in this chapter is to consider the relation of beliefs to their verifiers in various kinds of cases.

Let us begin by reconsidering the case in which A says that B is hot. There is, if this is true, an occurrence experienced by B but not by A, in virtue of which what A says is true. We interpreted this assertion by A as meaning: 'there is a hotness related to my percept of B's body as my hotness, when I am hot, is related to my percept of my body'. This interpretation, however, ignored the theory developed in the chapter on proper names, according to which 'hotness' (or at any rate a specific degree of hotness) is a proper name, not a universal of which there is one instance in A and another in B. We shall say, if we adhere to this theory, that 'A is hot' (pronounced by A) asserts a relation between a (which is A's percept of his own body) and h, which is hotness. The relation involved may be called 'compresence'. Then 'A is hot' (pronounced by A) means 'a and h are compresent'. Now if b is A's percept of B's body, b and h are compresent if A is hot, but not if B is hot while A is cold.

Therefore in order to interpret 'B is hot' (pronounced by A), A must somehow describe B's body, or B's percept of B's body, as opposed to A's percept of B's body. How is A to describe B's percept of B's body? He supposes it rather similar to his own percept of B's body, but with differences of perspective. Places in visual space, according to our present theory, are qualities, just as colours are; therefore the total of places in A's visual space (apart from different excellence of vision) is identical with, not merely similar to, the total of places in B's visual space. But we know empirically from perspective that the direction in which

A sees B's body is different from that in which B sees it. Hence the two complexes consisting of A's and B's percepts of B's body are different, both owing to differences of direction and owing to the differences of shape resulting from perspective. Thus when A says 'B is hot', he will have to *describe* B's percept of B's body (by means of the laws of perspective) and say that this is compresent with hotness.

Let us consider the following stages away from present experience:

(1) I am hot.
(2) I was hot.
(3) You are hot.
(4) The sun is hot.

When I judge (1), I am 'aware' of a circumstance, which is the 'verifier' of my judgement. When I judge (2), I am perhaps also 'aware' of the verifier, though in a different sense. When I judge (3), I am not 'aware' of the verifier; still less when I judge (4). In (3), 'hot' still means the quality I know from my own experience; in (4), it means an unknown cause of this quality, or, alternatively, the habitual coexistence of this quality with certain visual qualities.

For the present, let us take 'awareness' as an undefined term. The conception involved is the same as when I say that my hotness is part of my experience, but your hotness is not. Awareness, which we will denote by 'A', is a relation which may hold between two events in one person's experience; it is to be understood as including memory. In terms of A, we can define the person (if any) to whose biography a given event belongs. We do this by means of 'the R-family of x', defined in *Principia Mathematica* *96. This may be explained in popular language, designed to be intelligible to philosophers, as follows.

If 'P' means 'parenthood', the P-family of x is x's ancestors and descendants, and brothers and sisters, and cousins in any degree, and cousins of cousins, and himself – provided he has parents or children. But if x is something having no parents or children, then the P-family of x is not to include x, but to be the null class. In general, if R is any relation, let 'S' be 'R or its converse'. If x does not have the relation S to anything, the R-family of x is to be null; but if x has the relation S to anything, say y, let us call the journey from x to y an 'S-step'. Then the R-family of x consists of x together with all the terms that can be reached from x by a finite number of S-steps. Thus if 'P' is parent, the P-family of a person x is everything that is a parent or child of a parent or child of . . . of x.

Applying the above to 'awareness', denoted by 'A', we may take awareness to consist of noticing or remembering. Thus if x is an event in some person's biography, x's nearest relatives with respect to A will be events noticed or remembered by x and events which notice or remember x. If y is one of these, events noticed or remembered by y and events which notice or remember y will be relations of x in the second degree; and so on through any finite number of generations. I shall call an event 'personal' if it is aware of something or something is aware of it, i.e. if it belongs to the field of A. Thus if an event is personal its A-family contains the event itself and other terms, but if an event is not personal its A-family is the null class.

We may now define 'the person of x', or 'the person to whom the event x belongs', as 'the A-family of x'. We may define 'persons' as 'all A-families except the null class'. (An idealist will not have to make this exception, since he will hold that every event is the object or subject of an awareness.) We can define 'I' as 'the awareness-family of this'. On grounds which are empirical, and which have appeared in the course of our discussion, there is reason to believe that no two families ever have a common member, i.e. that there is nothing of which two different persons can be aware.

Thus 'I am hot' means 'hotness is a member of the aware-ness-family of this, and is compresent with this'. The latter clause is necessary to justify the present tense 'am' instead of 'was, am, or shall be'. The latter clause alone may sometimes be taken as what is meant by 'I am hot'.

In order to understand 'you are hot', we must understand 'you'. What is 'you'? I suppose that I am seeing you (as is said). In that case 'you' is related to an event in me, viz. the visual appearance of your body to me. This has a causal and also a perspective relation to an event in you, viz. the visual appearance of your body to you. The visual appearance of a human body to the person to whom it belongs has certain characteristic differences from its visual appearance to others – for example, it can contain neither eyes nor back, and the nose (if made to appear by closing one eye) looks more vast and portentous than to any one else. We can thus define two classes, one consisting of visual appearances of bodies to their owners, the other of visual appearances related by the laws of perspective to what I see when I 'see you'. (I am throughout assuming physics.) These two classes have only one common member, which is the appearance of your body to you. If we call this 'y', then 'you' may be defined as 'the awareness-family of y'.

Thus if y is that visual appearance which (a) is related by the laws of perspective to what I see when I 'see you', (b) has the characteristics which define a body viewed by its owner, then 'you are hot' means 'you are the awareness-family of y, and hotness is compresent with y'.

Of course if you are blind, or in the dark, or with your eyes shut, this definition will need to be modified. But the necessary modification offers no difficulty of principle, and is therefore uninteresting.

I have been assuming the theory of qualities developed in the discussion of proper names in Chapter 6, according to which there are not 'instances' of hotness (or at any rate of a given degree of hotness), but complexes of which hotness is an element. Space-time, on this view, depends upon qualities which are empirically unique, such as those used in defining latitude and longitude, and the complex 'hotness compresent with such-and-such a quality, or collection of qualities' takes the place of 'hotness in such-and-such a place'. This makes little difference after the definitions have been given.

We come now to 'the sun is hot'. This may be interpreted in two ways. It may mean only 'seeing-the-sun is usually compresent with feeling hot'; this is a generalization from experience. Or it may mean, as in physics: 'experiences of a certain sort, called sensations, have causes that are not in the experiencer; experiences of hotness have causes which all have a certain character called *heat*; the causal chains that start backwards from the experiences called *seeing-the-sun* meet in a certain region, and in this region there is heat'. We are not concerned to choose between these two interpretations, but only to consider both.

As regards the complexes which, on my view, take the place of 'instances' of hotness, I should use the relation 'compresence'. This relation subsists between any two things that I simultaneously experience, e.g. the sound of a piano and the sight of the piano player. But I suppose that it also holds between any two physical events which overlap in space-time. I now form a group of events all compresent with each other and not all compresent with anything outside the group; this I call a 'place' (or perhaps a 'point') in space-time. I assume the usual rules about places, but only as empirical generalizations – e.g. no place is earlier than itself, or to the left of itself, etc. Then an 'instance' of hotness is any place of which hotness is a member.

Starting from 'this', we can define 'I', 'here', 'now', etc., as was done in the chapter on egocentric particulars.

Let us now return to the question of 'verifiers'. If I say 'I am hot', the verifier is an event of which I am aware, namely hotness-here-now. But if I say 'you are hot', the verifier is hotness-*there*-now, of which I am not aware. This verifier cannot be any part of my reasons for believing that you are hot; these reasons must be derived from my experiences and prejudices. (Prejudice = synthetic *a priori*.) *My* reasons, in fact, must be derived from *me*.

When I say 'the sun is hot', interpreted as in physics, I travel further from experience, since 'hot' now means, not 'hotness', which I have experienced, but 'cause of hotness', which I have not experienced. The verifier of 'the sun is hot' is not only unknown, like that of 'you are hot', but unimaginable. My grounds for believing 'the sun is hot' (interpreted as in physics) are thus even more remote from the verifier.

The 'verifier' is defined as that occurrence in virtue of which my assertion is true (or false).

Formally, whenever an assertion goes beyond my experience, the situation is this: inference leads me to 'there is an x such that ϕx', and this, if true, is true in virtue of an occurence which would be asserted by 'ϕa'. But I know no such occurrence.

When I say 'I am hot', I am aware of the verifier, which is my hotness. When I say 'you are hot' or 'the sun is hot', I am not aware of the verifier.

In the case of 'I am hot', there is a simple kind of correspondence between the statement and the verifier. In this case, the correspondence-theory of truth holds *simpliciter*. This case covers all the *factual* premisses empirical knowledge. It does not cover the premisses used in inferring, e.g. induction.

In all other empirical assertions, such as 'you are hot', the correspondence on which truth depends is more complex. The assertion is of the form 'there is an x such that ϕx', and the 'fact' is that which, for a suitable a, would be asserted by 'ϕa'. But we cannot make the assertion 'ϕa' because we are not aware of a.

A great deal of metaphysics is involved in the belief that I can make assertions, such as 'you are hot', which go beyond my experience. I cannot imagine any way of discovering whether the metaphysics in question is true or false, but I think it is worthwhile to state the assumptions involved.

We have spoken of the assumptions as 'causal', but without investigating what we mean by this word, which, I am convinced, is capable of an important diversity of meaning. Let us consider various cases.

First: A and B have been frequently conjoined in experience, therefore when I see A I expect B. This raises the problem of induction, but not our present problem, which is that of transcending my experience.

Second: consider what makes me think that you have experiences that I do not have. The argument is obviously analogical, but is hard to state precisely. Suppose, e.g., you say 'I am hot', and I infer that you are hot. When I am hot, I say 'I am hot', and hear certain sounds (made by myself). I hear similar sounds when I am not speaking and not hot. I infer that they have a cause or antecedent similar to that which they have when I make them.

The argument, formally, is as follows. In a large class of cases, I know that events of kind B are preceded by events of kind A;

in another large class of cases, I do not know whether this is the case or not. In the absence of evidence to the contrary, I assume that it is the case. This is still induction, but it differs from the previous kind by the fact that there can be no evidence for or against it, except the indirect evidence that, accepted as a scientific hypothesis, it leads to no untoward consequences.

The above is the argument for the existence of other 'minds'. It remains to examine the argument for the physical world.

The simplest form of the argument for the physical world is the argument that 'things' exist when I do not see them – or rather, to avoid Berkeley, when no one sees them. Suppose, for example, that I keep my cheque-book in a drawer, so that it affects no one's senses except when the drawer is open. Why do I believe that it is there when the drawer is shut, and even when no one sees the drawer?

Some philosophers might argue that, when I say 'the book is in the drawer', I only mean 'if anyone opens the drawer he will see it' – where 'opening the drawer' must be interpreted as an experience, not as something done to a permanent drawer. This view, right or wrong, is one which would only occur to a philosopher, and is not the one I wish to discuss. What I wish to discuss is the view that *something* – which may be called the book – is occurring when no one sees it. I do not wish to discuss whether the view *is* true, but what kind of influence is involved in *supposing* it true.

Unsophisticated common sense supposes that the book, just as it appears when seen, is there all the time. This we know to be false. The book which can exist unseen must, if it exists, be the sort of thing that physics says it is, which is quite unlike what we see. What we more or less know is that, if we fulfil certain conditions, we shall see the book. We believe that the causes of this experience lie only partly within ourselves; the causes external to ourselves are what lead us to belief in the book. This requires belief in a kind of cause which completely and essentially transcends experience. What is the argument in favour of causes of this kind?

The belief from which we most naturally arrive at matter is, I think, the belief that in sensation we are passive. We experience sights and sounds, broadly speaking, involuntarily. Now the conception of 'cause' – however loath we may be to admit this fact – is derived from the conception of 'will'. Since *we* do not will what we see and hear, the cause of what we see and hear must, it is felt, be external to us. This is an argument which only has to be stated in order to be rejected. Is there any better argument for the physical world?

The only remaining argument, so far as I can see, is that the hypothesis of the physical world simplifies the statement of causal laws – not only of those that cannot be verified, but also of those that can. Of course there can be no argument *against* the physical world, since experience will be the same whether it exists or not. Therefore it is justified as a working hypothesis. But more than this cannot be claimed on the ground of simplicity.

This concludes the discussion of the relation between a singular belief and the fact in virtue of which it is true (or false). It will be seen that this fact is often quite remote from the grounds upon which we entertain the belief, and that the belief may be (in some sense) knowledge even when the fact is quite unknowable.

The relation between belief and fact is even more remote in the case of general beliefs, such as 'all men are mortal'. Here there is not a single verifier, but an indefinite multitude, though there could be a single 'falsifier'. We have not yet considered what is *expressed* by such beliefs as 'all men are mortal', but it is clear that there can be only a very remote correspondence between what is expressed and the multitude of verifiers. For the moment, I do not propose to discuss this problem; I mention it only in order to point out how much still remains to be considered.

CHAPTER 17

TRUTH AND EXPERIENCE

MY purpose in this chapter is to consider the relation between truth and experience, or, what comes to the same thing, between truth and knowledge. The most important question in this connexion is whether 'truth' is a wider concept than 'knowledge', and whether a proposition which is theoretically incapable of being proved or disproved, or rendered probable or improbable, by means of our experience, is nevertheless true or false. But a good many preliminaries are necessary before we can discuss this question.

'Truth', we have agreed, is a property primarily of beliefs, derivatively of sentences. Some beliefs can be 'expressed' by sentences containing no variables – e.g. 'I am hot'. Beliefs which transcend the experience of the believer – e.g. 'you are hot' – always involve variables in their expression. But some beliefs whose expression involves variables do not transcend experience, and among these some are basic. This is most evident in the case of memory – e.g. 'that book is *somewhere* in my shelves'. This can be replaced, after search, by 'that book is *here*', but in such a case as 'you are hot' this is impossible. If I believe 'something has the property f' but know no proposition 'a has the property f', I naturally suppose that, given some experience which I have not had, there would be a proposition of the latter sort describing this experience. There seems to be here an unconscious assumption that experience is purely contemplative, so that an event which I have not experienced might have remained unaltered if I had experienced it.

The question of truth which transcends experience may be put as follows: suppose a_1, a_2, ... a_n are all the names in my vocabulary, and that I have named everything I can name. Suppose fa_1, fa_2, ... fa_n are all false, is it nevertheless possible that 'there is an x for which fx' should be true? Or, alternatively, can I infer 'fx is false whatever x may be'?

We cannot discuss this question without first defining what is meant by the 'truth' of 'there is an x for which fx'. Such a proposition is called an 'existence-proposition'.

It is impossible to define 'truth' for existence-propositions except in terms of basic existence propositions. Any other definition will use existence-propositions. For example, in the above instance, 'consider there is a person, other than myself, whose vocabulary contains some name b which mine does not contain, and which is such that, for him, fb is a judgement of perception'. This is only a new and more complicated existence-proposition, even if, like Berkeley, we replace the hypothetical person by God.

It seems, therefore, that we must enumerate basic existence-propositions, and define 'true' existence-propositions as those deducible from these. But this leaves the question: 'in what sense are the basic existence-propositions true? It seems we shall have to say they are 'experienced'. For instance, when someone knocks on the door and you say 'who's there?' you know 'someone is there' and you wish to know a proposition of the form 'a is there'.

Suppose we assert 'there is an x such that fx' when, for every name we know, 'fa' is false. We cannot, in this case, get a *linguistic* statement without a variable. We cannot say: 'there is a name "a" such that "fa" is true', for this merely substitutes the name as variable, and is less likely to be true than the original statement. If I believe, for instance, that there are occurrences in the physical world which no one perceives, these occurrences must be nameless; the translation which substitutes a hypothetical name will therefore be false, even if the original belief was true.

It is clear that, unless our knowledge is very much more limited than there seems any reason to suppose, there must be basic existence-propositions, and that, in regard to some of these, every instance 'fa' that we can give is false. The simplest example is 'there are occurrences which I do not perceive'. I cannot in language express what makes such statements true, without introducing variables; the 'fact' which is the verifier is unmentionable.

Nevertheless, if 'there is an x such that fx' is true, it is true because of some occurrence, although, in the case supposed, we do not experience this occurrence. This occurrence may still be called the 'verifier'. There is no reason to suppose the relation of 'there is an x such that fx' to the verifier to be different when the verifier is not experienced from what it is when the verifier is experienced.* When the verifier is experienced, the knowledge-process is different, but that is another matter. When I experience an occurrence, it enables me to know one or more sentences of the form 'fa', from which I can deduce 'there is an x such that fx'. This new sentence has a different relation to the occurrence from that which 'fa' has; the relation of 'fa' to the occurrence is only possible when a is experienced. But this is a linguistic fact. The relation of 'there is an x such that fx' to the occurrence, unlike that of 'fa', does not demand that the verifier should be experienced. And the relation may be just the same when the occurrence is not experienced as when it is.

If I am asked 'what occurrence makes "there is an x such that fx" true?' I can answer by a description which involves existence-propositions, but I cannot answer by *naming* the occurrence. When I can name such an occurrence, I do more than is necessary for the truth of 'there is an x such that fx', since an indefinite multitude of other occurrences would do equally well. If I say 'there is at least one man in Los Angeles', any man in Los Angeles will do equally well as a verifier. But when I say 'there are invisible parts of the moon's surface', I am not acquainted with any verifier.

If there are basic existence-propositions, as we seem driven to conclude, their relation to perception must be very different from that of judgements of perception. In the case of memory, e.g. 'that book is *somewhere* in my shelves', there was once a judgement of perception. It would be possible, though I do not think it would be right, to argue that, at the time of perception, I inferred the existence-proposition, and now remember *it*.

* This subject will be considered further at the end of this chapter.

This would make the existence-proposition not basic. But there are other cases that are more stubborn.

Take events perceived by no one. I do not want to assert positively that we know of such events, but to inquire what is involved in supposing that we do. To make the matter concrete, let us imagine that I am walking just outside my house when a tile hits me on the head. I look up, and see the place on the roof from which it has apparently fallen. I am quite persuaded that it existed before it hit me. What is involved in this persuasion?

It is customary to appeal to causation, and to say that from perceived facts I infer unperceived facts. Obviously it is on occasion of perceived facts that I believe in unperceived facts, but I do not think this is an inference. Before we see the tile we say '*something* hit me', and this judgement is just as immediate as a judgement of perception. It would be possible, therefore, instead of a general principle of causal inference, to substitute a number of basic existence-propositions, each as immediate as perceptive propositions. From these, causation would be derived inductively.

This point is not very important. On the usual view, we know a judgement of perception p, and also 'p implies that there is an x such that fx'; on the view I am suggesting, when we know p we know that there is an x such that fx. The difference between the two views is negligible.

There is no reason why basic empirical knowledge should not be of the form 'there is an x such that fx'. To know this is less than to know 'fa'. If a has the property f, it may *cause* me to know 'there is an x such that fx' without causing me to know 'fa'. In 'you are hot', f is known; this therefore illustrates the above. In purely physical statements, such as 'sound is composed of air-waves', the 'f' involved is not very obvious. To interpret such statements, we must take theoretical physics in its (at present) most advanced form. Where does this touch experience?

(1) Physical events have a space-time order correlated (not very exactly) with that of percepts. (2) Certain trains of physical events are causal antecedents of certain percepts. We may hence conclude (*a*) that time is the same in the physical as in the psychological world; (b) that compresence (which we know as a

relation between any two parts of one experience) also exists in the physical world; (c) that if I have two qualitatively different experiences, their causes have differences which in some way correspond. This gives the experienced elements in physical propositions.

In any significant sentence, the constants must all be derived from experience. Space-time order in physics, for example, is derived from space-time order among percepts. If we see two stars close together, and the polar coordinates of the stars in physical space, with ourselves as origin, are (r, θ, ϕ), (r', θ', ϕ'), θ and θ', ϕ and ϕ' will be respectively very nearly equal, and will be very nearly identical in magnitude with the angular coordinates of the visual stars in our visual space. (I say 'very nearly' because light does not travel strictly in straight lines.)

In pure logic there are sentences containing no constants. These, if true, are true without any relation to experience. But such sentences, if knowable, are tautologies, and the meaning of 'truth' as applied to tautologies is different from its meaning as applied to empirical sentences. I am not concerned with the kind of truth belonging to tautologies, and shall therefore say no more on this subject.

So far we have been considering what 'there is an x such that fx' indicates; let us now consider what it expresses.

We agreed that 'p or q' expresses a state in which there is hesitation. Sometimes this is true of 'there is an x such that fx', but (I think) not always. If you find a man dead of a bullet wound, you judge that *somebody* shot him, and if you are a good citizen you desire to replace the variable by a constant; in this case, there is doubt, as in the case of 'p or q'. But sometimes you are quite content with 'there is an x such that fx', and have no wish to replace it by 'fa'. Examining footprints in the jungle, you may say 'a tiger has been here'; in this case, unless you are engaged in a tiger hunt, you have no wish to replace the variable by a perceived constant. Or suppose I say 'London has 7,000,000 inhabitants', I shall certainly not wish to replace this by 'the inhabitants of London are A and B and C and . . .' to 7,000,000 terms. The interesting question is: what is expressed, in such a case, by the sentence in which the variable occurs?

Suppose someone says to me 'I saw a fox in the street', and suppose I believe him. What does this involve as to my state of mind? I may have an image of a fox, more or less vague, and think 'he saw that'. This assumes that the image occurs as representative, since I do not think that he saw my image. Images, in fact, act as symbols, just as words do. Images are usually sufficiently vague to be capable of 'meaning' any member of a rather ill-defined class of possible or actual percepts. Such an image of a fox as I personally can form would fit any ordinary fox. It serves, therefore, almost exactly the same purpose as is served by the word 'fox'. Let us, then, suppose that the words which I hear act upon me without the intermediary of images. When I hear 'I saw a fox', certain kinds of action may result; what these are will depend upon whether I am engaged in fox-hunting or not. But we may say, broadly speaking, that different foxes call for very nearly the same actions. Therefore the heard words 'I saw a fox' are causally sufficient. We may put the matter as follows: let F_1, F_2, F_3 ... be different foxes, and suppose that seeing F_1 calls out the reaction A_1, F_2 calls out A_2, and so on. A_1, A_2, etc., are all complex actions; there may be a part A which they all have in common. This common part (with obvious limitations) may be called out by the word 'fox'. When I hear the words 'there's a fox', I understand them if they call forth the reaction A. (This is unduly simplified, but not in ways relevant to our problem.)

This makes it clear that, as regards what is expressed, the function of variables is exactly that of general words. If we take a pragmatic view of 'meaning', and define it in terms of the acts (or incipient acts) to which it gives rise, then 'there is an x such that fx' expresses that partial act which is common to 'fa', 'fb', 'fc', etc. What is expressed by 'there is an x such that fx' is therefore something smaller and simpler than what is expressed by 'fa'; moreover, it is a *part* of what is expressed by 'fa', so that whoever believes 'fa' in fact believes 'there is an x such that fx'.

(The situation is a little more complicated when a man has verbal knowledge which he does not know how to translate into perceptual terms. Most men know that rattlesnakes are dangerous, even if they cannot recognize one when they see it. In that case, a percept which is, in fact, of a rattlesnake, will not produce the appropriate reaction until someone says 'that is a rattlesnake'. In such a case the general word is more potent than the instances to which it is applicable. This only means, how-ever, that, in the case supposed, a man's verbal experience has outrun the experience of the things meant by words.)

The above theory has a bearing on the theory of analytic inference. An inference is defined as analytic when the con-clusion is part of the premisses. According to what we have been saying, *belief* in the conclusion is also part of *belief* in the pre-misses: whoever believes 'fa' is also believing 'there is an x such that fx'. Our theory of belief does not require that a belief should be expressed in words; therefore it is not surprising if, when a man has one belief which he expresses in words, he also has others, logically connected with it, which he may not express in words, and may not even know that he has.

We must now endeavour to reach more precision as regards the relation of a belief to its verifier when the verifier is not experienced. We said above that there is no reason to suppose the relation of 'there is an x such that fx' to its verifier to be different when the verifier is not experienced from what it is when the verifier is experienced. We have now to examine and amplify this statement.

In the first place, an existence-proposition has, in general, many verifiers, not one only; $fa, fb, fc \ldots$, if true, are statements which are true in virtue of different verifiers, each of which is a verifier of 'there is an x such that fx'.

In the second place, when no verifier is experienced, there is no sentence 'fa' corresponding to an occurrence which verifies 'there is an x such that fx'; this is merely because, *ex hypothesi*, there is no such name as a. When 'fa' expresses a judgement of perception, we can distinguish two steps: first, from the percept to the sentence 'fa'; second, from the sentence 'fa' to the sen-tence 'there is an x such that fx'. There are not these two steps in the case supposed. It may be that 'there is an x such that fx' is a basic proposition; it may be that it is a proposition which is true but cannot be known. These cases must be treated separately.

Take the case in which 'there is an x such that fx' is a basic proposition. Is there any reason why this should not itself express a fact of experience, just as 'fa' may? The word 'experience' is somewhat vague; perhaps it can only be defined in terms of basic propositions. A coroner's Court may decide that A was killed by B, or that he was killed by some person or persons unknown. The latter conclusion is based upon a number of propositions either proved in Court or generally accepted; among these, it is logically necessary that there should be at least one existence-proposition. In practice, the process is more or less as follows: we have judgements of perception, 'this is a bullet', 'this is in the brain', and a general proposition 'bullets in brains imply the firing of guns'. This last is not a basic proposition, but an inductive generalization. An inductive generalization is of the following form: 'whatever x may be, fx implies that there is a y such that gy'. The observed premisses of this generalization are of the form: $fa \cdot ga', fb \cdot gb', fc \cdot gc'$, etc., where a, a', b, b', c, c' are respectively simultaneous. In a new case we find fd, but we do not *find* any d' such that gd'; we, however, infer 'there *is* a simultaneous y such that gy'.

There is here a distinction between inductive inference in logic and inductive inference as an animal habit. In logic, we proceed, via the inductive principle, from $fa \cdot ga', fb \cdot gb', fc \cdot gc,$, etc., to 'whatever x may be, fx implies that there is a simultaneous y such that gy'. We then add the observed premiss fd, and conclude that in this case there is a y such that gy. But induction as an animal habit proceeds quite differently. The animal experiences $fa \cdot ga', fb \cdot gb', fc \cdot gc' \ldots$ and fd. On occasion of experiencing fd, he believes 'there is now a y such that gy', but he is unaware of the causes of his belief. When, in the course of evolution, he becomes an inductive logician, he notices the causes and says they are grounds. Since they are not, he might just as reasonably accept 'there is now a y such that gy' as a basic proposition; it is simpler than the inductive principle, and also more likely to be true. In this respect, therefore, the animal is to be preferred to the logician. This is a vindication of Hume.

However this may be, we must, I think, concede that there are existence-propositions that are basic. They have a correspondence with fact, though this is not of quite the same kind as in the case of propositions not containing variables. If 'fa' is a basic proposition, the fact corresponding to it is its cause. Now the belief 'there is an x such that fx' is part of the belief 'fa', when the latter belief exists; when it does not, the fact has had only part of the effect required to produce the belief 'fa', namely that part which produces the belief 'there is an x such that fx'. The reason may be merely that the causal chain from fact to belief is longer than when the fact causes the belief 'fa'.

The correspondence of truth and fact, here, is still causal, and of the kind connected with 'meaning' or 'significance'.

We now have to ask ourselves: is there a sense in which a proposition may be true although it cannot be known? Take, say, 'in the invisible part of the moon there is a mountain of which the height is between 6,000 and 7,000 metres'. Common sense would say unhesitatingly that this proposition is either true or false, but many philosophers have theories of truth which make this doubtful.

Let us call our proposition S. The question is: what, if anything, can be meant by the sentence: 'S is true'?

We may say that S is *probable*, because there are such mountains on the part of the moon that we can see. But probability is a different concept from truth, and I see no reason why what is probable should be either true or false, unless we can define truth independently of probability.

We cannot say that S is not significant, for it is correctly constructed out of terms of which we know the meaning. This is obvious, since, if we substitute 'visible' for 'invisible', the sentence becomes one asserted by astronomers; and 'invisible' means 'not visible' and no sentence is deprived of significance by the insertion of the word 'not'.

Common sense imagines travelling round the moon (which is only *technically* impossible), and holds that, if we did so, we should either see or not see the mountains in question. It is because of imagining oneself a spectator that one is so sure of S being significant. The astronomer may say: mountains on the further side of the moon would have gravitational effects, and might therefore conceivably be inferred. In both these cases, we are arguing as to what would happen in the event of a hypothesis which has not been verified in our experience. The principle involved is, in each case: 'in the absence of evidence to the contrary, we shall assume the unobserved portions of the universe to obey the same laws as the observed portions'. But unless we have an independent definition of truth concerning what is unobserved, this principle will be a mere definition, and the 'unobserved portions' will be only a technical device, so long as they remain unobserved. The principle only says something substantial if it means 'what I shall observe will be found to resemble what I have observed', or, alternatively, if I can define 'truth' independently of observation.

On what may be called the realist view of truth, there are 'facts', and there are sentences related to these facts in ways which make the sentences true or false, quite independently of any way of deciding the alternative. The difficulty is to define the relation which constitutes truth if this view is adopted. The question is serious, since, as we have seen, it is not only such things as the further side of the moon that are unobserved, but also cats and dogs and human beings other than ourselves.

A sentence which is true in virtue of an unobserved fact must contain at least one variable. The sentence 'there are men in Semipalatinsk' is true in virtue of particular facts, but as I do not know the name of any inhabitant of that region, I cannot adduce any of these facts. Each of these facts, however, has a determinate relation to my sentence, and each has the same relation to it. I do not think there is any real difficulty; the apparent difficulty is due to the trivial circumstance that what has no name cannot be mentioned. I conclude, therefore, that sentences containing variables may be true in virtue of a relation to one or more unobserved facts, and that the relation is the same as that which makes similar sentences true when they concern observed facts, e.g. 'there are men in Los Angeles'. Unobserved facts can be spoken of in general terms, but not with the particularity that is possible where observed facts are concerned. And there is no reason why 'truth' should not be a wider conception than 'knowledge'.

CHAPTER 18

GENERAL BELIEFS

WE have been concerned hitherto with beliefs as to particular matters of fact, when these result as directly as possible from perception; we have considered also, though less fully, beliefs in the verbal expression of which the word 'some' occurs, which we found important, especially, in connexion with memory. We have now to consider beliefs in the verbal expression of which either the word 'all' or the word 'none' occurs. As hitherto, I shall confine myself to extra-logical beliefs.

There is, in all such inquiries, a combination of logic and psychology. Logic shows us the goal we have to reach, but psychology must show us how to reach it. Our psychology of belief, while it must be able, at its conclusion, to embrace the refined abstractions of the logician, must, at its outset, be applicable to animals and young children, and must show logical categories as a natural development out of animal habits. In this we are very much helped by our decision that belief is essentially pre-linguistic, and that, when we express a belief in words, we have already taken the most difficult of the steps that lead from the animal to the logician.

The psychology to be offered in this chapter, as in previous chapters, is more or less schematic, and is not asserted to be correct in detail. What is asserted is that something of the general kind that is suggested is necessary in order to pass from animal habits to what logic demands. Accuracy as to the detail is matter for the psychologist, and must depend upon investigations somewhat remote from theory of knowledge. So far as psychology is concerned, I am content if I can persuade the psychologist of the nature and importance of the problems that I indicate.

General beliefs – by which I mean such as, in their verbal expression, involve 'all' or 'none' or some synonym – have their pre-intellectual origin in habits of a certain kind. In those who possess language, such habits may be purely verbal. The word 'primrose' may suggest the word 'yellow'; the word 'Apostles' may suggest the word 'twelve'. Scholastic education produces a mass of knowledge of this sort, which may be almost wholly unrelated to what the sentences employed signify. We, however, are in search of something pre-linguistic, and must therefore, to begin with, ignore habits concerned with words.

Consider the behaviour of a dog. When he sees his master put on a hat, he expects to be taken for a walk, and shows his expectations by leaps and barks. A certain smell suggests rabbit; so does a rabbit-hole, or any place where he has frequently found rabbits. The smell of a female on heat will stimulate incredible exertions. I am told that horses are terrified by the smell of a bear-skin even if they have never seen a bear. The above kinds of behaviour are partly instinctive, partly the result of experience. The smell of a rabbit or a female has an instinctive effect, but the master's hat has an effect generated by previous occurrences. In both kinds of cases alike, if the dog were miraculously endowed with language and the mental habits of a philosopher, he would be led to enunciate a general proposition. He would say 'wherever there is this smell, there is something edible', and 'my master's putting on his hat is an invariable antecedent of his going out'. If you asked him how he knew this, he would say, in the latter case, that he had observed it, and in the former, that it was a synthetic *a priori* intuition. He does not say this, because he cannot talk; but we say very similar things in very similar circumstances.

Let us consider some rather easy general propositions, such as 'any neighbourhood that contains a smell of a certain sort also contains bacon'. Let 'fx' mean 'there is a certain kind of smell in the neighbourhood x', and let 'gx' mean 'there is bacon in the neighbourhood x'. Whenever we eat bacon, we experience both fx and gx, and when we experience fx alone we usually find that, by a suitable effort, we can arrive at also experiencing gx. This state of affairs in time generates a habit of believing gx whenever we believe fx. So far, however, we are not believing any general proposition. The psychologist who observes us can arrive at a general proposition: 'whenever Mr So-and-so believes fx, he also believes gx.' But this is not the general proposition we want, which is 'whenever fx is true, gx is also true'. For Mr So-and-so, however, this latter general proposition results from his observation, exactly as the psychological proposition results from the observation of the psychologist. Whatever is to be said for or against the one general proposition is to be said equally for or against the other.

Let us try to consider in more detail the proposition 'whenever there is fx there is gx'. Consider, first, the various values of the function f, say fa, fb, fc, ... Each of these is a proposition which can be believed: fa, for instance, says 'the neighbourhood a has a certain smell (that of bacon)'. The smell is strictly a class of smells, since two pieces of bacon do not smell exactly alike. Let us call the class of smells in question σ, and the class of bits of bacon β. Or, to avoid the assumptions of physicalism, let β be the class of visual perceptions called 'seeing bacon'. We may somewhat alter our original proposition so as to simplify our discussion; we can take it as saying 'whenever I smell bacon, I see it then or soon afterwards'. To make this precise, let us fix on a time-interval t which we consider short – say five minutes. Then our statement becomes: 'whenever a member of the class σ occurs, there is a slightly later member of the class β, such that the time-interval from σ to β is less than t', where t is a given constant time-interval. This is rather complicated; let us see whether anything simpler is possible.

When I begin my reflections, I observe that, on certain specific occasions, I have experienced fa and expected ga, experienced fb and expected gb, etc. I observe also that my expectations have not been disappointed. The time t which appeared in our previous statement is now replaced by the time taken for an expectation to be disappointed. This of course varies with the character of the expectation, and, in our case, with the intensity of the smell. It will be remembered that we distinguished expecting, like recollecting, as a species of belief: e.g. the proposition 'there is a loud bang at time t' may be expected before t, perceptively judged at t, and recollected after t. The tense of the verb – 'will be', 'is', 'was' – expresses the difference of bodily state in the believer, according as he expects, perceives, or recollects. Tense applies *primarily* only to matters within my perceptive experience, and expresses the species of belief involved, not a character of what the belief 'indicates'. If we want to say, in a Spinozistically timeless manner, 'Caesar *is* murdered on the Ides of March', we have to invent a special language and use 'is' in a sense different from that which it ordinarily bears.

Let us now return to our bacon. The person or animal who or which, whenever he or she or it experiences a member of σ, expects a member of β, has not begun to believe a general proposition, though his, her, or its behaviour in the presence of a member of σ is what it would be if he, she, or it were believing a general proposition. The difference of behaviour between the above and the belief in a general proposition arises when no member of σ is present. If I believe 'where there is σ a there is a β', and if I desire a β, I may be led to search for a σ; this is exemplified by a geologist prospecting for gold, who will search only where there are certain obvious indications of the likelihood of gold. The geologist requires the explicit general proposition as a guide to action. It is the explicit general proposition that concerns us in this chapter, but we shall understand it better by considering its animal ancestry.

When I believe a proposition about the future, it may or may not involve the physical state called 'expectation', just as a belief about the past may or may not involve recollection. If I think 'some day the sun will grow cold', I have no state of expectation; if, having seen lightning, I think 'there is going to be thunder', I have a state of expectation. Expectation, as a physical state, is only possible as regards experiences in the immediate future. In what follows I use 'expectation' as the analogue of memory, and not to cover any belief about the future.

Animal induction differs from scientific induction in various ways; one of these is that the former, but not the latter, involves expectation. When, in the experience of an animal, an event of kind A has been quickly followed by an event of kind B, if B is emotionally interesting the animal comes to expect B whenever A occurs. How many experiences are necessary depends upon the degree of emotion aroused by B; if B is very pleasurable or very painful, one experience may suffice. As soon as the animal has acquired the habit of expecting B when it sees A, it behaves, *in the presence of A*, as a man would who believed the general proposition 'A is always followed by B'. But the animal is at no time believing anything that can only be expressed in words by mentioning both A and B. It sees A, and it expects B; these two, though *we* see them to be causally connected, are separate beliefs in the animal. We, when we reflect upon our own animal behaviour, may observe that A has always hitherto been followed by B, or we may observe the *two* laws 'A causes expectation of B' and 'expectation of B is followed by B'. These two laws will begin to be true at a later time than our first experience of the one law that A is followed by B, since a certain number of experiences of the one law are necessary to cause instances of the law that A causes expectation of B. Any one of the three laws may fail at any moment, but I am considering the case in which this does not occur.

The importance of the above is that it shows the limitations of animal induction. This never leads to belief in the general proposition 'A is followed by B', but only, when A occurs, to the expectation 'B will occur'. Belief in general laws, however inductive and however mistaken, requires a higher intellectual development than is required for what may be called 'inductive behaviour' in the presence of the stimulus A. Speaking pragmatically, there is the essential difference that belief in the general law, as opposed to animal habit, can influence action in the absence of the stimulus A.

In a scientific induction, expectation in the above limited sense is not involved. Take one of the earliest of such inductions, the Egyptian discovery of the periodicity of eclipses. Here the events foretold were too distant to be 'expected' in the physical sense. In a scientific induction, two events A and B are observed to occur together or in close temporal succession, but no physical expectation is generated, or if it is, it is regarded as irrelevant. The *hypothesis* that A is always accompanied or followed by B precedes the *belief* that this is the case, and the belief never acquires the dogmatic and immediate quality of animal expectation. I cannot help thinking, however, that our obstinate belief in induction has some connexion with animal expectation. But this is a purely psychological question, of no essential importance to our inquiry.

We must now attempt to analyse what is 'expressed' by the words 'A is always followed by B'. What is expressed cannot be merely that, when I experience A, I expect B, for this is another general law, which would have to be similarly analysed, and we should thus be led into an endless regress. What is expressed must be a belief involving both A and B, not a merely causal relation between a belief involving only A and another belief involving only B.

Suppose I am believing that all men are mortal, what sort of thing must be occurring in me? I think that a belief of this kind is sometimes affirmative, sometimes negative, where these terms are to be interpreted psychologically. A belief is affirmative when what is considered is accepted, and is negative when what is considered is rejected. Thus 'all men are mortal', when affirmative, will involve some connexion between the predicates 'man' and 'mortal', but when negative may be represented by the question 'an immortal man?' followed by the answer 'no'. The psychology is somewhat different in these two cases. Let us take the affirmative first.

It might be thought that 'whatever is human is mortal' could be interpreted, on the subjective side, as only a relation between the two predicates 'human' and 'mortal'. We might say: the beliefs 'A is human', 'B is human', etc., all, considered as events in the believer, have something in common; this something is what is 'expressed' by the predicate 'human'. Similarly there is something 'expressed' by the predicate 'mortal'. We might be tempted to say that one of these predicates implies the other, and to use this as an analysis of what is 'expressed' by 'all men are mortal'.

This Aristotelian interpretation, however, overlooks the fact that the connexion is not between the predicates as such, but only between the predicates as predicated of one subject. 'A is human' involves 'A is mortal', but not 'B is mortal'. We cannot therefore eliminate the hypothetical subject and the hypothetical propositional form in interpreting 'all men are mortal'.

When I believe 'all men are mortal', I believe, if I am a logician, 'for all possible values of x, if x is human x is mortal'. It is not the case that, for all possible values of x, I believe that if x is human x is mortal. For if this were the case, I should have as many beliefs as there are possible values of x; and if a is a possible value of x, I should be believing 'if a is human, a is mortal'. But I may have never heard of a, and therefore be incapable of this belief. Thus the belief that all men are mortal is *one* belief, and the generality is part of the belief. Moreover, it is intensional in the sense that I can have the belief without knowing all the men there are. As soon as I understand the words 'human' and 'mortal', the subject-predicate form, and the 'if-then' form, I have everything, except generality, that is required for understanding 'all men are mortal'.

We have already seen that general propositions cannot be explained as habits, although they are genetically connected with habits. This is obvious for three reasons. First: a general proposition is required in order to state that a given person has a given habit; we have to be able to say 'Mr A always responds to stimulus A by the action B'. If, therefore, we attempt to use habit to explain general propositions, we shall be involved in an endless regress. Second: general propositions not only can be understood, but can influence our actions, in the absence of the stimulus to the associated habit. Suppose I believe 'all wild giraffes live in Africa', that does not mean merely that whenever I see a wild giraffe I think 'I must be in Africa'; it means also that, when I am thinking of starting on a big-game hunting expedition, I think 'if I want to hunt giraffes, I shall have to go to Africa'. Third: when I discover a general proposition by scientific methods, the knowledge that I obtain ante-dates any habit connected with it. The belief that metals conduct electricity may generate a habit, but was not generated by a habit.

In order to make any further advance in the analysis of what is 'expressed' by a general proposition, we must, I think, adopt the alternative interpretation, mentioned above, in which the proposition is interpreted as denying an existence-proposition. 'No A is B' denies 'Some A is B'; 'All A is B' denies 'Some A is not B'. Thus from this point of view 'No A is B' is simpler than 'All is B'. We will therefore consider it first.

In connexion with factual premisses, we considered the man who is asked 'do you hear anything?' and replies 'No, I hear nothing'. This man, we said, has committed himself to the stupendous generalization: 'everything in the universe is not a sound now heard by me'. However true this may be as regards what is 'indicated', it is impossible to believe that it is true of what is 'expressed'. Let us see whether we can arrive at a less unplausible interpretation of what is 'expressed'.

Consider a series of judgements of perception 'I hear A', 'I hear B', 'I hear C', etc. These all have something in common, namely a stimulation of the auditory centres and a certain kind of sensation. What they all have in common is what is meant by the word 'hear'. This is expressed by 'I hear something', which, on the side of expression, is simpler than 'I hear A'.

We saw in an early chapter that there are two kinds of affirmation: one of these belongs to judgements of perception, occurs only in the object-language, and has no correlative negation; the other, which can only occur in languages of higher order, arises when a proposition is first considered and then accepted. This second kind has a correlative negation, when the proposition, after being considered, is rejected. Rejection of a proposition is, psychologically, inhibition of the impulses which belief in the proposition would generate; it thus always involves some tension, since the impulses connected with belief are not absent, but are counteracted by an opposing force.

Let us apply this to the man who gives a negative answer to the question whether he hears anything. We have already seen what is expressed by 'I hear something'. The question causes the man to consider this proposition, and after considering it he rejects it; he expresses his rejection in the words 'I hear nothing'. This seems an intelligible and psychologically credible account of what happens in such a case.

In the case of an affirmative general proposition, 'All A is B', there is an extra complication, but no new difficulty of principle. Let us take again 'all men are mortal'. This is to be interpreted as 'are some men not mortal? No'. The process may be amplified as follows. When we judge 'A is a man but not mortal', we accept 'A is a man' but we reject 'A is mortal'. The various acts of this kind, putting B, C, etc., in place of A, all have something in common; what they have in common is a belief expressed in the words 'some man is not mortal'. When we reject this belief, we are in a state expressed by the words 'all men are mortal'. These words thus express a double negation, or, speaking psychologically, the inhibiting of an inhibition. So far as I remember, pre-verbal forms of this operation were studied by Pavlov in dogs.

We must now inquire into what is 'indicated' by a general belief, and how, if at all, we can know that a general belief is true.

As regards what is 'indicated' by a general belief, we must remember that, as we saw in an earlier chapter, the world can, in theory, be completely described without the use of any logical words. 'Had we but world enough and time', we could dispense with general propositions. Instead of 'all men are mortal', we could say 'Socrates is mortal', 'Plato is mortal', and so on. In fact, however, this would take too long, and our vocabulary of names is insufficient. We must therefore use general propositions. But the subjective character of logical words appears in this, that the state of the world which makes a general proposition true can only be indicated by means of a general proposition. If 'all men are mortal' is to be true, there must be an occurrence which is A's death, another which is B's death, and so on throughout the catalogue of men. There is nothing in the world which is 'all men's deaths', and therefore there is no *one* verifier of 'all men are mortal'.

According to modern logic, 'all men are mortal' is a statement, not only about men, but about everything. This is certainly a *possible* interpretation, and certainly the most convenient for logic. But it is difficult not to believe that the statement *can* be interpreted so as to be only about men. Let us examine this question.

If I wish to make 'all men are mortal' a statement which is only about men, I must first have an extensional definition of 'men'. Suppose I say: 'A, B, C ... Z is a complete list of men'. Then, in order to prove that all men have a certain predicate,

I need only observe that this predicate belongs to A and B and C and ... and Z; the rest of the universe is irrelevant. This is all very well if men are a conventional collection; but if 'men' are defined as those objects which possess a certain predicate, how am I to know that my list A, B, C ... Z is complete? In fact, in the case of men, I know that any list that can be framed is incomplete. This, it may be said, is merely due to my limitations; an omniscient Being could be sure that the list is complete. Yes, but only in virtue of knowledge about everything: He would know, concerning each thing outside the list, that it was *not* human, and this knowledge would be essential.

This, however, does not seem quite conclusive. Ignoring means of knowing, let us suppose that, in fact, A, B, C ... Z are all the men there are, and let us suppose that there are occurrences correctly described as A's death, B's death, C's death, ... Z's death. Then, in fact, it is true that all men are mortal. Thus the number of occurrences required to insure the truth of 'all men are mortal' is the same as the number of men, and no more. Other occurrences are necessary in order that we may *know* our list to be complete, but not in order that it may *be* complete. We may conclude, therefore, that the occurrences required to make a statement about all men true are as numerous as men, but not more numerous. These occurrences collectively are the verifier of the statement in question.

Let us consider some case where we seem more certain of the truth of our general proposition, say 'all dodos are mortal'. We know this, it may be said, because all dodos are dead. It might be objected that perhaps there are dodos in other planets, or that evolution, having produced the dodo once, may produce it again, and next time may make it immortal, like the phoenix. We will therefore amend our general proposition, and say only: 'all dodos living on the surface of the earth before 1940 were mortal'. This seems fairly indubitable.

The proposition at which we have now arrived is strictly analogous to 'there is no cheese in the larder', which we considered at an earlier stage. It requires, for its proof, a survey of the earth's surface, leading to a set of negative propositions of the form 'this is not a living dodo', applied to every terrestrial portion of space-time large enough to have any chance of being a dodo. These negative propositions, as we saw, depend upon negative propositions such as 'this is not blue'. The generality is strictly enumerative, and is rendered possible by the fact that our defining predicate contains a space-time determination. It is the peculiarity of such predicates that, given favourable circumstances, they can be shown empirically to be equivalent to a list. But that this is empirically possible is itself an empirical fact, connected with the properties of space-time which we considered in connexion with proper names.

According to the above, what is 'indicated' by a general statement of the form 'All A's are B's' is a collection of occurrences, one for each A. This collection is the 'verifier' of the general statement: when every member of the collection occurs, the statement is true; when there is any member of it that does not occur, the statement is false.

We come now to the question how, if at all, we can know empirical general propositions. We have seen that some among such statements can be known by means of a census; this happens when the objects concerned are confined by definition to a region of space-time which is in our neighbourhood and none of it in the future. But this is an exceptional case, and probably, when our knowledge of space-time is adequately analysed, will be found to be ultimately no real exception. Certainly in all other cases it is impossible for us to know that we have made a complete census, and our knowledge of a general proposition must therefore, if it exists, be obtained by other methods.

I think that, if we are to be allowed to know any empirical generalizations except those derivable from a census, the word 'know' will have to be used rather more liberally than hitherto. We could be said to 'know' a proposition if it is in fact true and we believe it on the best available evidence. But if this evidence is not conclusive, we shall never know whether the proposition is in fact true, and shall therefore never know whether we know it. It is hoped that inductive evidence may make an empirical generalization probable. This takes us, however, into a region that lies outside the scope of the present work, and I shall therefore say no more on the subject.

CHAPTER 19

EXTENSIONALITY AND ATOMICITY

THE analysis of such propositions as 'A believes p', 'A doubts p', etc., raises two problems of great logical importance. In general, in these chapters, I have kept silent on logical topics, but in the present connexion they are unavoidable. A brief excursion into logic is therefore necessary before we can return to our main theme.

The two logical problems that arise in connexion with propositional attitudes are that of extensionality and that of atomicity. Of these, the former has been much discussed by recent logicians, while the latter has been almost wholly ignored.

Before stating the 'thesis of extensionality', as it is called by Carnap, it is necessary to say something about the theory of truth-functions and about the theory of classes.* The theory of truth-functions is the most elementary part of mathematical logic, and concerns everything that can be said about propositions by means of 'or' and 'not'. Thus 'p and q' is the negation of 'not-p or not-q'. The most general relation between p and q which allows us, given p, to infer q, is 'not-p or q'. Or suppose you want the most general relation which, given p and q, will enable you to infer r, this will be 'not-p or not-q or r'. The law of excluded middle is 'p or not-p'; the law of contradiction is the negation of 'p and not-p'. Two propositions are said to be 'equivalent' when both are true or both are false, i.e. when we have 'either p and q, or not-p and not-q'. Two propositions which are equivalent are said to have the same 'truth-value'.

Instead of starting with 'not-p' and 'p or q' we may start with a single undefined function 'p and q are not both true'. We denote this by '$p \mid q$' and call it the stroke-function. It is obvious that '$p \mid p$' is equivalent to 'not-p', for if p and p are

---

* In what follows I shall repeat, in a somewhat more elementary form, some things already said in Chapter 13, Section c.

not both true, then p is not true, and vice versa. Again: 'p or q' is equivalent to 'not-p and not-q are not both true', i.e. to '$p \mid p$ and $q \mid q$ are not both true', i.e. to '$(p \mid p) \mid (q \mid q)$'. Thus 'or' and 'not' can be defined in terms of the stroke-function. It follows that everything that can be defined in terms of 'or' and 'not' can be defined in terms of the stroke-function.

It is evident, and easily proved, that, given any proposition built up out of other propositions by means of the stroke, its truth-value depends only upon the truth-values of the constituent propositions. This follows from the fact that 'p and q are not both true' is true if p is false and also if q is false, and is false if p and q are both true; what propositions p and q may be is irrelevant, so long as their truth-values are unchanged. Functions of which this holds are called 'truth-functions'. All the functions required in the theory of deduction are truth-functions.

The first part of the principle of extensionality, the truth or falsehood of which we are to examine, says that all functions of propositions are truth-functions, i.e. that, given any statement which contains as a part a proposition p, its truth-value is unchanged if we substitute for p any other proposition q having the same truth-value as p.

I come now to 'propositional functions'. A 'propositional function' is an expression containing one or more undetermined constituents $x, y, \ldots$, and such that, if we settle what these are to be, the result is a proposition. Thus 'x is a man' is a propositional function, because, if you decide on a value for x, the result is a proposition – a true proposition if you define that x is to be Socrates or Plato, a false proposition if x is to be Cerberus or Pegasus. The values for which it is true constitute the class of men. Every propositional function determines a class, namely the class of values of the variable for which it is true.

Two propositional functions are said to be 'formally equivalent' if, for every possible value of the variable, the resulting propositions are equivalent. Thus 'x is a man' and 'x is a featherless biped' are formally equivalent; so are 'x is an even prime' and 'x is a real cube root of 8'. When two propositional functions are formally equivalent they determine the same class.

Predicates may be identified with propositional functions with one variable, dyadic relations with those with two, triadic relations with three, etc. When I say 'humans are mortal', that means 'if x is human, x is mortal, for all possible values of x'. It is obvious that, if humans are mortal, so are featherless bipeds. It is obvious also that, if there are n humans, there are n featherless bipeds. These propositions illustrate the fact that, if two propositional functions are formally equivalent, a great many statements that are true of either are also true of the other. The second part of the principle of extensionality states that this is always the case, i.e. that, in any statement about a propositional function, any formally equivalent function may be substituted without changing the truth-value of the statement.

Carnap states the 'thesis of extensionality' in a somewhat weakened form, which, slightly simplified, may be enunciated as follows: it is possible to construct a language, into which any statement in any language can be translated, and having the following two properties: (1) if a proposition p occurs as part of a larger proposition q, the truth-value of q is unchanged if we substitute for p any proposition having the same truth-value; (2) if a propositional function occurs in a proposition, the truth-value of the proposition is unchanged by the substitution of any formally equivalent propositional function (i.e. one which is true for the same values of the variable).

Carnap's innovation is to state the principle, not as one which must be true in any language, but as one which is true in a certain possible language into which all statements in other languages can be translated.

The first of the two properties asserted by the principle implies, for instance, that any true statement of which 'Socrates is mortal' is a part will remain true if we substitute 'Anglesey is an island', and any true proposition of which 'Homer was an Irishman' is a part (for instance, 'if Homer was an Irishman I'll eat my hat') will remain true if we substitute 'Brian Boru was a Greek'. The second property implies that, wherever the words 'human beings' occur, we can substitute 'featherless bipeds' without affecting the truth or falsehood of what is said – assuming that, in fact, the class of human beings is identical with that of featherless bipeds.

Prima facie, the thesis of extensionality is not true of propositions asserting propositional attitudes. If A believes p, and p is true, it does not follow that A believes all true propositions; nor, if p is false, does it follow that A believes all false propositions. Again: A may believe that there are featherless bipeds that are not human beings, without believing that there are human beings who are not human beings. Consequently those who maintain the thesis of extensionality have to find some way of dealing with propositional attitudes. The thesis is sought to be maintained for several reasons. It is very convenient technically in mathematical logic; it is obviously true of the sort of statements that mathematicians want to make; it is essential to the maintenance of physicalism and behaviourism, not only as metaphysical systems, but even in the linguistic sense adopted by Carnap. None of these reasons, however, gives any ground for supposing the thesis true. The grounds that have been given for supposing the thesis true will be examined shortly.

The thesis of atomicity is stated by Wittgenstein as follows (*Tractatus*, 2.0201): 'Every statement about complexes can be analysed into a statement about their constituent parts, and into those propositions which completely describe the complexes.' The relevance of this thesis to the analysis of propositional attitudes is obvious. For in 'A believes p', p is complex; therefore, if Wittgenstein's principle is true, 'A believes p', which appears to be a statement about the complex p, must be analysed into a statement about the parts of p together with propositions describing p. Put more loosely, this means that p as a unit does not enter into 'A believes p', but only its constituents enter in.

The thesis of atomicity has a technical form, and it is important to logic to know whether, in this form, it is true. Certain preliminary explanations are necessary before this technical principle can be stated.

The object-language, as we saw, contains a certain store of proper names, predicates, dyadic relations, triadic relations, etc. Any n-adic relation can be combined with any n proper names (which need not all be different) to make a proposition.

Suppose n_1, n_2, n_3 ... are proper names, P_1, P_2, P_3 ... are predicates, R_1, R_2, R_3 ... are dyadic relations, S_1, S_2, S_3 ... are triadic relations, etc.

Then P_1 (n_1) stands for 'n_1 has the predicate P_1'

R_1 (n_1, n_2) stands for 'n_1 has the relation R_1 to n_2'

S_1 (n_1, n_2, n_3) stands for 'n_1, n_2, n_3 (in that order) stand in the relation S_1', and so on.

All the propositions obtained in this way are called 'atomic propositions'.

Now let us take any two atomic propositions p and q, and combine them by the stroke, so as to obtain $p \mid q$. The propositions so obtained, together with atomic propositions, give us an enlarged total of propositions. If we combine any two of this enlarged total by means of the stroke, we obtain a still larger total. Let us go on in this way indefinitely. The whole set of propositions so obtained we call 'molecular propositions', because combinations of atomic propositions compose them in more or less the kind of way in which combinations of atoms compose molecules.

Having now reached the assemblage of molecular propositions by means of the sole operation of the stroke, we introduce a new operation for constructing propositions, which is called 'generalization'. Take any atomic or molecular proposition which contains some constituent a, and let us call it ϕa. The same proposition with b substituted for a will be called ϕb, and, if c is substituted, ϕc. Let us substitute for a not some definite term, but a variable x. We thus obtain a propositional function ϕx. It may happen that this is true for all possible values of x; again, it may happen that it is true for at least one value of x. The propositions asserting that either of these is the case are two new propositions. If they contain a constant constituent b, we can apply generalization in turn to b, and so on until no constants remain. Take, e.g., 'if Socrates is a man, and all men are mortal, then Socrates is mortal'. This is not a proposition of logic, because it mentions Socrates and man and mortal, whereas propositions of logic mention nothing particular. It is also not a molecular proposition, because it contains the word 'all'. It is on the road from a molecular proposition to a proposition of logic. The latter is: 'whatever x, α, and β may be, if x has the predicate α and everything that has the predicate α has the predicate β, then x has the predicate β'.

To show in detail the process of generalization involved, let us consider the following statement: 'either Socrates is human but not mortal, or Socrates is not human, or Socrates is mortal'. This is a logically necessary molecular proposition. Now when a proposition is true of Socrates, it is true of some one. Therefore the above statement remains true if, the first time that 'Socrates' occurs, we substitute 'some one' for 'Socrates'. (We might make this substitution for either of the other occurrences, for any two, or for all three; but the first alone suits our present purpose.) We thus arrive at the following proposition: 'there is someone who has the property that either he is human but not mortal, or that Socrates is not human, or that Socrates is mortal'. (The someone in question, we happen to know, is Socrates, but we are ignoring this piece of knowledge.) We now divide the proposition a little differently, and say 'someone is human but not mortal, or Socrates is not human, or Socrates is mortal'. Here we have three alternatives; therefore if the first is false, one of the other two must be true. Now if 'someone is human but not mortal' is false, then 'all men are mortal' is true. Thus we arrive at 'if all men are mortal, then either Socrates is not a man or Socrates is mortal', which is equivalent to 'if all men are mortal, then if Socrates is a man Socrates is mortal'. We have reached this point, from our original molecular proposition, by using once the process of putting 'someone' in place of 'Socrates', which is the logical process by which, given that a has some property α, we infer 'something has the property α'.

So far, the new propositions that we have manufactured have been logical consequences of the earlier ones. From this point on, however, we are concerned with processes of manufacturing propositions which are not logical consequences of those from which they are derived. Our last statement still contained three 'constants', namely 'Socrates', 'man', and 'mortal'. To each of these we apply the process of generalization, substituting x for Socrates, a for man, and β for mortal, and asserting the result for all values of the variables. We thus obtain 'for all possible values of x, α, β, if all α's are β's, and x is an α, then x is a β'. This is a proposition of logic, of which our original proposition was an instance. But the point in which I am interested at the moment is not that we have arrived at a *true* proposition, but merely that we have arrived at a proposition.

The principle by which propositions of varying degrees of generality are manufactured from molecular propositions is as follows:

Let $\phi\,(a_1, a_2, a_3 \ldots P_1, P_2, P_3 \ldots R_1, R_2, R_3 \ldots)$ be a molecular proposition which contains the proper names a_1, a_2, a_3 ... the predicates P_1, P_2, P_3 ... the dyadic relations R_1, R_2, R_3 ... and so on. All these are called the 'constituents' of the proposition in question. Any one or more of these constituents may be replaced by a variable, and the result asserted for some value or for all values of the variable. This gives us a large assemblage of general propositions all manufactured out of (not deduced from) the original molecular proposition. Take as a very simple instance, 'Socrates is wise'. This leads, by the above process, to the following ten propositions:

Something is wise
Everything is wise
Socrates has some predicate
Socrates has all predicates
Something has some predicate
Everything has some predicate
There is some predicate that everything has
Something has all predicates
Every predicate belongs to something
Everything has all predicates

The process of substituting either some value or all values of a variable is called 'generalization'. It is not convenient to confine this term to the case of all values.

The technical form of the principle of atomicity, as I said before, asserts that all propositions are either atomic, or molecular, or generalizations of molecular propositions; or at least,

that a language of which this is true, and into which any statement is translatable, can be constructed. This must be true if
Wittgenstein's principle of atomicity is true. The converse does
not hold. As I shall explain in a moment, a less sweeping and
more defensible form of the principle leads equally to the technical form. It is in its technical form that the principle is important in logic. I think that Wittgenstein himself would now
accept the modification in question, since I understand that he
no longer believes in atomic propositions. As we saw in an earlier
chapter, what is useful in logic is atomic *forms*, and the modified
principle allows them to be substituted for the original atomic
propositions, in which it was considered necessary that each word
should stand for something destitute of complexity.

The weakening of Wittgenstein's thesis, which makes it more
plausible, is as follows. A name N may be in fact the name of a
complex, but may not itself have any logical complexity, i.e.
any parts that are symbols. This is the case with all names that
actually occur. Caesar was complex, but 'Caesar' is logically
simple, i.e. none of its parts are symbols. We might maintain
that Wittgenstein's thesis is not to be applied to everything that
is in fact complex, but only to things named by complex names.
E.g., though 'Caesar' is simple, 'the death of Caesar' is complex. Instead of the phrase 'every statement about complexes',
which appears at the beginning of Wittgenstein's enunciation,
we shall substitute: 'every statement about complexes of which
the complexity is made explicit in the statement'. This meets the
difficulty that would otherwise arise whenever we speak of something which is in fact complex, but which we do not know to
be so, or at any rate do not know how to analyse.

Even in this weakened form, the principle forbids the occurrence of p as a unit in 'A believes p', since a proposition must
be explicitly complex, except in those unusual cases in which it
has a proper name, such as the *Pons Asinorum*; and even then,
we only arrive at what is asserted in 'A believes p' when we
substitute the proposition for its name.

If either the thesis of extensionality or that of atomicity is to
be maintained, it is necessary to distinguish between the 'p' in
'A believes p' and the 'p' in an ordinary truth-function such as

'p or q'. If the two are identical, it is impossible to construct a purely extensional logic, and it is probably impossible to maintain physicalism in Carnap's sense. The attempt to distinguish between the two ps was first made by Wittgenstein (*Tractatus*, 5.54 ff.). He says:

'In the general propositional form, propositions occur in a proposition only as bases of the truth-operations.

'At first sight it appears as if there were also a different way in which one proposition could occur in another.

'Especially in certain propositional forms of psychology, like " thinks, that p is the case", or "A thinks p", etc.

'Here it appears superficially as if the proposition p stood to the object A in a kind of relation.

'(And in modern epistemology (Russell, Moore, etc.) those propositions have been conceived in this way.)

'But it is clear that "A believes that p", "A thinks p", "A says p", are of the form " 'p' says p": and here we have no coordination of a fact and an object, but a coordination of facts by means of a coordination of their objects.

'This shows that there is no such thing as the soul – the subject, etc. – as it is conceived in contemporary superficial psychology.'

I adopted Wittgenstein's view in the second edition of *Principia Mathematica* (Vol. I, Appendix C), and so did Carnap in *Der logische Aufbau der Welt*. In *The Logical Syntax of Language** he makes a slight change: he says that intensional as well as extensional languages are possible, and that we must only say that every statement in an intensional language can be translated into an extensional language. Even this he does not regard as certain, though he considers it plausible. On this question of propositional attitudes, however, he repeats what Wittgenstein says. 'Charles says (or thinks) A', he says, is, as it stands, intensional, but can be translated into 'Charles says (or thinks) "A"'. Here we are told: 'let "A" be an abbreviation (not a designation) of some sentence'. We are also told that syntactical designations are to be formed with inverted commas. All this adds nothing to what occurs in the *Tractatus Logico-Philosophicus*.

* § 67, p. 245 ff.

I have come to doubt whether this view, even if true, can be maintained on Wittgenstein's grounds. I propose, therefore, to examine Wittgenstein's arguments controversially.

The kernel of the passage just quoted from Wittgenstein is: ' "A believes that p", "A thinks p", "A says p", are of the form " 'p' says p " '. Let us try to state this point of view clearly.

In general, when a word occurs in a sentence, we are not speaking about the word, but about what it means; when we wish to speak about the word, we put it in inverted commas. Thus the sentence ' " Socrates " is the name of Socrates' is not a tautology; you learn a proposition of this sort when you are introduced to a person of whom you have never heard. When the word 'Socrates' is not in inverted commas, you are speaking of the man, not the word. Now in like manner, when we assert a proposition, it is maintained that we are not saying anything about the words, but about what the words mean; and if we want to say anything about the words, we must put them in inverted commas. But there is a difference between propositions and single words. Single words, at least such as are object-words, have a meaning which is external to language; but propositions, since they can be false, must, except when they express perceptions, have some less direct relation to objects. Thus the distinction between 'p' and p is not so simple as that between 'Socrates' and Socrates.

The important distinction, in this discussion, is not between 'p' and p, but between what p *expresses* and what it *indicates*. This distinction is not confined to propositions; it exists also in the case of object-words. If I exclaim 'fire!' I express my own state and indicate an occurrence different from my state. The single word is a complete sentence. This is a prerogative of object-words; other words can only be parts of sentences. I maintain that the use of an object-word as a complete exclamatory sentence is its primary use, from which its use as part of a larger sentence is derivative. It is *quâ* sentence that an object-word has the two aspects of expression and indication.

The distinction between significant and nonsensical strings of words compels us to recognize that a significant sentence has a non-linguistic property – namely 'significance' – which has nothing to do with truth or falsehood, being more subjective. We may identify the significance of a sentence with what it expresses, which is a state of the speaker. Such a state may be called a 'believing', if the sentence is indicative. Two believings that can be expressed by the same sentence are said to be instances of the same 'belief'.

From what has just been said, it follows that there are *three* ways, not two, in which a sentence may occur.

First: we may be concerned with the actual words; this is the proper occasion for the use of inverted commas. For example, we may assert: Caesar said '*jacta est alea*'. A person who knows no Latin can know that Caesar said this; it is not necessary that he should know what Caesar meant. Therefore the words '*jacta est alea*' occur here as words, not as having meaning.

Second: we may be concerned with what the sentence expresses, and be indifferent as to what it indicates; this happens if we assert: Caesar said that the die was cast. Here the words 'the die was cast' occur as having significance; Caesar did not use these words, but Latin words expressing the same state. If we asserted: Caesar said 'the die is cast', our assertion would be false, since it would imply that he spoke English. Thus when we say: 'Caesar said that the die was cast', the significance of the words 'the die was cast' is relevant, but not the indication, since it is entirely irrelevant whether, in fact, the die was cast or not.

Third: we may be concerned, not only with what a sentence expresses, but also with what it indicates. I may say: 'The die was cast, as Caesar truly said'. Here, when I say 'the die was cast', I make an assertion, which is true if the sentence indicates something, and false if it indicates nothing. In every complete sentence in the indicative, the indication is relevant, but in subordinate sentences it may happen that only what is expressed is relevant. This happens, in particular, as regards the p in 'A believes p'.

We can now decide what we are to think of Wittgenstein's view that 'A believes p' is of the form: ' "p" says p'. Or rather, we can decide whether we should say 'A believes p' or 'A believes "p"'. Let us put for 'p' the sentence 'B is hot'. When we say that A believes that B is hot, we are saying (roughly) that A is in a state which will lead him, if he speaks, to say 'B is hot' or something having the same significance. We are not saying that these words are in A's mind; he may be a Frenchman who, if he spoke, would say '*B a chaud*'. We are, in fact, saying nothing about the *words* 'B is hot', but only about what they signify. Therefore there should be no inverted commas, and we should say: 'A believes p'.

Should we say 'p is true' or '"p" is true'?

It is generally assumed that we should say the latter, but I think this assumption is wrong.

Consider 'it is true that B is hot'.

This asserts a complicated relation between a class of believings and an event. It means: any person who is in one of a certain class of states [to wit, those expressed by the words 'B is hot'] has a certain relation to a certain event [to wit, B's being hot, or not-hot, as the case may be].

Here the words 'B is hot' enter only through the significance of the phrase, not as words. Therefore we should say: 'p is true'.

The difficulty of the subject, I repeat, arises from the fact that sentences, and some words, have *two* non-verbal uses, (*a*) as indicating objects (*b*) as expressing states of mind. Words may occur through their significance, and not *as* words, without occurring as *indicating*: this happens when they occur as *only expressing*. Single words other than object-words *only* express and do not indicate. That is why, unlike object-words, they cannot be complete sentences.

The above makes it clear that 'p' may occur in two different non-verbal ways, (*a*) where both indication and expression are relevant, and (*b*) where only expression is relevant. When the sentence occurs by itself, as an assertion, we have (*a*); when we say 'A believes p', we have (*b*), since the occurrence we are asserting can be completely described without reference to the truth or falsehood of p. But when we assert 'p or q' or any other truth-function, we have (*a*).

The principle of extensionality, if the above analysis is correct, applies to all occurrences of 'p' in which its indication is relevant, but not to those in which only the expression is relevant; i.e. it applies to (*a*), not (*b*). This statement, I think, is a tautology. The principle of extensionality in its general form must, if I am not mistaken, be rejected.

It has been suggested to me by Mr N. Dalkey that in 'A believes that B is hot', the words 'that B is hot' *describe* what is *expressed* by 'B is hot' when this is a complete sentence. This view is attractive, and may be right. According to this view, the words 'that B is hot' do not really refer to B, but describe A's state. The case is analogous to that in which I say 'A smells a smell of roses'. Here roses only come in as describing A's state; I might give a name, say S, to the smell, and say 'A smells S'. Similarly I might (in theory) substitute for 'that B is hot', words descriptive of the state of mind and body existing in those who are engaged in believing that B is hot. This view makes it necessary to draw a sharp distinction between '*p*' and 'that *p*'. Whenever it is really '*p*' that occurs, we can preserve the principle of extensionality; but when it is 'that *p*' that occurs, the reason for the failure of the principle is that '*p*' is not, in fact, occurring.

We have now to consider the principle of atomicity. I shall not now consider it generally, but only in relation to such sentences as 'A believes *p*'. In its general form it requires a consideration of analysis, and of the question whether proper names for complexes are theoretically indispensable, which I propose to leave to a later stage. For the present I wish only to consider whether such sentences as 'A believes *p*' can, in a suitable language, be expressed within the hierarchy of atomic, molecular, and generalized sentences explained earlier in this chapter.

The question is: can we interpret 'A believes *p*' so that *p* does not appear as a subordinate complex?

For '*p*' let us again take 'B is hot'. We agreed in an earlier chapter that to say A believes this is to say that he is in one of a number of describable states, all which have something in common. One of such states is that in which A exclaims 'B is hot!', but there is no reason to suppose that any words are necessarily present to A when he is believing that B is hot.

To say 'A exclaims "B is hot!"' is to assert a series of movements in A's speech-organs; this is a purely physical occurrence, which can be completely described without introducing any subordinate complex. It would seem that every other state of A which is a believing that B is hot could be similarly described. The question remains, however: what do all these states have in common?

I think that what they have in common is only causal. This, however, is a difficult question, and one which, I believe, it is not necessary for us to answer with any precision. It seems to me that no answer which is at all likely to be correct can interfere with the conclusion that 'A believes p' can be analysed without introducing a subordinate complex p, at any rate when p is a simple sentence such as 'B is hot'. If p is a general sentence, such as 'all men are mortal', the matter is more difficult. I shall, therefore, for the moment, content myself with the provisional conclusion that, so far, we have found no good argument against the principle of atomicity.

We thus reach the conclusions (1) that the principle of extensionality is not shown to be false, when strictly interpreted, by the analysis of such sentences as 'A believes p'; (2) that this same analysis does not prove the principle of atomicity to be false, but does not suffice to prove it true.

CHAPTER 20

THE LAW OF EXCLUDED MIDDLE

In general, in this book, I am avoiding logical questions, but in this chapter, as in the last, I shall be concerned with a logical topic, namely the law of excluded middle. As everyone knows, Brouwer has challenged the law, and has done so on epistemological grounds. He, in common with many others, holds that 'truth' can only be defined in terms of 'verifiability', which is obviously a concept belonging to theory of knowledge. If he is right, it follows that the law of excluded middle, and the law of contradiction also, belong to epistemology, and must be reconsidered in the light of whatever definition of truth and falsehood epistemology permits. We considered truth and falsehood in a preliminary manner in Chapter 16, and discussed the attempt to define them epistemologically. It is fairly obvious that, if an epistemological definition is adhered to, the law of excluded middle, in its usual form, cannot be true, though the law of contradiction may be. We have to consider, in this chapter and the next, whether to sacrifice the law of excluded middle or to attempt a definition of truth which is independent of knowledge.*

The difficulties of either view are appalling. If we define truth in relation to knowledge, logic collapses, and much hitherto accepted reasoning, including large parts of mathematics, must be rejected as invalid. But if we adhere to the law of excluded middle, we shall find ourselves committed to a realist metaphysic which may seem, in the spirit if not in the letter, incompatible with empiricism. The question is fundamental, and of the greatest importance.

Before attempting to decide it, let us develop the alternatives. Brouwer is not concerned with phrases that are syntactically

---

* What is said in this chapter is intended to clarify the question. It is only in the next chapter that a serious attempt is made to reach a decision.

nonsensical, such as 'quadruplicity drinks procrastination'. He is concerned with sentences that are grammatically and logically correct, but epistemologically incapable of being proved or disproved. We must be clear as to the point at issue before we begin to discuss it.

Brouwer argues that 'true' is a useless conception unless we have ways of discovering whether a proposition is true or not. He therefore substitutes 'verifiable' for 'true', and he does not call a proposition 'false' unless its contradictory is verifiable. There thus remains an intermediate class of propositions, which are syntactically correct, but neither verifiable nor the contradictories of verifiable propositions. This intermediate class Brouwer refuses to call either true or false, and in regard to them he regards the law of excluded middle as mistaken.

No one has yet gone so far as to define 'truth' as 'what *is* known'; the epistemological definition of 'truth' is 'what *can* be known'. The word 'verifiable' is commonly used, and a proposition is verifiable if it *can* be verified. This at once introduces difficulties, since possibility is an awkward concept. If the definition is to be definite, the particular kind of possibility that is intended will have to be elucidated. In mathematics, Brouwer and his school have done this, with a considerable measure of success; but so far as I know, they have given little thought to more ordinary propositions, such as historical hypotheses concerning which there is no evidence either way. Much is to be learnt from Carnap's *Logical Syntax of Language*, but mainly by way of suggestion. He holds that a general proposition, such as 'all men are mortal', which is inherently incapable of being completely proved, is to be taken (provisionally) as true if many instances of its truth are known, and none of its falsehood.

A definition of 'truth' as 'what can be known' will have to advance step by step from basic propositions. I shall assume, in accordance with what was said in Chapter 11, that my present factual premisses consist of: (1) a very small number asserting present percepts; (2) a considerably larger number of negative propositions derived from present percepts as we arrive at 'this is not red' when we see a buttercup; (3) memories, in so far as no argument exists to throw doubt on them; (4) the law of contradiction, but not the law of excluded middle. The law of excluded middle will be true, to begin with, of a certain class of propositions, namely those that can be confronted with percepts. If you are letting off fireworks on the fifth of November, and you say 'look out, there's going to be a bang', either there is a bang, or the fireworks are damp and there isn't. In such a case, your statement is true or false. There are other cases, derived from this kind, to which the law of excluded middle applies; the definition of the class of cases is much the same problem as the epistemological definitions of 'truth'.

It is to be observed that, when the law of excluded middle fails, the law of double negation also fails. If p is neither true nor false, it is false that p is false; if the principle of double negation held, this would imply that p is true, whereas, by hypothesis, p is neither true nor false. Consequently, in this logic, 'it is false that p is false' is not equivalent to 'p is true'.

To give ourselves a chance, we will, at least to begin with, allow inductive generalizations from basic propositions. These may turn out to be false if a negative instance occurs; until that happens, we shall, following Carnap, provisionally accept them as true. In either case, we shall regard them as subject to the law of excluded middle. We will allow also the testimony of others, subject to common sense provisos. We can now build up science; and having accepted inductive generalizations, we will admit as true such of their consequences as cannot be disproved. For example, we will say that eclipses occurred in prehistoric times as astronomy leads us to suppose; but we say this with the degree of hesitation appropriate to the inductive generalizations that constitute the laws of astronomy.

We can thus assert and deny all propositions that, as empiricists, we see reason to assert or deny. The difficulties come (a) in logic and mathematics (b) as to extra-logical propositions in regard to which there is no evidence either way.

Let us consider a definite extra-logical proposition as to which there is no evidence. Take 'it snowed on Manhattan Island on the first of January in the year 1 A.D'. Let us call this proposition 'P'. What do we know about P? Having accepted inductive generalizations, history tells us that there was a year I A.D., and geology assures us that Manhattan Island existed then. We know that snow often falls there in winter. We therefore *understand* P just as well as if it related to a snowfall of which there is historical record. In theory, a Laplacean calculator could infer the weather of former times, just as the astronomer infers the eclipses. In practice, however, this is impossible, not only because the calculations would be too difficult, but because more data would be required than could ever be obtained. We must therefore admit that we have not any evidence as to whether P is true or false, and that, so far as we can see, we are never likely to have any. We must conclude, if 'truth' is to be defined epistemologically, that P is neither true nor false.

Our reluctance to accept this conclusion comes from our obstinate belief in a 'real' world independent of our observation. We feel that we *might* have been there, and we should then have seen whether it was snowing, and the fact of our looking on would have made no difference to the snow. We are ready enough to concede that the whiteness of the snow's appearance has to do with our eyes, just as the cold feeling has to do with our temperature nerves; but we suppose these sensations to have an outside cause, which is the snow as dealt with in physics. And this, we believe, except where certain very delicate quantum observations are concerned, is just the same whether we know of it or not.

But all this was already conceded when we accepted inductive generalizations, and allowed ourselves to believe that Manhattan Island probably existed at the date in question. If we are going to allow inductions of this sort, there seems no reason for refusing to extend the law of excluded middle to every proposition for or against which there is any evidence, however slender. Now there might easily be evidence that the climate of Manhattan Island has not changed much in the last two thousand years, and in that case weather records give the probability of snow on any given day of the year. We shall therefore conclude that P is either true or false, for, though we cannot *decide* the question, we know something of the likelihood of each alternative.

There will still be propositions as to which there is no evidence whatever, for instance: 'there is a cosmos which has no spatio-temporal relation to the one in which we live'. Such a cosmos can be imagined by a writer of scientific romances, but by the very nature of the hypothesis there can be no inductive argument either for or against it. When we feel that there must be or not be such a cosmos, I think that we imagine a Deity contemplating all the worlds that He has made, and thereby we surreptitiously restore the link with our own world which, in words, we have denied.* If we rigidly exclude both this conception and that of a miraculous heightening of our own perceptive faculties, it is perhaps possible to suppose that our hypothesis has no meaning. In that case, it is neither true nor false, but it is not a proposition, and therefore fails to show that there are propositions which do not obey the law of excluded middle.

We must face the question: in what circumstances, if any, does a sentence which is syntactically correct fail to have a meaning? We suggested, a moment ago, that perhaps the sentence: 'something has no spatio-temporal relation to my present percept', is devoid of meaning; for that is what the rejection of the imagined cosmos amounts to. It seems to follow that the contradictory of the above sentence, namely: 'everything has some spatio-temporal relation to my present percept', is also devoid of meaning; but this seems far less plausible. If this is to be meaningless, it must be because of the word 'everything'. The word 'everything', it may be said, implies that the whole universe can be laid out for inspection, whereas, in fact, new percepts perpetually occur, and all totality is illusory except that of an enumerated set of objects.

This question of totality is very important. Can we define a total conceptually, as we define the class of men or the class of natural numbers? Some think that we can do so if the class is finite, but not otherwise. I cannot see, however, that this is a relevant consideration, except when a general word is a mere abbreviation for 'these objects in this given collection'. In that case, the general word is unnecessary. Whenever, as in the case of men, actual enumeration is impossible, the question whether

---

* cf. *The Star Maker*, by Olaf Stapledon.

the collection is finite or infinite seems irrelevant. 'All men are mortal' raises the same problems, in this connexion, as 'all integers are odd or even'.

When we say 'all men are mortal', are we saying anything, or are we making meaningless noises? I am not asking whether the sentence is true, but whether it is significant. Let us first exclude some untenable views. (1) We cannot try to reduce the proposition to a prescription, to wit: 'if I see a man, I shall judge him to be mortal'. For the occasions on which I shall see a man are just as impossible to enumerate as men are. I might, with my dying breath, say 'all the men I have met were mortal', because then they could be enumerated; but until then the collection is only defined conceptually. (2) We cannot say: 'a statement about a collection is legitimate when there is a *possible* set of experiences which would cover the whole collection, but not otherwise'. For we shall find, if we attempt to define 'possible experiences', that we are taken into just the hypothetical conceptual realm from which we wished to escape. How are we to know whether an experience is 'possible'? Obviously this will require knowledge that transcends *actual* experience. (3) We cannot confine 'all men are mortal' to past experience, for in that case it would have to mean 'all the men who have died hitherto were mortal', which is a tautology. (4) It is sometimes thought possible to interpret general statements – especially inductive generalizations – as practical advice. Thus 'all men are mortal' will mean: 'next time you meet a man, I should advise you to behave as if he were mortal, for if you chop his head in two in the hope that he is immortal, you will be hanged'. But this advice is only sound because the man *is* mortal. If you seriously doubt whether all men are mortal, you may do well to go about making experiments on the subject. The pragmatic interpretation, in fact, is only an evasion.

If we exclude such sentences as 'all men are mortal', which deal with collections defined conceptually, general propositions will be confined to history, or rather to collections composed of objects which now exist or have existed. We can say 'all the men in this room will die', but not 'all the children of the men in this room will die'. This is surely absurd.

It seems to me that, when we understand the words 'man' and 'mortal', we can understand 'all men are mortal', without having to be acquainted with each individual man. And in like manner, I should say, we can understand 'all integers are odd or even'. But if this view is to be maintained, there must be such a thing as understanding 'all-ness', independently of enumeration. This is really a question of understanding what is hypothetical. The analysis of general propositions is very difficult, since it seems quite clear that we can know propositions about all of a collection without knowing its several members. We say that 'I hear nothing' may be a basic proposition; yet it is for logic a statement about everything in the universe. We have seen in Chapter 18 how to avoid this difficulty.

When we were discussing snow in 1 A.D., we allowed ourselves to accept inductive generalizations. It is questionable whether, when we are doubting the law of excluded middle, we have any right to do this, except at most in the way of inferring percepts. Inductions in the physical sciences are always phrased in realist terms, i.e., they suppose that what you observe can happen without your observation, and does happen in suitable circumstances. If we arrive at an uninhabited island and find luxuriant vegetation, we shall infer that it has rained there, although no one has seen the rain. Now it is obvious that, from the standpoint of inductive verification, two hypotheses which only differ as to unobserved occurrences are precisely on a level. From the epistemological point of view, therefore, we may suppose that there are no unobserved occurrences, or that there are a few, or that there are many; we can, as physicists do, insert whatever number and kind of unobserved occurrences will make it easiest to formulate the laws of observed occurrences. They serve the same sort of purpose as may be served by complex numbers in a calculation which begins and ends with real numbers.

Is there any sense in asking whether these unobserved occurrences really occur? According to Carnap, there is only a linguistic question: 'reality' is a metaphysical term for which there is no legitimate use. Well and good, but let us be consistent. I have not myself observed what I have learnt from testimony or from history; I have observed only what has come within my own experience. Therefore, on the view in question, the hypotheses that testimony is not merely noises or shapes, and that the world existed before the earliest moment that I can remember, are mere linguistic conveniences.

This view is one which, in fact, no one accepts. If a doctor says to you 'your wife has cancer', you feel no doubt that what you hear expresses a thought; you also have no doubt that, if the doctor is right, your wife is having and will have painful experiences which will not be yours. Your emotions would be quite different if you thought the whole thing merely a linguistic abbreviation for describing certain experiences of your own. This, of course, is no argument. But I notice that those who take the sort of view that I am combating always avoid applying it as against other human beings, and are content to apply it to such matters as the glacial epoch, which have very little emotional content. This is illogical. If the glacial epoch is only a linguistic convenience, so are your parents and your children, your friends and your colleagues. It is, of course, still possible to accept testimony. You may say: 'Mr A, so far as I know, is a series of noises and shapes; but I have found, odd as it may seem, that if I interpret the noises as those which I should make to express certain thoughts or percepts, they frequently turn out to be true. I have therefore decided to behave as if Mr A were an intelligent being'. But your emotions will not be what they would be if you believed that he 'really' had intelligence.

When we ask: 'do any occurrences not observed by me really occur?' we are asking a question which, at least as regards other human beings, has a very great emotional content, and can hardly, it would seem, be totally devoid of significance. We are interested in other people's loves and hates, pleasures and pains, because we are firmly persuaded that they are as 'real' as our own. We mean *something* when we say this. A person in a novel manifests himself, but deceptively: the emotions which he expresses have not been actually felt. 'Real' people are different; but how?

I am not concerned, at the moment, to argue that unobserved events occur; I am only concerned to argue that the question whether they occur or not is more than a linguistic question. I take the question, to begin with, in connexion with the percepts, thoughts, and feelings of other people, because in that case what we are inferring is closely analogous to what we know from our own experience. In the case of unobserved matter, there is not only the fact that it is unobserved, but that it must be very different from anything of which we have experience, since it cannot have any sensible qualities. This additional problem is avoided by considering the experiences of other people. If we see a man apparently suffering, the hypothesis that he *is* suffering adds something, and is not merely the adoption of a different linguistic convention from that of the solipsist.

It is no use to say: 'but this does not take you outside experience; it only takes you outside *your* experience'. You do not know that this is true unless you know that the other man has experiences, and is not merely what you perceive; but this is the very piece of knowledge that was to be justified. Epistemology cannot *begin* by accepting testimony, for the correctness of testimony is certainly not among basic propositions.

I conclude, then, that there is a substantial meaning in the hypothesis that something occurs which I do not experience, at least when this is something analogous to my experiences, e.g. the experiences which I attribute to other people.

This, however, does not settle the question whether there is any meaning in the hypothesis of physical phenomena which are observed by no one, which we must now consider.

There are here certain distinctions to be made. On empirical grounds we believe that there cannot be visual objects except where there are eyes and nerves and a brain, but there is no *logical* difficulty in the hypothesis of such objects existing elsewhere. In fact, every person who is philosophically and scientifically naïve believes that what we see when we look at something is still there when we are no longer looking. This is what is called naïve realism – a doctrine which must be held to be false in fact, but not logically impossible. The problem in connexion with physics is: having admitted that where there is no sentient percipient there cannot be anything having the sensible qualities that we know from experience, is there any meaning in the hypothesis that there is *something* there? There are in fact two questions: First, is there significance in the hypothesis that something not experienced exists? Second, is there significance in the hypothesis that something exists which is as unlike objects of perception as we should have to suppose occurrences to be where there are no percipients?

As to the first, I see no difficulty. The fact that we experience a phenomenon is not an essential part of our understanding of the phenomenon, but only a cause of our knowledge that it occurs, and there is no logical obstacle to the hypothesis that the phenomenon could exist unperceived. In fact, we all hold that we have many sensations which we do not notice, and these are, strictly speaking, not experienced.

There is more difficulty as to the second question, namely: is there any significance in the hypothesis of physical phenomena as different from our percepts as they would have to be if they were neither visual nor auditory nor of any of the familiar kinds? The question is not quite that of the Kantian *Ding-an-Sich*, which is outside time; the kind of occurrences concerning which we are inquiring are certainly in time, and they are in space of a sort, though not quite of the sort to which we are accustomed in percepts. Physical space – i.e. the space of physics – is not directly sensible, but is definable by relation to sensible spaces. It would seem, therefore, that a proposition concerning a purely physical phenomenon can be enunciated in terms which are known through experience; if so, the proposition is certainly, in one sense, significant, even if we do not know how to discover whether it is true or false. If it is significant to say 'everything that exists is sensible', the contradictory of this, namely 'something non-sensible exists', must also be significant. If it be maintained that 'sensible' has no meaning, we can substitute 'visual or auditory, or etc.' It seems, therefore, that we cannot deny significance to the hypothesis of occurrences having none of the qualities which we believe to be causally dependent upon a sensorium.

It remains to inquire in what sense, if any, such a hypothesis can be regarded as either true or false.

This brings us to the question of 'fact' as what makes

propositions true. According to the correspondence theory of truth, as Tarski points out, the proposition 'it is snowing' is true if it is snowing. This has, *prima facie*, nothing to do with knowledge. If you do not realize that it is snowing, that does not make the proposition 'it is snowing' any less true. You may find several inches of snow on the ground when at last you do look out, and say 'it must have been snowing for hours'. Surely it would have been snowing just the same if you had not been going to look out afterwards? All the time that you were not looking out, the proposition 'it is snowing' was true, although you did not know that it was. This is the view of realism and of common sense. And it is this view which has made the law of excluded middle seem self-evident.

Let us set to work to state this view in such a way as to avoid all avoidable difficulties. First, as to 'facts': they are not to be conceived as 'that grass is green' or 'that all men are mortal'; they are to be conceived as occurrences. We shall say that all percepts are facts, but according to the realist view they are only some among facts. They may be defined as facts that some one knows without inference; but on the realist hypothesis there are other facts which can only be known by inference, and perhaps yet others which cannot be known at all.

Percepts, in this view, may be defined as events having a certain kind of spatio-temporal relation to a living body with suitable organs. Suppose, for example, you are measuring the velocity of sound, and for this purpose you occasionally fire a gun, while a man a mile away waves a flag as soon as he hears the report. Throughout the intervening space – if we are to believe the physicists – there are events, namely air-waves. When this train of events reaches an ear, it undergoes various modifications, much as sunlight undergoes modifications when it sets up the manufacture of chlorophyll in plants. One of the events resulting from the impact of sound-waves on an ear, provided the ear is attached to a normal brain, is what is called 'hearing' the sound. After this event, the chain of causation runs out of the brain into the arm, and leads to the waving of the flag. What is odd about the brain and the sensation is the character of the causal laws that operate at this point in the chain: they involve

habit, and 'mnemic' causation. To say that we 'know' a percept is to say that it has set up a certain habit in the brain. Only
events in the brain can set up habits in the brain; therefore only
events in the brain can be known in the kind of way in which we
know percepts.

Some such view as the above is assumed technically in physics
and physiology. I do not mean that physicists and physiologists
are necessarily prepared to defend it theoretically, or that their
results are not compatible with other views. I mean only that the
language they naturally use is one which implies some such
outlook.

I do not know whether there is any argument which shows
that this view is false. Various idealistic philosophies have
attempted to prove it untenable, but in so far as they appealed
to logic I shall take it for granted that they failed. The argument
from epistemology, which unlike that from logic, is as powerful
as it ever was, does not attempt to show that the view in question
is false, but only that it is gratuitous, in the sense that it sins
against Occam's razor by assuming the existence of unnecessary
entities. What we know, says the epistemological argument,
is percepts; the sound-waves, the brain, etc., are mere convenient hypotheses in the interconnecting of percepts. They
enable me, when I have fired my shot, to calculate how long
(according to the visual perceptions which I call 'seeing a stop-
watch') it will be before I have the percept which I call the
waving of the flag. But there is no more need to suppose that
these hypotheses have any 'reality' than there is to suppose that
parallel lines 'really' meet in a point at infinity, which also is
for some purposes a convenient way of speaking.

This epistemological scepticism has a logical foundation,
namely the principle that it is never possible to deduce the
existence of something from the existence of something else.
This principle must be stated more clearly, and without the use
of the word 'existence'. Let us take an illustration. You look out
of the window, and observe that you can see three houses. You
turn back into the room and say 'three houses are visible from
the window'. The kind of sceptic that I have in mind would say
'you mean three houses *were* visible'. You would reply 'but

they can't have vanished in this little moment'. You might look again and say 'yes, there they are still'. The sceptic would retort: 'I grant that when you looked again they were there again, but what makes you think they had been there in the interval?' You would only be able to say 'because I see them whenever I look'. The sceptic would say 'then you ought to infer that they are caused by your looking'. You will never succeed in getting any evidence against this view, because you can't find out what the houses look like when no one is looking at them.

Our logical principle may be stated as follows: 'no proposition about what occurs in one part of space-time logically implies any proposition about what occurs in another part of space-time'. If the reference to space-time is thought unduly suggestive of physicalism, it can easily be eliminated. We may say: 'the perceptive propositions derivable from one perceived event never logically imply any proposition about any other event'. I do not think this can be questioned by any one who understands the logic of truth-functions.

But outside pure mathematics the important kinds of inference are not logical; they are analogical and inductive. Now the kind of partial sceptic whom we have been having in mind allows such inferences, for he accepts physicalism whenever it enables us to prophesy our own future percepts. He will allow the man measuring the velocity of sound to say 'in five seconds I shall see the flag wave'; he will only not allow him to say 'in five seconds the flag will wave'. These two inferences, however, are exactly on a level as regards induction and analogy, without which science, however interpreted, becomes impossible. Our logical foundation thus becomes irrelevant, and we have to consider whether induction and analogy can ever make it probable that there are unperceived events.

At this point there is danger of a fallacy, so simple that it ought to be easy to avoid, but nevertheless not always avoided. A man may say: 'everything that I have ever perceived was perceived; therefore there is inductive evidence that everything is perceived'. The argument would be the same if I said: 'everything I know is known; therefore probably everything is known'.

We are left, then, with a substantial question: assuming the legitimacy of induction and analogy, do they afford evidence for unperceived events? This is a difficult but by no means insoluble question. I shall, however, not discuss it now, since it assumes as conceded, what is for us at present the essential point, that the difference between a theory which allows unperceived events and one which does not is a difference which need not be merely linguistic.

Although the above discussion has been so far very inconclusive, I find myself believing, at the end of it, that truth and knowledge are different, and that a proposition may be true although no method exists of discovering that it is so. In that case, we may accept the law of excluded middle. We shall define 'truth' by reference to 'events' (I am speaking of non-logical truth), and 'knowledge' by relation to 'percepts'. Thus 'truth' will be a wider conception than 'knowledge'. It would be a practically useless conception, but for the fact that knowledge has very vague boundaries. When we embark upon an investigation, we assume that the propositions concerning which we are inquiring are either true or false; we may find evidence, or we may not. Before the spectroscope, it would have seemed impossible ever to ascertain the chemical constitution of the stars; but it would have been a mistake to maintain that they neither do nor do not contain the elements we know. At present, we do not know whether there is life elsewhere in the universe, but we are right to feel sure that there either is or is not. Thus we need 'truth' as well as 'knowledge', because the boundaries of knowledge are uncertain, and because, without the law of excluded middle, we could not ask the questions that give rise to discoveries.

In the following chapter, I shall continue the discussion of the questions we have just been considering, but the discussion will be intensive and analytical rather than discursive. Before proceeding to minute analysis, I wished to make clear the bearing of the question at issue upon matters of general interest. This course involves some unavoidable repetition, which I must ask the reader to excuse.

CHAPTER 21

TRUTH AND VERIFICATION

In recent philosophy we may distinguish four main types of theory as to 'truth' or as to its replacement by some concept which is thought preferable. These four theories are:

I. The theory which substitutes 'warranted assertibility' for 'truth'. This theory is advocated by Dr Dewey and his school.

II. The theory which substitutes 'probability' for 'truth'. This theory is advocated by Professor Reichenbach.

III. The theory which defines 'truth' as 'coherence'. This theory is advocated by Hegelians and certain logical positivists.

IV. The correspondence theory of truth, according to which the truth of basic propositions depends upon their relation to some occurrence, and the truth of other propositions depends upon their syntactical relations to basic propositions.

For my part, I adhere firmly to this last theory. It has, however, two forms, between which the decision is not easy. In one form, the basic propositions must be derived from experience, and therefore propositions which cannot be suitably related to experience are neither true nor false. In the other form, the basic propositions need not be related to experience, but only to 'fact', though if they are not related to experience they cannot be known. Thus the two forms of the correspondence theory differ as to the relation of 'truth' to 'knowledge'.

Of the above four theories, I have discussed the third in Chapter 10; the first and second, which have a certain affinity, I shall discuss in a later chapter. For the present, I shall assume that 'truth' is to be defined by correspondence, and examine the two forms of this theory, according as 'experience' or 'fact' is taken as that with which truth must correspond. I will call these two theories the 'epistemological' and the 'logical' theory respectively. I do not mean to suggest that the 'logical' theory is

more logical than the other, but only that it is the one technically assumed in logic, which is involved in certain difficulties
if the theory is rejected.

Over a great part of the field, the two theories are identical.
Everything that is true according to the epistemological theory
is also true according to the logical theory, though not vice versa.
All the basic propositions of the epistemological theory are also
basic in the logical theory, though again not vice versa. The
syntactical relations of basic propositions to other true propositions are the same in both theories. The propositions that can be
known empirically are the same in both theories. There are
differences, however, in regard to logic; in the logical theory all
propositions are either true or false, whereas in the epistemological theory a proposition is neither true nor false if there is no
evidence either for or against it. That is to say, the law of excluded middle is true in the logical theory, but not in the epistemological theory. This is the most important difference between
them.

It will be observed that the correspondence used in defining
'truth', in both theories, is only to be found in the case of basic
propositions. Such a proposition as 'all men are mortal',
assuming it true, derives its truth from 'A is mortal', 'B is
mortal', etc., and each of these derives its truth from such propositions as 'A grows cold', 'B grows cold', etc. These propositions, for certain values of A and B, can be derived from
observation; they are then basic propositions in both theories.
They will (if true) be basic propositions in the logical theory,
even when they are not observed; the logical theory will hold
that there is a 'fact' which would make the statement 'A grows
cold' true, even if no one is aware of this fact – or, alternatively,
that there is an opposite fact, or rather set of facts, from which it
would follow that A is immortal.

In the epistemological theory, basic propositions are defined
as in Chapter 10. In the logical theory, they must have a definition
not referring to our knowledge, but such that, with this new
logical definition, 'experienced basic propositions' become
identical with 'basic propositions' in the epistemological theory.
The logical definition is to be obtained by observing the logical

form of epistemologically basic propositions, and omitting the condition that they must be experienced, while retaining the condition that they must be true (in the sense of the logical theory).

In the epistemological theory, we say that a 'basic' sentence is one that 'corresponds' to an 'experience', or 'expresses' an 'experience'. The definition of 'corresponding' or 'expressing' is in the main behaviouristic. 'Experience' can be surveyed, but on our present view it can hardly be defined. On the alternative 'logical' view, 'experiences' can be defined as a certain sub-class of 'facts'.

Sentences which express experiences are of certain logical forms. When they express such experiences as supply the data of physics, they are always atomic. As regards the data of psychology, there are difficulties in maintaining that this is the case, but we have seen reason to think these difficulties not insuperable. There are recollections involving logical words such as 'or' and 'some'; more generally, there are 'propositional attitudes', such as believing, doubting, desiring, etc. The question of propositional attitudes is complex, and involves considerable discussion, but our analysis of belief has been intended to show that the basic propositions in regard to them are not essentially different from those required in physics.

Assuming the logical forms of epistemologically basic sentences decided, we can proceed to consider the logical theory of basic sentences. But it must be said that the point of view we are now to consider is disputable. Its main merit is that it allows us to believe in the law of excluded middle.

If the law of excluded middle is assumed, any sentence which is epistemologically basic will remain true-or-false if any word in it is replaced by another word of the same logical type. But when a sentence is epistemologically basic, the fact to which it corresponds, and in virtue of which it is true, is experienced. When one or more of the words in the sentence are changed, there may be no experience which is expressed by the new sentence; there may also be no syntactical relation to any epistemologically basic sentence in virtue of which the new sentence has derivative truth or falsehood. Therefore we must either abandon the law of excluded middle or enlarge our definition of truth.

If, reverting to the epistemological theory, we abandon the law of excluded middle, we can define derivative truth in terms of 'verifiability': a sentence is 'verifiable' when it has one of certain assigned syntactical relations to one or more epistemologically basic sentences. A sentence which has no such syntactical relation will be neither true nor false. (Certain syntactical relations to basic sentences make a sentence 'probable'; in this case, also, we shall be obliged, on our present plan, to deny that the sentence is true-or-false.)

Per contra, we may adhere to the law of excluded middle, and seek a logical as opposed to an epistemological definition of 'basic sentences'. This course requires, first, a definition of 'significant' sentences. For this purpose we set up the following definitions:

A sentence is 'verifiable' when either (*a*) it is epistemologically basic, or (*b*) it has certain syntactical relations to one or more epistemologically basic propositions.

A sentence is 'significant' when it results from a verifiable sentence S by substituting for one or more words of S other words of the same logical type.

The law of excluded middle will then be asserted to apply to every significant sentence.

But this will require a new definition of 'truth'.

We said in the epistemological theory that the truth of a 'basic' sentence is defined by correspondence with an 'experience'. We may, however, substitute 'fact' for 'experience', and in that case, an unverifiable sentence may be 'true' because it corresponds with a 'fact'. In that case, if the law of excluded middle is to be retained, we shall have to say that, whenever there is a verifiable sentence '$f(a)$' containing a certain word 'a', which is verified by the appropriate fact about a, if 'b' is a word of the same type as 'a', there is a fact indicated by the sentence '$f(b)$' or there is a fact indicated by the sentence 'not-$f(b)$'.

Thus the law of excluded middle involves us in much difficult metaphysics.

If the law of excluded middle is to be retained, we shall have to proceed as follows:

(1) 'Fact' is undefined.

(2) Some facts are 'experienced'.

(3) Some experienced facts are both 'expressed' and 'indicated' by sentences.

(4) If 'a' and 'b' are words of the same logical type, and '$f(a)$' is a sentence expressing an *experienced* fact, then either '$f(b)$' indicates a fact or 'not-$f(b)$' indicates a fact.

(5) 'Data' are sentences expressing and indicating experienced facts.

(6) 'Verifiable' sentences are those having such syntactical relations to data as make them deducible from data – or, we may add, more or less probable in relation to data.

(7) 'True' sentences are such as either indicate facts, or have the same syntactical relations to sentences indicating facts as verifiable sentences have to data.

On this view, verifiable sentences are a sub-class of true sentences.

It seems fairly clear that the law of excluded middle cannot be preserved without the metaphysical principle (4) above.

There are difficulties in both theories of truth. The epistemological theory of truth, consistently developed, limits knowledge to a degree that seems excessive, and that is not intended by its advocates. The logical theory involves us in metaphysics, and has difficulties (not insuperable) in defining the correspondence which it requires for the definition of 'truth'.

Whichever theory we adopt, it should, I think, be conceded that *meaning* is limited to experience, but *significance* is not.

As regards meaning: we may, on the usual grounds, ignore words that have a dictionary definition, and confine ourselves to words of which the definition is ostensive. Now it is obvious that an ostensive definition must depend upon experience; Hume's principle, 'no idea without an antecedent impression', certainly applies to learning the meaning of object-words. If our previous discussions have been correct, it applies also to logical words; 'not' must derive its meaning from experiences of rejection, and 'or' from experiences of hesitation. Thus no essential word in our vocabulary can have a meaning independent of experience. Indeed any word that *I* can understand has a meaning derived from *my* experience.

As regards significance: this transcends my personal experience whenever I receive information; it transcends the experience of all mankind in works of fiction. We experience 'Hamlet', not Hamlet; but our emotions in reading the play have to do with Hamlet, not with 'Hamlet'. 'Hamlet' is a word of six letters; whether it should be or not be is a question of little interest, and it certainly could not make its quietus with a bare bodkin. Thus the play 'Hamlet' consists entirely of false propositions, which transcend experience, but which are certainly significant, since they can arouse emotions. When I say that our emotions are about Hamlet, not 'Hamlet', I must qualify this statement: they are really not about anything, but we think they are about the man named 'Hamlet'. The propositions in the play are false because there was no such man; they are significant because we know from experience the noise 'Hamlet', the meaning of 'name', and the meaning of 'man'. The fundamental falsehood in the play is the proposition: the noise 'Hamlet' is a name. (Let no one make the irrelevant remark that perhaps there was once a Prince of Denmark called 'Hamlet'.)

Our emotions about Hamlet do not involve belief. But emotions accompanied by belief can occur in very similar circumstances. St Veronica owes her supposed existence to a verbal misunderstanding, but is none the less capable of being an object of veneration. In like manner the Romans revered Romulus, the Chinese revered Yao and Shun, and the British revered King Arthur, though all these worthies were literary inventions.

We saw in Chapter 14 that a belief such as 'you are hot' involves a variable in its complete expression. Can we say that every belief of mine which transcends my personal experience involves at least one variable? Let us take an instance as unfavourable as possible to this hypothesis. Suppose I am standing with a friend looking at a crowd. My friend says 'there's Jones'. I believe him, but cannot see Jones, whom I am supposing is known to me as well as to my friend. I shall suppose that my friend and I attach the same meaning to the word 'Jones'; fortunately it is not necessary in the present connexion to discuss what this meaning is. The word 'there' is, for our purposes, the crucial one. As used by my friend, it is a proper name for a certain visual direction. (We have discussed in Chapter 7 the sense in which 'there', which is an egocentric particular, can be regarded as a proper name.) My friend may elucidate the word 'there' by pointing; this enables me to know *approximately* what direction he is calling 'there'. But whatever he may do or say, the word 'there', to me, is not a proper name, but only a more or less vague description. If I see Jones, I may say: 'oh yes, *there* he is'. I am then uttering a proposition which my friend's statement had failed to convey to me. The heard word 'there' as used by my friend means to me only 'somewhere within a certain region', and thus involves a variable.

Let us try to define the word 'experience', which is often used very loosely. It has different, though connected, meanings in different connexions. Let us begin with a linguistic definition.

Linguistically, a word has a meaning which lies within 'experience' if it has an ostensive definition. The word "Hamlet" does not have a meaning which lies within experience, because I cannot point to Hamlet. But the word '"Hamlet"' does have a meaning which lies within experience, because it means the word "Hamlet", which I *can* point to. When a word has an ostensive definition, we will call it an 'experience-word'. Among such words are included all genuine proper names, all the apparatus of predicates and relations that have no dictionary definitions, and also some few logical words as expressing states of mind such as rejection or hesitation.

The above definition is satisfactory while we are concerned with language, but elsewhere is too narrow. Understanding a word in virtue of an ostensive definition is merely one kind of habit, and 'experience' may, in some of its uses, be identified with 'habit'. Or, to speak more exactly, we may say that the difference between an event which is 'experienced' and one which merely occurs is that the former, but not the latter, gives rise to a habit.

The above definition has both advantages and disadvantages. In considering what these are, we must remember that the main question we are concerned with is whether we have any knowledge as to what is not experienced, and that it is in order to make this question precise that we are seeking a definition of 'experience'. Now everyone would agree that 'experience' is confined to animals, and perhaps plants, but is certainly not to be found in inanimate matter. Most people, if asked to mention the difference between a man and a stone, would probably reply that the man, but not the stone, is 'conscious'. They would probably concede that a dog is 'conscious', but would be doubtful about an oyster. If asked what they mean by 'conscious', they would hesitate, and perhaps in the end would say that they mean 'aware of what is happening about us'. This would lead us to the discussion of perception and its relation to knowledge. People do not say that a thermometer is 'aware' of the temperature, or a galvanometer of an electric current. Thus we find that 'awareness', as the term is commonly used, involves something more or less of the nature of memory, and this something we may identify with habit. In any case, habit is what mainly distinguishes the behaviour of animals from that of inanimate matter.

Reverting to our definition of 'experience', we may observe that an event which we are said to 'experience' must continue to have effects after it has ceased, whereas an event which merely happens exhausts its effects in the moment of its happening. As it stands, however, this is lacking in precision. Every event has indirect effects to the end of time, and no event has direct effects except at the moment. 'Habit' is a concept which is intermediate between complete ignorance and complete knowledge. It is to be supposed that, if our knowledge were adequate, the behaviour of living bodies could be reduced to physics, and habit would be reduced to effects on the brain which might be compared to water-courses. The route taken by water in flowing down a hillside is different from what it would be if no rain had ever fallen there before; in this sense, every river may be regarded as embodying a habit. Nevertheless, since we can understand the effect of each rainfall in digging a deeper channel, we have no occasion to use the notion of habit in this connexion. If we had equal knowledge of the brain, it is to be supposed that we could equally dispense with habit in explaining animal behaviour. But this would be only in the sense in which the law of gravitation enables us to dispense with Kepler's laws: habit would be deduced, not assumed, and in being deduced would be shown to be not a wholly accurate law. Kepler could not explain why planetary orbits are not exact ellipses, and similar limitations apply to theories of animal behaviour which begin with the law of habit.

In the present state of our knowledge, however, we cannot avoid using the notion of habit; the best we can do is to remember that 'habit', and all concepts derived from it, have a certain provisional and approximate character. This applies in particular to memory. An adequate physiology and psychology would deduce memory, as Newton deduced Kepler's laws, as something approximately true, but subject to calculable and explicable inaccuracies. Veridical and misleading memories would be brought under the same laws. But this is a distant ideal, and for the present we must do our best with concepts which we believe to be provisional and not quite accurate.

With these provisos, we may, I think, accept the view that an event is said to be 'experienced' when it, or a series of similar events of which it is one, gives rise to a habit. It will be observed that, according to this definition, every event that is remembered is experienced. An event may, however, be experienced without being remembered. I might know by experience that fire burns, without being able to recollect any particular occasion on which I had been burnt. In that case the occasions on which I had been burnt would have been experienced but not remembered.

Let us now try, first, to state positively the relation of empirical knowledge to experience, as it results from our previous discussions. When this has been done, we can proceed to defend our view against those of certain other philosophers.

Dependence upon my experience is complete in the case of all beliefs in the verbal expression of which there are no variables, i.e. no such words as 'all' or 'some'. Such beliefs must express my perceptive experience, the only extension being that the experience may be recollected. The experience concerned must be mine and no one else's. Everything that I learn from others involves variables, as we saw in discussing the man who says 'there's Jones'. In such a case, the belief conveyed to the auditor is never that expressed by the speaker, though it may, in favourable cases, be logically deducible from it. When a man, in my hearing, makes a statement 'fa', where 'a' is the name of something that I have not experienced, if I believe him I believe, not 'fa' (since for me 'a' is not a name), but 'there is an x such that fx'. Such a belief, although it transcends *my* experience, would not be excluded by any of the philosophers who wish to define 'truth' in terms of 'experience'.

It may be said: when a man exclaims 'there's Jones' and I believe him, the cause of my belief is his exclamation, and the cause of his exclamation is his perception; therefore my belief is still based upon perception, though indirectly. I have no wish to deny this, but I want to ask how it is known. In order to bring out the point at issue, I shall assume it true that my friend said 'there's Jones' because he saw Jones, and that I believed Jones was there because I heard my friend say so. But unless my friend and I are both philosophers, the two words 'because' in this statement must both be causal, not logical. I do not go through a process of reasoning in arriving at the belief that Jones is there; given the stimulus, the belief arises spontaneously. Nor does my friend go through a process of reasoning in passing from the percept to the utterance 'there's Jones'; this also is spontaneous. The causal chain is thus clear: Jones, by reflecting sun light, causes a percept in my friend; the percept causes the utterance 'there's Jones', the utterance causes an auditory percept in me, and the auditory percept causes in me the belief 'Jones is somewhere in the neighbourhood'. But the question we have to ask is: what must I know in order that, as a reflective philosopher, I may know that this causal chain affords a *ground* for my belief?

I am not now concerned with common sense reasons for doubt, such as mirrors, auditory hallucinations, etc. I am willing to suppose that everything happened as we naturally think it did, and even, to avoid irrelevances, that in all similar cases it has so happened. In that case, my beliefs as to the causal antecedents of my belief that Jones is in the neighbourhood are true. But true belief is not the same thing as knowledge. If I am about to become a father, I may believe, on grounds of astrology, that the child will be a boy; when the time comes, it may turn out to be a boy; but I cannot be said to have *known* that it would be a boy. The question is: is the true belief in the above causal chain any better than the true belief based on astrology?

There is one obvious difference. The prophecies based on the above casual chain, when they can be tested, turn out to be true; whereas astrological prophecies as to the sex of a child will, in a series of cases, be false as often as they are true. But the hypothesis that the light-waves proceeding from Jones, the percept and utterance of my friend, and the sound-waves proceeding from him to me, are mere auxiliary fictions in the causal inter-connexion of my percepts, has the same consequences as the realist hypothesis, and is therefore equally tenable if my percepts are the sole ground of my empirical knowledge.

This, however, is not the main objection. The main objection is that, if it is meaningless to suppose that there are unexperienced events, the light-waves and sound-waves involved in the realist hypothesis are meaningless. Unless we assume a plenum of Leibnizian monads, all causation between human beings will have to be telepathic: my friend experiences himself saying 'there's Jones', and after a time, without anything relevant having happened meantime, I hear what he has said. This hypothesis seems preposterous, and yet, if we deny that there can be truth about unexperienced events, we shall be forced to adopt it. Thus if we assert that it is meaningless to say that there are events which no one experiences, we cannot avoid conflicting grossly with scientific common sense – just as grossly, in fact, as if we were solipsists.

Nevertheless, the hypothesis that only experienced events occur is not logically refutable, any more than the solipsist hypothesis. We need only suppose that, in physics, all those events that are not experienced are mere logical fictions, introduced for convenience in interconnecting the events that are experienced. In this hypothesis, we accept the experiences of others, and therefore admit testimony, but we do not admit unperceived events. Let us consider whether anything is to be said in favour of this hypothesis from the standpoint of the meaning of 'truth'.

The main argument will be derived from the difficulty of defining the correspondence which is to constitute basic truth in cases in which no percept is involved. Between a certain percept and the utterance 'there's Jones' there is a causal connexion which we more or less understand; this connexion constitutes the correspondence in virtue of which the utterance is 'true'. But where no percept is involved, no such simple type of correspondence is possible.

It will be remembered, however, that propositions which go outside the experience of the speaker always involve variables, and that such propositions necessarily derive their truth (when they are true) from a correspondence of a different kind from that involved in the case of propositions not involving variables. The statement 'there are men in Los Angeles' is verified by any one of a number of facts, namely that A is there and is a man, that B is there, etc. No one of these has any special claim to be *the* verifier of the statement. On purely logical grounds, therefore, we should not expect the same kind of correspondence, or truth of the same 'type', in the case of unperceived events as in that of events that are perceived.

Let us take the statement 'you are hot', which we considered in Chapters 15 and 16. We decided that, in order to interpret this, we must be able to describe some occurrence x which is part of your present biography but of no one else's, and then add 'hotness is compresent with x'. In order to make sure that x belongs to no other biography, we must use some quality of the sort employed in defining spatio-temporal position. We suggested your percept of your body, but your percept of my body would do equally well. By means of the laws of perspective and my location of my percept of your body among my other percepts, I can approximately infer the character of your visual percept of your body. If R is the perspective relation that I use in this inference, while a is my visual percept of your body and C is the relation of compresence, 'you are hot' means 'there is an x which has the relation R to a and the relation C to hotness'. Here all the constants – i.e. all the terms except x – are derived from experience. The correspondence with fact (supposing the proposition true) is of the only kind possible for existence-propositions. From 'I am hot' I can infer 'someone is hot'; this has the same sort of correspondence with fact as 'you are hot' on the above interpretation. The difference lies not in the kind of correspondence, but in the circumstance that in the one case the verifying fact is a percept of my own and in the other it is not.

Let us now take a statement about something that no one experiences, such as sound-waves or light-waves. I am not arguing that such statements can be known to be true; I am only concerned to assign a significance to them. Suppose you and I are at a considerable distance from each other along some measured road. You fire a pistol, and I first see the smoke and then hear the report. You move along the road while I stand still; I find by experiment that the time between my seeing the flash and hearing the report is proportional to your distance from me. So far I have introduced nothing that transcends my experience. Your movement may be taken as the movement of my percept of you, your position on the road may be taken as the position of my percept of you on my percept of the road, and your distance from me may be taken to be the number of percepts of measuring-posts between my percept of my body and my percept of yours. Equality of distance between successive measuring posts is easily interpreted subjectively, since the space concerned may be taken to be the space of my percepts, not physical space.

The essential transition involved is that from perceptual to physical space. To eliminate testimony, which is not essential in the present connexion, I shall suppose, not that you fire a pistol, but that I have placed a series of time-bombs at the various measuring posts, and that I measure the intervals between seeing and hearing the various explosions. What is the nature of the inference from these subjective experiences to physical space?

It must be understood that I am not discussing any inference performed by common sense. Common sense believes in naïve realism, and makes no distinction between physical and perceptual space. Many philosophers, although they have realized that naïve realism is untenable, nevertheless retain some opinions logically connected with it, more particularly in this matter of different kinds of space. The question that I am discussing is this: having realized all that is implied in the rejection of naïve realism, how can we enunciate the hypothesis that there is physical space, and what sort of principle would (if true) justify us in believing this hypothesis?

Part, at least, of the hypothesis involved is that a cause and its effect, if separated by a finite time-interval, must be connected by a continuous intermediate causal chain. There is evidently a causal relation between seeing and hearing the explosion; when I am on the spot, they are simultaneous; we therefore assume that, when they are not simultaneous, there has been a series of intermediate occurrences, which, however, were not perceived, and are therefore not in perceptual space. This point of view is reinforced by the discovery that light, as well as sound, travels with a finite velocity.

We may therefore take, as a principle which will serve for the purposes of discussion: if, in my experience, an event of kind A is always followed, after a finite interval, by an event of kind B, there are intermediate events which interconnect them. Some such principle is certainly involved in scientific procedure; its exact form is, for our purposes, unimportant.

This is an instance of a more general question: given an existence-proposition of which I do not experience any verifier, what is involved in supposing that I can know it? The problem is, in part, not essentially different in the case of 'there are sound-waves in air' and 'there are people in Semipalatinsk'. In the latter case, it is true, I *could* experience verifiers by taking a journey, whereas in the former case I could not. But so long as I do not actually take the journey, this difference is not decisive. Each proposition is believed, not on sensible evidence alone, but on a combination of sensible evidence with some non-demonstrative form of inference.

Perhaps all non-demonstrative inferences can be reduced to induction? The argument would be as follows: I infer people in Semipalatinsk, and subsequently verify my inference. Many instances of such verification make me feel confidence in similar inferences even when unverified. But is it possible for an inductive inference to be not merely unverified, but unverifiable? This is the case of sound-waves, which can never be perceived. Do these require some further principle than induction?

It might be said: the hypothesis of sound-waves enables us to predict occurrences which *are* verifiable, and thus receives indirect inductive confirmation. This depends upon the general assumption that, as a rule, untrue hypotheses will have some consequences that can be shown by experience to be false.

At this point, there is a substantial difference between hypotheses about what can be experienced and hypotheses about what cannot. The hypothesis that whenever I have seen an explosion I shall soon hear a noise is one which, if false, will sooner or later be proved false by my experience. But the hypothesis that the sound reaches me by means of sound-waves might be false without ever leading to any consequence that experience would show to be false; we can suppose that the sound-waves are a convenient fiction, and the sounds which I hear occur *as if* borne by sound-waves, but in fact without non-sensible antecedents. This hypothesis cannot be rejected on grounds of induction; if it is to be rejected, it must be on grounds of some other kind, for example, on the basis of the principle of continuity mentioned above.

We may distinguish four assemblages of events: (1) those that I experience, (2) those in which I believe on the basis of testimony, (3) all those ever experienced by human beings, (4) those assumed in physics. Of these I know empirically that portion of (1) that I now perceive or remember; from these I can arrive at my future or forgotten experiences by assuming induction. I can arrive at (2) by means of analogy, if I assume that speech or writing which I hear or see 'means' what it would if I spoke or wrote it. Given this assumption, I can by induction arrive at (3). But how about (4)?

It may be said: I believe in (4) because it leads to a harmonious body of theory, at all points consistent with (1), (2), and (3), and giving a simpler statement of the laws governing the occurrence of (1), (2), and (3), than can be obtained otherwise. As to this, however, it should be said that (1) alone, or (2) alone, or (3) alone, allows an equally harmonious theory by merely supposing the events in excluded groups to be convenient fictions. The four hypotheses – (1) alone, (2) alone, (3) alone, or (4) – are empirically indistinguishable, and if we are to adopt any except (1) alone we must do so on the basis of some non-demonstrable principle of inference, which cannot be rendered either probable or improbable by any empirical evidence. Since no one accepts (1) alone, I conclude that there are no true empiricists, and that empiricism, though not logically refutable, is in fact believed by no one.

The argument that an unverifiable existence-proposition, such as those of physics, is unmeaning, is to be rejected. Every constant in such a proposition has a meaning derived from experience. Many such propositions – e.g. 'the good, when they die, go to heaven' – have a powerful effect both on emotion and on action. Their type of relation to fact, when they are true, is just the same as in the case of verifiable existence-propositions or general propositions. I conclude that there is no ground in the analysis of significance for rejecting them, and that empiricism affords only such grounds against (4) as apply equally against (2) and (3). I therefore accept the law of excluded middle without qualification.

To sum up the result of this long discussion: what we called the epistemological theory of truth, if taken seriously, confines 'truth' to propositions asserting what I now perceive or remember. Since no one is willing to adopt so narrow a theory, we are driven to the logical theory of truth, involving the possibility of events that no one experiences and of propositions that are true although there can never be any evidence in their favour. Facts are wider (at least possibly) than experiences. A 'verifiable' proposition is one having a certain kind of correspondence with an experience; a 'true' proposition is one having exactly the same kind of correspondence with a fact – except that the simplest type of correspondence, that which occurs in judgements of perception, is impossible in the case of all other judgements, since these involve variables. Since an experience is a fact, verifiable propositions are true; but there is no reason to suppose that all true propositions are verifiable. If, however, we assert positively that there are true propositions that are not verifiable, we abandon pure empiricism. Pure empiricism, finally, is believed by no one, and if we are to retain beliefs that we all regard as valid, we must allow principles of inference which are neither demonstrative nor derivable from experience.

CHAPTER 22

SIGNIFICANCE AND VERIFICATION

IN Chapter 21, I considered what may have been thought a parody of empiricism, and decided against it. I did not mean to decide against all possible forms of empiricism, but only to bring out certain implications of what is generally accepted as scientific knowledge, which seem to me to be insufficiently realized by most modern empiricists. It will serve to give precision to what I am asserting to compare it with opinions with which I am very nearly in agreement. For this purpose, I shall, in the present chapter, examine in detail certain parts of Carnap's 'Testability and Meaning'.* This is an important and careful analysis; in particular, his distinction between 'Reduction' and 'Definition' throws much light on the theory of scientific method. In so far as I have any disagreement with Carnap's views, this arises almost entirely from my belief that he begins rather too late in his analyses, and that certain prior problems, to which the present work is mainly devoted, are more important than he would be inclined to admit. This opinion I shall now proceed to defend controversially.

Carnap begins with a discussion of the relation between the three concepts 'meaning', 'truth', and 'verifiability'. (What he calls 'meaning' is what I have called 'significance', i.e. it is a property of sentences.) He says:

'Two chief problems of the theory of knowledge are the question of meaning and the question of verification. The first question asks under what conditions a sentence has meaning, in the sense of cognitive, factual meaning. The second one asks how we get to know something, how we can find out whether a given sentence is true or false. The second question presupposes the first one. Obviously we must understand a sentence, i.e. we must know its meaning, before we can try to find out whether it

* *Philosophy of Science*, vols. iii and iv, 1936 and 1937.

is true or not. But, from the point of view of empiricism, there is a still closer connexion between the two problems. In a certain sense, there is only one answer to the two questions. If we knew what it would be for a given sentence to be found true then we would know what its meaning is. And if for two sentences the conditions under which we would have to take them as true are the same, then they have the same meaning. Thus the meaning of a sentence is in a certain sense identical with the way we determine its truth or falsehood; and a sentence has meaning only if such a determination is possible.'

Carnap regards as oversimplified the thesis 'that a sentence is meaningful if and only if it is verifiable, and that its meaning is the method of its verification'. This formulation, he says, 'led to a too narrow restriction of scientific language, excluding not only metaphysical sentences but also certain scientific sentences having factual meaning. Our present task could therefore be formulated as that of a modification of the requirement of verifiability. It is a question of a modification, not of an entire rejection of that requirement.'

The cruder view is stated, for example, by Schlick:* 'Stating the meaning of a sentence amounts to stating the rules according to which the sentence is to be used, and this is the same as asking the way in which it can be verified (or falsified). *The meaning of a proposition is the method of its verification* [my italics]. There is no way of understanding any meaning without ultimate reference to ostensive definitions, and this means, in an obvious sense, reference to "experience" or "possibility of verification".'

In this passage, Schlick falls into a fallacy from failure to distinguish between words and sentences. All necessary *words*, as we have seen, have ostensive definitions, and are thus dependent on experience for their meaning. But it is of the essence of the use of language that we can understand a sentence correctly compounded out of words that we understand, even if we have never had any experience corresponding to the sentence as a whole. Fiction, history, and all giving of information depend upon this property of language. Stated formally: given the experience necessary for the understanding of the name '*a*' and

* 'Meaning and Verification', *Philosophical Review*, vol. 45, July 1936.

the predicate 'P', we can understand the sentence '*a* has the predicate P' without the need of any experience corresponding to this sentence; and when I say that we can understand the sentence, I do not mean that we know how to find out whether it is true. If you say 'Mars contains inhabitants as mad and wicked as those of our planet', I understand you, but I do not know how to find out whether what you say is true.

Again, when it is said that 'the meaning of a proposition is the method of its verification', this omits the propositions that are most nearly certain, namely judgements of perception. For these there is no 'method of verification', since it is they that constitute the verification of all other empirical propositions that can be in any degree known. If Schlick were right, we should be committed to an endless regress, for propositions are verified by means of other propositions, which, in turn, must derive their meaning from the way in which they are verified by yet other propositions, and so on *ad infinitum*. All those who make 'verification' fundamental overlook the real problem, which is the relation between words and non-verbal occurrences in judgements of perception.

The process of verification is never sufficiently examined by those who make it fundamental. In its simplest form, it occurs when I first expect an event and then perceive it. But if an event occurs without my having first expected it, I am just as capable of perceiving it and forming a judgement of perception about it; yet in this case there is no process of verification. Verification confirms the more doubtful by means of the less doubtful, and is therefore essentially inapplicable to the least doubtful, viz. judgements of perception.

Let us now return to Carnap. He says 'if we knew what it would be for a given sentence to be found true then we would know what its meaning is'. Here, on grounds which I have given previously, we must distinguish sentences containing variables from such as contain only constants. Let us take first the case in which there are only constants; consider, for example, some subject-predicate sentence 'P(*a*)', where the predicate 'P' and the name '*a*' both have ostensive definitions. This implies that I have had experiences which were expressed in sentences 'P(*b*)',

'P(c)', 'P(d)' ... by means of which I acquired the habit of associating 'P' with P; it also implies that I have had experiences which were expressed in sentences 'Q(a)', 'R(a)', 'S(a)' ... by means of which I acquired the habit of associating 'a' with a. But it is assumed that I have never had an experience which I should express in the sentence 'P(a)'. However, I am supposed 'to know what it would be for this sentence to be found true'. I do not see what this can mean except that we can *imagine* the percept which would lead us to pronounce the sentence 'P(a)' as a judgement of perception. This is certainly a *sufficient* condition for understanding the sentence, but I am not sure that it is a *necessary* one. For example, if we hear 'P(a)' asserted, we may act appropriately without any intermediary between hearing and acting, and we must then be said to understand the sentence.

Let us now take the much commoner case in which the sentence concerned contains at least one variable. According to what has been said in previous chapters, it is doubtful whether a proposition which is not a judgement of perception can ever contain no variable; thus perhaps the case discussed in the last paragraph never occurs. In any case, when it *seems* to occur the sentence concerned will be found, usually if not always, to be an existence-sentence: 'there is an x such that ...'

In the case of a sentence of the form 'there is an x such that ...', to say 'what it would be for the sentence to be found true' is not easy, and involves another sentence of the same form. Take the case of a murder, committed, according to the verdict of the coroner's Court, by some person or persons unknown. (We will, for simplicity, omit 'or persons'.) In what sense do we know 'what it would be for this sentence to be found true'? The simplest hypothesis is that some new witness comes forward and says he saw the murder committed by Mr A. I shall omit the possibility of perjury. We have thus, while we are considering the possibility of a new witness, a whole series of hypothetical percepts: B or C or D ... or Z seeing A do it; A or C or D ... or Z seeing B do it; A or B or D or ... Z seeing C do it; and so on – where A, B, C ... Z are all the men there are. Thus to know what it would be for the sentence to be found true is to know what it would be for some man to see some other man committing the murder, i.e. to know what is meant by another sentence of the same form.

Speaking generally, the sentence 'there is an x such that fx' may be found true if 'fa' or 'fb' or 'fc', or etc., is a judgement of perception. The sentence has a multitude of possible verifiers, and therefore we cannot, in advance, describe its verification except by another existence-sentence.

At this point, however, it is necessary to recall what we said in connexion with memory, to the effect that we may, in virtue of past perception, know an existence-proposition without knowing the definite perceptive proposition which existed on the occasion that gave rise to our present vague recollection. If memory is accepted – as I think it must be – as an independent source of knowledge (independent logically, not causally, since all memories are causally dependent on previous percepts), then a sentence must be considered verified if it either expresses or follows from a present recollection. In that case, there will be a kind of verification which consists in arriving at an existence-proposition expressing a memory-belief. This kind of verification, however, in view of the fallibility of memory, is inferior to that by perception, and we shall always endeavour, as far as we can, to supplement it by perceptive verification.

I omit, for the moment, the case of universal propositions such as 'all men are mortal'. For the moment, I am only concerned to show that the phrase 'what it would be for a sentence to be found true' is one of which the interpretation is far from simple.

Between the method that I advocate in theory of knowledge and that advocated by Carnap (in company with many others), there is a difference in starting-point which is very important and (I think) insufficiently realized. I start from sentences about particular occurrences, such as 'this is red', 'that is bright', 'I-now am hot'. The evidence in favour of such a sentence is not other sentences, but a non-verbal occurrence; the whole of the evidence is contained in a single such occurrence, and nothing that happens at any other time or place can confirm or confute this evidence. Previous occurrences are concerned *causally* in my use of language: I say 'red' because of a habit generated by past experiences. But the manner in which the habit was formed is irrelevant to the meaning of the word 'red', which depends upon what the habit *is*, not upon how it came about.

Every sentence of the above kind is logically independent of all the others, severally and collectively. Whenever, therefore, one such sentence is said to increase or diminish the probability of another such sentence, this must be in virtue of some principle of interconnexion, which, if believed, must be believed on evidence other than that of perception. The most obvious example of such a principle is induction.

The sentences that Carnap has in mind must, in view of what he says about them, be of a different kind. Some quotations will help to make this clear.

'We distinguish the *testing* of a sentence from its confirmation, thereby understanding a procedure – e.g. the carrying out of certain experiments – which leads to a confirmation in some degree either of the sentence itself or of its negation. We shall call a sentence *testable* if we know such a method of testing it; and we shall call it *confirmable* if we know under what conditions the sentence would be confirmed' (p. 420).

'A predicate "P" of a language L is called *observable* for an organism (e.g. a person) N, if, for suitable arguments, e.g. "b", N is able under suitable circumstances to come to a decision with the help of few observations about a full sentence, say "$P(b)$", i.e. to a confirmation of either "$P(b)$" or "not-$P(b)$" of such a high degree that he will either accept or reject "$P(b)$"' (p. 454).

These passages make it obvious that Carnap is thinking of sentences having some degree of generality, since various different occurrences may have a bearing on their truth or falsehood. In the first passage, he speaks of experiments which confirm in some degree the sentence or its negation. He does not tell us what it is that we learn from each experiment. Yet unless each experiment taught us *something*, it is difficult to see how it could have any bearing on the truth or falsehood of the original sentence. Further: the original sentence must have had a bearing upon events at various different times, since otherwise the experiments, which occurred at different times, could not have increased or diminished the probability of its truth. The sentence must therefore have had a greater degree of generality than the sentences embodying the results of the several experiments. These latter, therefore, must be of a logically simpler form than the sentence which they confirm or confute, and our theory of knowledge ought to begin with them rather than with the sentence that they are to prove or disprove.

Very similar remarks apply to the second quotation. Carnap speaks of 'few observations' as being necessary to decide the truth of 'P(b)'. Now if more than one observation is possible, b must be capable of occurring more than once, and cannot therefore be an event, but must have the character of a universal. I am convinced that this consequence is not intended by Carnap, but I do not see how it can be avoided – except, perhaps, by the theory of proper names advocated in Chapter 6, which Carnap would be compelled to reject in view of the importance that he attaches to space-time.

Even if we adopt the theory of Chapter 6 as to proper names, we do not really escape from the difficulty as to repetition. Suppose I see, on two different occasions, a given shade of colour C. My percept is in each case a complex, from which C has to be disengaged by analysis, and if I am to use both occasions to give me knowledge of C, I shall need a judgement of identity: 'this shade of colour that I see is identical with a certain shade that I remember seeing'. Such a judgement takes me beyond any present perception, and cannot have any high degree of certainty. Thus on any theory the possibility of repetition, which Carnap assumes, involves difficulties which he does not seem to realize, and shows that the kind of sentence that he is considering is not the kind from which a discussion of empirical evidence ought to start, since it is both less simple and less certain than sentences of another kind, of which the existence is implied in Carnap's discussion, although he does not seem to be aware of this implication.

All use of language involves a certain universality in fact, but not necessarily in knowledge. Consider, for example, the definition of 'predicate'. A predicate is a class of similar noises connected with a certain habit. We may say: 'let P be a class of similar noises. Then P is, for a given organism N, a "predicate",* if there is a class E of similar events such that the occurrence of any member of the class E causes in N an impulse to make a noise of the class P'. The class of noises P will only have this property for N if N has frequently experienced members of E and P in conjunction. Repetition and universality, *in fact*, are of the essence of the matter, for language consists of habits, habit involves repetition, and repetition can only be of universals. But *in knowledge* none of this is necessary, since we use language, and can use it correctly, without being aware of the process by which we acquired it.

To come to another point: Carnap defines what he means by an observable *predicate*, but not, in general, what is to be meant by a *sentence* of which the truth can be tested by observation. For him, a predicate 'P' is observable if there is a sentence '(b)' which can be tested by observation; but this does not help us to know whether '$P(c)$' can be tested by observation. I should say that, unless there were a number of sentences of the form '$P(b)$' which had already been tested by observation, the word 'P' would have no meaning, since the habit that constitutes meaning would not have been generated. What is proper matter for observation, I should say, is rather a sentence than a word: "P" and "c" may both have a meaning, which must be derived from experience, but there may be no observation bearing on the truth or falsehood of the sentence "$P(c)$". Whether this is the case, is, to my mind, the important question. And I should add that, in the kind of sentence which is fundamental for empirical data, only one single occurrence can give any ground for asserting or denying "$P(c)$". As soon as repetition is possible, we have passed beyond what is basic.

The word 'observable', like all words involving possibility, is dangerous. As it stands, Carnap's definition says that "P" is 'observable' if certain observations *could* occur. But we cannot, at the outset, know what observations are possible although they do not in fact occur. It seems necessary, therefore, to substitute 'observed' for 'observable', and say that the predicate "P" is

* Or, more exactly, a predicate having an ostensive definition.

observed if observations actually occur which help to decide about "P(*b*)" for some *b*.

Further: Carnap's definition, as it stands, is purely causal: the observations *cause* the observer to believe P(*b*) or not-P(*b*). Nothing is said – and I do not see how, from his point of view, anything can be said – to show that there is any *reason* (as opposed to *cause*) why these observations should lead to this belief.

It would thus seem that the definition of an 'observable' predicate "P" reduces to: 'A observes "P" if there is a "*b*" such that circumstances lead A to assert "P(*b*)" or "not-P(*b*)"'. In other words, since all A's assertions must be the result of circumstances, 'A observes "P" if A asserts "P(*b*)" or "not-P(*b*)"'. This makes the whole theory come to nothing.

Throughout the above discussion, I have not been contending that what Carnap says is mistaken, but only that there are certain prior questions to be considered, and that, while they are ignored, the relation of empirical knowledge to non-linguistic occurrences cannot be properly understood. It is chiefly in attaching importance to these prior questions that I differ from the logical positivists.

The most important of these prior questions is: can anything be learnt, and if so what, from a single experience? Carnap and the whole school to which he belongs think of knowledge as scientific knowledge, and as beginning with such propositions as 'metals conduct electricity'. Such propositions clearly require a number of observations. But unless each single observation yields *some* knowledge, how can a succession of observations yield knowledge? Every induction is based upon a number of premisses which are more particular than the conclusion: 'copper conducts electricity' is more particular than 'metals conduct electricity', and is itself an induction derived from 'this is copper and conducts electricity', 'that is copper and conducts electricity', and so on. Each of these is in itself an induction, based, ultimately, upon a series of single observations. Every single observation tells the observer *something*. It may be difficult to express in words exactly what can be learnt from one observation, but it is not impossible; I am at one with the logical positivists in rejecting the notion of ineffable knowledge. I do not see how it can be denied that our knowledge of matters of fact is built up, by means of inference, from premisses derived from single observations.

It is because I regard single observations as supplying our factual premisses that I cannot admit, in the statement of such premisses, the notion of 'thing', which involves some degree of persistence, and can, therefore, only be derived from a plurality of observations. The view of Carnap, which allows the concept of 'thing' in the statement of factual premisses, seems to me to ignore Berkeley and Hume, not to say Heraclitus. You cannot step twice into the same river, because fresh waters are continually flowing in upon you; but the difference between a river and a table is only a matter of degree. Carnap might admit that a river is not a 'thing'; the same arguments should convince him that a table is not a 'thing'.

Carnap advances an argument, which must be examined in this connexion, to prove that 'there is no fundamental difference between a universal sentence and a particular sentence with regard to verifiability but only a difference in degree'. His argument is:

'Take for instance the following sentence: "There is a white sheet of paper on this table". In order to ascertain whether this thing is paper, we make a set of simple observations and then, if there still remains some doubt, we may make some physical and chemical experiments. Here as well as in the case of the law, we try to examine sentences which we infer from the sentence in question. These inferred sentences are predictions about future observations. The number of such predictions which we can derive from the sentence given is infinite; and therefore the sentence can never be completely verified.'

The question of certainty or complete verification is not the one I wish to discuss. In all the arguments known to me on this subject, except those of Reichenbach, the question whether a proposition is certain is mixed up with the question whether it is a factual premiss. I am prepared to admit that what we take to be perceptive judgements, like recollections (though in a less degree), are fallible; this, however, is irrelevant to the question:

'what form ought we to give to the propositions that we admit as factual premisses?'

It is obvious that, if nothing can be learnt from one observation, then nothing can be learnt from many observations. Therefore our first question must be: 'what can be learnt from one observation?' What can be learnt from one observation cannot contain words applicable to classes of things, such as 'paper' and 'table'. We saw in an earlier chapter that 'there is a dog' cannot be a factual premiss, but 'there is a canoid patch of colour' can be.* A factual premiss must not contain words which are condensed inductions, such as 'dog', 'paper', 'table'.

Carnap's argument, quoted above, really involves appeal to such factual premisses as I consider essential, but makes this appeal by the way, and as though it were unimportant. 'In order to ascertain whether this thing is paper, we make a set of simple observations.' What do we learn from any one of these observations? On this point Carnap is silent. Again he says: 'We try to examine sentences which we infer from the sentence in question. These inferred sentences are predictions about future observations.' This admits that sentences are possible which state what is to be learnt from a single observation, and makes it obvious that such sentences give the factual premisses from which we infer that 'this is paper'.

As regards the 'certainty' of factual premisses, what is to be said is as follows.

First: we give to our factual premisses such a form that no two groups of them can be mutually inconsistent, and also no one such premiss can be rendered in any degree probable or improbable by any number of others. The interconnecting of factual premisses, by means of which they are made to confirm or disconfirm each other, depends upon principles of inference, notably induction, which are never demonstrative, which yield only probabilities, and which, therefore, are not disproved when what they show to be probable does not happen.

Second: the whole of the reason for believing a factual premiss. in so far as it is a premiss, is the event to which it refers. The evidence for it, that is to say, is a unique occurrence, not a

---

* It is assumed that 'canoid' is used in defining 'dog', not vice versa.

sentence or proposition or belief; the evidence is complete at the moment of the occurrence, was previously non-existent, and cannot afterwards be strengthened by any further evidence.

Third: if we are to hold, as many philosophers do, that a factual premiss may be rejected on the basis of later evidence, this must be because we accept *a priori* non-demonstrative forms of inference, which experience can neither confirm nor confute, but which we regard, in some circumstances, as more certain than the evidence of the senses.

Finally: factual premisses may not be certain, but there is nothing more certain by which they can be shown to be false.

CHAPTER 23

WARRANTED ASSERTIBILITY

I T will be remembered that, at the beginning of Chapter 21, four theories of truth were distinguished, of which I advocate the fourth, which is the correspondence theory. The third, that of coherence, was discussed and rejected in Chapter 10. The second, which substitutes 'probability' for 'truth', has two forms, in one of which I can accept it, while in the other I must regard it as mistaken. In the form in which it merely says that we are never quite certain that a given proposition, expressed in words, is true, I accept it; but in the form in which it contends that the concept 'truth' is an unnecessary one, I reject it. It seems to me that '"p" is probable' is strictly equivalent to '"p is true" is probable', and that when we say '"p" is probable', we need some probability that this statement is *true*. I see no reason why an advocate of probability, as all that is practically attainable, should reject 'truth' as it appears in the above statements. I shall therefore not controvert Professor Reichenbach's views, since I believe that, by a small modification, they can be rendered consistent with my own.

The first of our four theories, on the contrary, differs radically from the theory that I advocate, and must therefore be discussed. This is the theory of Dr Dewey, according to which 'warranted assertibility' should take the place of 'truth'. I have already discussed this theory in *The Philosophy of John Dewey*, which is Volume I of 'The Library of Living Philosophies'. The reader is referred to this volume for detail, and, what is more important, for Dr Dewey's answers to my objections. In the present chapter I wish to confine myself to the general principle, and to consider it as uncontroversially as is compatible with giving my reasons for rejecting it.

It appears from Dr Dewey's reply in the above-mentioned volume that I have unintentionally misunderstood and parodied his opinions. I am most anxious to avoid doing so if I possibly can, the more so as I am convinced that there is an important difference between his views and mine, which will not be elicited unless we can understand each other. It is because the difference goes deep that it is difficult to find words which both sides can accept as a fair statement of the issue. This, however, is what I must attempt.

So far as I can understand Dr Dewey, his theory is, in outline, as follows. Among the various kinds of activities in which mankind can engage, there is one called 'inquiry', of which the general purpose, like that of many other kinds of activity, is to increase the mutual adaptation of men and their environment. Inquiry uses 'assertions' as its tools, and assertions are 'warranted' in so far as they produce the desired results. But in inquiry, as in any other practical operation, better tools may, from time to time, be invented, and the old ones are then discarded. Indeed, just as machines can enable us to make better machines, so the temporary results of an inquiry may be the very means which lead to better results. In this process there is no finality, and therefore no assertion is warranted for all time, but only at a given stage of inquiry. 'Truth' as a static concept is therefore to be discarded.

The following passage in Dr Dewey's reply to me (loc. cit., p. 573) may serve to elucidate his point of view:

'The exclusive devotion of Mr Russell to discourse is manifested in his assumption that *propositions* are the subject-matter of inquiry, a view assumed so unconsciously that it is taken for granted that Peirce and I likewise assume it. But according to our view – and according to that of any thorough-going empiricist – *things and events* are the materials and object of inquiry, and propositions are *means* in inquiry, so that as conclusions of a given inquiry they become means of carrying on further inquiries. Like other means they are modified and improved in the course of use. Given the beliefs (I) that propositions are from the start the objects of inquiry and (II) that all propositions have either truth or falsity as their inherent property, and (III) then read these two assumptions into theories – like Peirce's and mine – which deny both of them, and the product is just the doctrinal confusion that Russell finds in what we have said'.

First, a few words of personal explanation. Any reader of the present work will, I hope, be convinced that I do not make *propositions* the ultimate subject-matter of inquiry, since my problem has been, throughout, the relation between *events* and the propositions that they cause men to assert. I do not, it is true, regard *things* as the object of inquiry, since I hold them to be a metaphysical delusion; but as regards *events* I do not, on this point, disagree with Dr Dewey. Again: as regards scientific hypotheses, such as quantum theory or the law of gravitation, I am willing (with some qualifications) to accept his view, but I regard all such hypotheses as a precarious superstructure built on a foundation of simpler and less dubious beliefs, and I do not find, in Dr Dewey's works, what seems to me an adequate discussion of this foundation.

As to truth and falsehood, I should interpret the facts as regards inquiries and changing hypotheses somewhat differently. I should say that inquiry begins, as a rule, with an assertion that is vague and complex, but replaces it, when it can, by a number of separate assertions each of which is less vague and less complex than the original assertion. A complex assertion may be analysable into several, some true, some false; a vague assertion may be true or false, but it is often neither. 'An elephant is smaller than a mouse' is vague, and yet definitely false; but 'a rabbit is smaller than a rat' is not definitely either true or false, because some young rabbits are smaller than some old rats. When Newton's theory of gravitation was replaced by Einstein's, a certain vagueness in Newton's concept of acceleration was removed, but almost all the assertions implied by Newton's theory remained true. I should say that this is an illustration of what always happens when an old theory gives way to a better one: the old assertions failed to be definitely true or false, both because they were vague, and because they were many masquerading as one, some of the many being true and some false. But I do not see how to state the improvement except in terms of the two ideals of precision and truth.

One difficulty, to my mind, in Dr Dewey's theory, is raised by the question: what is the goal of inquiry? The goal, for him, is not the attainment of truth, but presumably some kind of harmony between the inquirer and his environment. I have raised this question before (in the above-mentioned volume), but have not seen any answer to it. Other activities, such as building houses or printing newspapers or manufacturing bombs, have recognizable purposes. In regard to them, the difference between a good tool and a bad one is obvious: a good tool minimizes the labour involved in achieving the purpose. But 'inquiry' is neutral as between different aims: whatever we wish to do, some degree of inquiry is necessary as a preliminary. If I wish to telephone to a friend, I must inquire his number of the telephone book, taking care to use the most recent edition, since its truths are not eternal. If I wish to govern the country, I must inquire in previously unfamiliar circles as to how to become a political boss. If I wish to build ships, either I or some one in my employ must inquire into hydrostatics. If I wish to destroy democracy, I must inquire into crowd psychology. And so on. The question is: what happens as the result of my inquiry? Dr Dewey rejects the traditional answer, that I come to *know* something, and that, as a consequence of my knowledge, my actions are more successful. He eliminates the intermediate stage of 'knowing', and says that the only essential result of successful inquiry is successful action.

Taking man as he appears to science, and not as he may appear to a Cartesian sceptic, there are here two questions to be discussed. First: what sort of psychological occurrence is to be described as a 'believing'? Second, is there any relation between a 'believing' and its environment which allows us to call the believing 'true'? To each of these questions I have tried to give an answer in previous chapters. If there are such occurrences as 'believings', which seems undeniable, the question is: can they be divided into two classes, the 'true' and the 'false'? Or, if not, can they be so analysed that their constituents can be divided into these two classes? If either of these questions is answered in the affirmative, is the distinction between 'true' and 'false' to be found in the success or failure of the effects of believings, or is it to be found in some other relation which they may have to relevant occurrences?

I am prepared to admit that a belief as a whole may fail to be 'true' or 'false' because it is compounded of several, some true, and some false. I am also prepared to admit that some beliefs fail, through vagueness, to be either true or false, though others, in spite of vagueness, are either true or false. Further than this I cannot go towards agreement with Dr Dewey.

In Dr Dewey's view, a belief is 'warranted' if, as a tool, it is useful in some activity, i.e. if it is a cause of satisfaction of desire. This, at least, would have seemed to me to be his opinion. But he points out (loc. cit., p. 571) that consequences are only to be accepted as tests of validity '*provided* these consequences are operationally instituted and are such as to resolve the specific problem evoking the operations' [his italics]. The second half of this proviso is clear in its meaning. If I go to a place under the mistaken belief that my long-lost uncle lives there, but on the way I meet my long-lost aunt, and in consequence she leaves me her fortune, that does not prove that 'my long-lost uncle lives there' had 'warranted assertibility'. But the first half of the proviso, which insists that the consequences must be 'operationally instituted', is one of which the meaning remains to me somewhat obscure. The passage in Dr Dewey's *Logic* (Preface, p. iv) where the phrase occurs does not elucidate it. But in his reply to me (loc. cit., p. 571) there is a passage which I will quote in full, as it is designed to remove my errors in interpretation:

'The proviso about the kind of consequences that operate as tests of validity was inserted as a caution against just the kind of interpretation which Mr Russell gives to my use of consequences. For it explicitly states that it is necessary that they be *such as to resolve the specific problem* undergoing investigation. The interpretation Mr Russell gives to consequences relates them to personal desire. The net outcome is attribution to me of generalized wishful thinking as a definition of truth. Mr Russell proceeds first by converting a doubtful *situation* into a personal doubt, although the difference between the two things is repeatedly pointed out by me. I have even repeatedly stated that a personal doubt is pathological unless it is a reflection of a *situation* which is problematic. Then by changing doubt into private discomfort, truth is identified with removal of this discomfort. The only desire that enters, according to my view, is desire to resolve as honestly and impartially as possible the problem involved in the situation. 'Satisfaction' is satisfaction of the conditions prescribed by the problem. Personal satisfaction may enter in as it arises when any job is well done according to the requirements of the job itself; but it does not enter in any way into the determination of validity, because, on the contrary, it is determined by that validity.'

I find this passage very puzzling. Dr Dewey *seems* to speak as if a doubtful situation could exist without a personal doubter. I cannot think that he means this; he cannot intend to say, for example, that there were doubtful situations in astronomical and geological epochs before there was life. The only way in which I can interpret what he says is to suppose that, for him, a 'doubtful situation' is one which arouses doubt, not only in some one individual, but in any normal man, or in any man anxious to achieve a certain result, or in any scientifically trained observer engaged in investigating the situation. *Some* purpose, i.e. *some* desire, is involved in the idea of a doubtful situation. If my car won't go, that creates a doubtful situation if I want it to go, but not if I want to leave it where it is. The only way to eliminate all reference to *actual* desire is to make the desire purely hypothetical: a situation is 'doubtful' in relation to a given desire if it is not known what, in that situation, must be done to satisfy that desire. When I say 'it is not known', I must mean, in order to avoid the sort of subjectivity that Dr Dewey deprecates, that it is not known to those who have the relevant training. Thus suppose I find myself in a situation S, and I desire a situation S', and I believe (rightly or wrongly) that there is something that I could do which would transform S into S', but the experts cannot tell me what to do, then S is, in relation to my desire, a 'doubtful' situation.

Eliminating all reference to personal doubt and desire, we may now say: S is 'doubtful' is relation to S' if mankind do not know of any human action A which will transform S into S', but also do not know that no such action is possible. The process of inquiry will consist in performing a series of actions A, A', A'', ... in the hope that one of them will transform S into S'.

This, of course, implies that S and S' are both described in terms of universals, since, otherwise, neither can occur more than once. A, A', A'', ... must also be so described, since we wish to arrive at some such statement as: 'whenever you are in the situation S, and wish to be in the situation S', you can secure your desire by performing the action A', where A must be a *kind* of action, since otherwise it could only be performed once.

Thus when we take Dr Dewey's elimination of subjective desire seriously, we find that his goal is to discover causal laws of the old sort 'C causes E', except that C must be a situation plus an act, and E another situation. These causal laws, if they are to serve their purpose, must be 'true' in the very sense that Dr Dewey wishes to abolish.

One important difference between us arises, I think, from the fact that Dr Dewey is mainly concerned with theories and hypotheses, whereas I am mainly concerned with assertions about particular matters of fact. As explained in the preceding chapter, I hold that, for any empirical theory of knowledge, the fundamental assertions must be concerned with particular matters of fact, i.e. with single events which only happen once. Unless there is *something* to be learnt from a single event, no hypothesis can ever be either confirmed or confuted; but what is to be learnt from a single event must itself be incapable of being confirmed or confuted by subsequent experience. This whole question of how we learn historical facts by experience seems to me to be ignored by Dr Dewey and the school of which he is the leader. Take, for instance, the statement 'Caesar was assassinated'. This is true in virtue of a single event which happened long ago; nothing that has happened since or will happen in the future can in any way affect its truth or falsehood.

The distinction between truth and knowledge, which was emphasized in connexion with the law of excluded middle, is relevant at this point. If I wish to 'verify' the statement 'Caesar was assassinated', I can only do so by means of *future* events – consulting books of history, manuscripts, etc. But these are only to the purpose as affording evidence of something other than themselves. When I make the statement, I do not mean 'whoever looks up the encyclopaedia will find certain black marks on white paper'. My seeing these black marks is a unique event on each occasion when I see them; on each occasion I can know that I have seen them; from this knowledge I can infer (more or less doubtfully) that Caesar was assassinated. But my perception of the black marks, and my inference from this perception, are not what make the assertion about Caesar *true*. It would be true even if I made it without any grounds whatever. It is true because of what happened long ago, not because of anything that I am doing or shall do.

The broad issue may be stated as follows. Whether we accept or reject the words 'true' and 'false', we are all agreed that assertions can be divided into two kinds, sheep and goats. Dr Dewey holds that a sheep may become a goat, and vice versa, but admits the dichotomy at any given moment: the sheep have 'warranted assertibility' and the goats have not. Dr Dewey holds that the division is to be defined by the *effects* of assertions, while I hold, at least as regards empirical assertions, that it is to be effected by their *causes*. An empirical assertion which can be *known* to be true has percepts, or a percept, among its proximate or remote causes. But this only applies to knowledge; so far as the *definition* of truth is concerned, causation is only relevant in conferring meaning upon words.

The above discussion has been mainly concerned to clarify the issue. The grounds of my own opinions have been, for the most part, given in previous chapters.

CHAPTER 24

ANALYSIS

I AM concerned, in this chapter, with propositions of the form 'P is part of W'. I wish to inquire whether these are ever part of the fundamental apparatus of empirical knowledge, or whether they are always to be deduced from a definition of the whole W, which, incidentally, will mention the part P whenever 'P is part of W' is true. Something has already been said on this subject in Chapters 3 and 8, but I wish now to examine it on its own account.

The operation by which, from examination of a whole W, we arrive at 'P is part of W', is called 'analysis'. It has two forms: logical analysis, and analysis into spatio-temporal parts. One of the matters to be considered is the relation between these two forms of analysis.

From the earliest times, many philosophers have objected to analysis: they have maintained that analysis is falsification, that a whole does not really consist of parts suitably arranged, and that, if we mention any part singly, the act of isolation so alters it that what we have mentioned is not what is an organic part of the whole.

The principle of atomicity, which we considered in an earlier chapter, represents the opposite extreme from that of the monists. The principle of atomicity may be said to forbid synthesis. Linguistically, it forbids the giving of proper names to complex wholes, at any rate when they are recognized to be complex.

For my part, I reject both these extremes.

Those who deny the legitimacy of analysis are compelled to maintain that there is knowledge not expressible in words. For it is difficult to deny that sentences consist of words, and that, therefore, sentential utterances can be analysed into series of verbal utterances. If this is to be denied, it is necessary to deny that a sentence is a string of words, and in that case it becomes something ineffable.

Those, on the other hand, who believe in analysis, not infrequently follow language too slavishly; I have been guilty of this fault myself. There are two ways in which language may guide us in analysis: one is by considering words and sentences as sensible facts, the other is by considering the different kinds of words, as is done in grammar. Of these the first, I should say, is wholly innocuous, while the second, though it has its uses, is very dangerous, and a copious source of error.

To begin with language as composed of sensible facts. Sentences are composed of words, printed words are composed of letters. The man who has a book printed causes separate bits of type to be put together in a certain order; yet, if he is a philosopher, his book may be saying that no series of material objects can represent thought. Now it may be the case – I hope it is – that these philosophers have better ideas in their heads than they succeed in putting into their books, but it is quite certain that the ideas in their books *can* be expressed by series of material objects, for, if not, the compositors would find their task impossible. Thought, in so far as it is communicable, cannot have any greater complexity than is possessed by the various possible kinds of series to be made out of twenty-six kinds of shapes. Shakespeare's mind may have been very wonderful, but our evidence of its merits is wholly derived from black shapes on a white ground. Those who say that words falsify sensible facts forget that words *are* sensible facts, and that sentences and words, as facts, are composed of discrete parts, which can be separately named, and are so named by every child learning to spell. It is therefore undeniable that *some* sensible facts can be analysed into parts.

The analysis of a printed word into letters is easier than the analysis of most sensible facts; it is the purpose of print to make the analysis easy. But the difference is only one of degree, and some natural phenomena invite analysis just as much as print does. A black dog in snow, a rainbow, a seagull against a stormy sea, are very noticeable. I believe even the most monistic of philosophers would notice a tiger, and not stop to argue that it could not be validly considered except in relation to its background. Analysis of the sensible present occurs almost inevitably where there is a sharp contrast, such as a sudden noise, or black against white. Rapid movement, which is very noticeable, comes under the same head. In such cases, we become aware, not simply of a whole, but of a complex of parts. If this were not the case, we should never have acquired the notion of spatio-temporal order.

It is customary nowadays to dismiss contemptuously the atomic view of sensation as it appears in Hume and his followers. We are told that the sensible world is a continuous flux, in which divisions are unreal, the work of the mind purely conceptual, and so on. This is said as something obvious, for which only a stupid man would demand evidence. Now the word 'sensation' or 'sensible', as is often pointed out, stands for something hypothetical – broadly speaking, for what *could* be noticed without change in the environment or the sense-organs. What is not hypothetical is what *is* noticed, not what *could* be noticed; and what *is* noticed has, I maintain, just that atomicity and discreteness which the critics of Hume reject. They do not, as empiricists should, start from data, but from a world that they have inferred from data but use to discredit the kind of thing that can be a datum. In theory of knowledge, what is fundamental is noticing, not sensation.

I shall take for granted, henceforth, that we can, within a perceived whole, perceive parts as interrelated. It is not necessary to suppose that the parts are 'simple', nor is it clear what this supposition would mean. For the purpose of expressing in words what we perceive in such a case, the smallest parts that are noticed should be given proper names, and then we can state how they are related.

Such analysis as I have been considering hitherto is spatio-temporal, but there is another kind of analysis that raises much more difficult problems; it is that which proceeds from considering different kinds of words, and which inquires whether anything corresponds in the non-verbal world. The matter may be put as follows: given a complex whole, there are not only parts, but the parts are arranged in a pattern. The description of the whole will employ some relational word to indicate the pattern; what is there, in the non-verbal world, corresponding to this relational word?

The problem is suggested by the distinction between the parts of speech. But common language is not sufficiently logical for this distinction to be taken over as it stands. We must first construct an artificial logical language before we can properly investigate our problem.

Logical languages have been invented by logicians for the purposes of logic. They need no actual proper names, since logic never speaks about anything in particular. Our purpose is slightly different, but by the help of logic we can easily construct the sort of language we need. What we require, at the moment, is a language that will symbolize, as accurately and systematically as possible, all that part of our knowledge which belongs to the primary language; and when we have constructed our language, we have to consider what light its structure throws on the structure of the percepts in virtue of which its propositions are true.

Our language must, in the first place, contain proper names for all perceived objects which are perceived as units. When we perceive a *Gestalt* without analysing it, we must be able to name it – e.g. to say 'that is a swastika'. But when, in geometry, we have a figure consisting of several lines, each of which is separately noticed, we seem not to need a proper name for the whole figure. Nevertheless, if there is such a thing as a judgement of analysis, where the analysis is of the sort we have already considered, i.e. of spatio-temporal whole and part, it needs a proper name for the whole and other proper names for the parts. Suppose, for instance, you want to say, not in general, but in a particular case, that a certain face consists of its two eyes, it nose, and its mouth (ignoring other parts), you will have to proceed as follows: Let us call the face F, the eyes respectively E_1 and E_2, the nose N, and the mouth M. Then F consists of E_1, E_2, N, M arranged so that E_1 and E_2 are ovals on a level, N is a narrow isosceles triangle which descends vertically from half way between E_1 and E_2, and M is a horizontal line with its middle point vertically below N. (This is not a very accurate description of a face, but it suffices to illustrate linguistic necessities.)

It will be seen that F, here, seems somewhat superfluous, since the state of affairs can be described completely by means of E_1, E_2, N, and M. Whether there is or is not any need for the proper name 'F' is a question which, for the moment, I will leave open.

In the above description of a particular face, we have had to use other words besides the proper names. We have had to state the spatial relations of the parts. Let us simplify the matter by reducing the eyes and nose to lines. Then we may say: E_1 and E_2 are equal parts of one horizontal line; if E_0 is the middle point between E_1 and E_2, N is part of the vertical line descending from E_0, M has its middle point on this line, and is part of a horizontal line below N. This statement has a geometrical accuracy which is lacking in perception, but that is not important at the moment. We can perhaps, in the visual field, take 'horizontal' and 'vertical' as predicates, like 'blue' and 'red'. But we need statements such as 'E_1 is to the left of E_2', 'E_1 is above N', 'N is above M'. There is no possible way of describing what we see without relational statements of this sort.

Let us consider this from a scientific point of view. Complete information about the visual field at any moment would consist of propositions stating the colour of each place in it. The visual field has an absolute origin, the point upon which we are focusing, and absolute position in the field is defined by two angular coordinates, which we may call θ, ϕ.* Thus the visual field is completely specified if we know, for a variable x which may take all values that are shades of colour, the value of x that satisfies

$$x = f(\theta, \phi)$$

for every θ and ϕ, where '$f(\theta, \phi)$' means 'the shade of colour at (θ, ϕ)'. This is a triadic relation between x and θ and ϕ, and it does not seem possible to describe the visual field more simply.

Let us consider the following sentence: 'as I was leaving the theatre, I heard cries of "fire" and was violently pushed by a panic-stricken mob.' This cannot quite report a judgement of perception, for 'panic-stricken' is hardly a quality of perceptible

* I am, for the sake of simplicity, ignoring depth as a visual quality.

data. But we only have to omit the words 'by a panic-stricken mob' to have a possible judgement of perception. What, exactly, does it assert? It asserts the simultaneity of the following three percepts: (1) my visual field was such-and-such (what in fact it is when one is close to the exit); (2) I heard the sound 'fire' repeatedly; (3) I experienced a strong sensation of pressure in the back. We may simplify this, and substitute the simultaneity of the following: (1) I saw and felt my hand touching the door; (2) I heard the sound 'fire'; (3) I felt a violent pressure of the sort that one refers to the back. Here a visual, an auditory, and two tactual data are said to be simultaneous. The word 'simultaneous' is difficult, but I think that, when we are discussing data, it means 'parts of one perspective experience'. And when A, B, C, D are simultaneous, that does not mean merely that A and B, B and C, C and D are simultaneous in pairs; for anything perceptible lasts for a finite time, and therefore simultaneity among perceptibles is not transitive. Thus in our case there must have been one experience, or, in a sense, one perception, which embraced the visual, the auditory, and the two tactual data.

It may be said that the simultaneity of a number of events can be inferred from their all having happened at the same time. Let us look into this. A watch or clock is (*inter alia*) a device for giving names to a number of very brief events. Let us suppose a clock which indicates not only seconds, minutes, and hours, but the day of the month and the month of the year. We may even let it indicate the year. In that case, such-and-such an appearance of the clock is an event which lasts for exactly a second and never recurs. Let us suppose that you are such an expert in perceiving *Gestalt* that you can distinguish any two different appearances of the clock without having to notice the separate hands. You can then give the proper name 'A' to the appearance of the clock at exactly 10.45 p.m. on 1 December 1940. You may observe successively, concerning the events B, C, D, E, that B was simultaneous with A, that C was so, that D was so, and that E was so; but you cannot infer that B, C, D, and E were simultaneous with each other, since they may all have been very brief; they might, for instance, have been the four words 'fly for your lives', which can easily be uttered successively in a second.

If, now, your clock, instead of changing its appearance only once a second, changes it as often as is compatible with the perception of jerks rather than continuous motion, you will be unable to make *successive* observations while its appearance remains unchanged, and therefore you cannot know that two events were both simultaneous with one appearance of the clock unless they and this appearance were all parts of one experience; and when I say that they were parts of one experience, I mean that there is a perceptive proposition in the primary language which asserts their togetherness or simultaneity. The clock, therefore, however elaborate, does not help us out. We must admit that we can perceive several events as simultaneous, and obviously there is no theoretical limit to the number of such events.

What follows from the above is that we must allow, within the primary language, for the possibility of *n*-adic relations, where *n* is any finite number. There must, that is to say, be words which are not proper names, but predicates, or dyadic relations, or triadic relations, or etc.

What has been said so far in this chapter is preliminary to the main question, which, as already stated, is this: can we state all that we know without the use of any basic propositions of the form 'P is part of W'? In asking this question, it is supposed that 'P' and 'W' are proper names. It will be remembered that, in Chapter 8, we concluded that *all* judgements of perception are of this form, and that what, in such propositions, we naturally call 'this', is a complex which the judgement of perception partially analyses. It is assumed, in saying this, that we can experience a whole W without knowing what its parts are, but that, by attention or noticing, we can gradually discover more and more of its parts. It is not assumed that this process must stop short of complete analysis, nor is it assumed that it can be carried to the point at which the parts that have been arrived at are incapable of further analysis. But it is assumed that the whole W can preserve its identity throughout the process of analysis: that, e.g., in perception we can begin with 'W!' as an exclamatory use of an object-word, and arrive, by attention, at 'P is part of W', without any change in the denotation of the name 'W'.

In the above account there is a suggestion of a chronological process of analysing, which is perhaps not logically essential to the theory that names for wholes are indispensable. When we study a perceptual datum, which, at first, appears as a vague whole, we may gradually arrive at an enumeration of interrelated parts; but in such a case it may be said that the datum changes as a result of attention. This is certainly true, for example, in the case of a visual datum which we observe first carelessly, and then attentively. Attention, in such a case, involves changes in the eyes, which change the visual object. It may be said that all analysing is of this sort, and that the whole whose parts are known is never identical with the previous whole which was perceived vaguely. I do not think it is necessary for the theory we are considering to deny this. We can, I think, confine ourselves to the finished product of our analysing, and ask ourselves: can this result be expressed without reference to whole-and-part?

Our question is: when we *do* perceive that a whole has parts, do our data always consist of propositions about the parts and their relations, or must they sometimes contain propositions in which the whole is mentioned? This is again the question of atomicity. Consider (say) a circle, which we will call A, and a

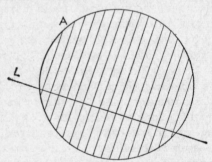

straight line, L, which passes through it. We can say 'L divides A into two parts', but we may be interested in A as a whole, and in the fact that it is divided, without being in the least interested in the separate parts. Consider, for instance, a thin cloud cutting the full moon in two. We remain aware of the moon as a whole, much more vividly than of the parts.

Or consider a somewhat different case. We see a distant object approaching along a road; at first we *only* see it as a whole, but gradually we see it clearly enough to make out that it is a dog. When this happens, our visual object is, of course, not the same as it was before, but we believe it to be connected with the same physical object, which has, from the first, interested us as a whole. Hence when we come to see the parts, we see them *as* parts, not as separate items arranged in a certain pattern. It seems to me that, in such a case, what we perceive cannot be accurately expressed without propositions of the form 'P is part of W', where 'P' and 'W' are proper names for percepts, and P, at least, is only part of our total percept.

To take another instance: a child who is being taught, by modern methods, to read the word 'CAT', learns to make, in succession, the sounds 'k', 'a', 't'. (I mean the sounds these letters stand for, not the names of the letters.) At first, the interval between the sounds is too long for the child to be conscious of their succession as forming a whole, but at last, as the rapidity increases, there comes a moment when the child is aware of having said the word 'cat'. In that moment, the child is aware of the word as a whole composed of parts. Before that, he was not aware of the whole; when he can read fluently, he ceases to be aware of the parts; but in the first moment of understanding, whole and parts are equally present in consciousness. What the child is aware of in this moment cannot be expressed without such propositions as 'the sound "k" is part of the sound "cat"'.

I think that all judgements of perception involve analysis of a perceptual whole; what is given is a pattern, and the realization that it consists of interrelated objects results from analysis. Without propositions of the form 'P is part of W', the process would not be explicable. It seems, therefore, that such propositions must occur in the primary language.

Every judgement of perception which contains more than one object-word expresses an analysis of a perceived complex whole; the perceived whole is, in one sense, known by being perceived, but the kind of knowledge which is opposed to error requires something more than perception. A judgement of perception which contains more than one object-word, and is expressed in a sentence which is not equivalent to several separate sentences, must contain at least one word of which the meaning is relational. There is no theoretical limit to the complexity of the object of perception or of the structure affirmed in judgements of perception which the object verifies. It is upon the complexity of the object of perception that our knowledge of both space and time depends.

Assuming, as it seems from the above that we must, that there are wholes composed of interrelated parts, and that the knowledge expressed in judgements of perception requires, for its verbalization, names for such wholes, there remains a difficult question, namely: in what circumstances do interrelated terms form a whole, which needs a name for the verbal expression of what we know?

The argument demands that the total of our experience at any one time should always be such a whole, and so must certain complex parts of this total. The parts of such a total are bound together by the relation of compresence. For reasons explained in Chapter 21, we hold that the relation of compresence may hold outside experience as well as within it; indeed, if there is the un-experienced world that physics supposes, its space-time will depend upon unexperienced compresence. Perhaps wholes, of the indispensable sort, are always constituted by compresence. Let us examine this possibility.

In the following pages, I shall be concerned to develop a *possible* view on the element of analysis in judgements of percep-tion. I am not concerned to maintain that this view is *necessary*.

Let us give the name 'W' to my total perceptual field at some given moment. At *that* moment, I can give the pseudo-name 'this' to W, and also to certain parts of W, but not to anything larger than W. The psuedo-name 'I-now' applies to the whole of W at the moment when W exists, and not to any part of W. According to the theory of Chapter 6, W is a bundle of com-present qualities. To these qualities we can give names. Let 'Q' be the name of one of them. Then 'I-now perceive Q' is to be translated into 'Q is part of W'.

If this is to be satisfactory, it is necessary that, among the qualities constituting W, there should be at least one which does not recur, or one subordinate complex which does not recur. For the sake of simplicity, I shall suppose that I am always watching a clock which indicates not only minutes and hours, but the day of the month, the month of the year, and the year of our Lord. If now I give the name 't' to the aspect of this clock which is part of W, 't' will designate a group of qualities which has no temporal relation to itself, i.e. occurs only once. Any other aspect of the clock will be earlier or later than t, and we shall say that the total perceptual field of which this other aspect is a part is correspondingly earlier or later than W.

According to the above, the values of t form a numerically measurable series, and two different values of t cannot be compresent unless they are so nearly equal that they can be parts of one specious present, i.e. of one W. All this is empirical.

We now have to consider what parts of W can be wholes requiring names for the expression of judgements of perception. The total W may be analysed into a number of qualities, but this analysis will not, by itself, enable us to explain such judgements of perception as 'A is to the left of B'. These demand the analysis of W into what we should be tempted to call 'substantial' rather than 'conceptual' parts. They demand, that is to say, an investigation of *spatial* analysis within a given perceptual whole.

Let us again, as on former occasions, confine ourselves to the visual field and ignore depth. We may then say, with a simplification which is innocuous, that there are in the visual field a number of differing qualities of up-and-downness and a number of differing qualities of right-and-leftness. Any one of the former we will denote by 'θ' and any one of the latter by 'ϕ'. Apart from differences in excellence of vision, we may suppose that each quality θ and each quality ϕ exists in everybody's field of vision whenever his eyes are open and it is not dark.

We now require a relation of 'overlapping', which plays a part in the construction of perceptual space analogous to that played by compresence in private time. I do not define this relation, but I maintain that, if Q and Q' are two qualities, 'Q and Q' overlap' can be a judgement of perception. For example: red and bright red can overlap; so can a given degree of pressure with the quality by which we distinguish a touch on one part of the body from a touch on another. Two different θ-qualities cannot overlap; no more can two different ϕ-qualities. Two different colours cannot overlap; no more can two touch-qualities belonging to different parts of the body. Any visual quality can overlap with any θ and with any ϕ.

Two different values of θ have to each other an asymmetrical spatial relation, that of above or below; two different values of ϕ have an asymmetrical spatial relation, that of right or left. A given value of θ will have a relation of right or left, but not of up or down, to itself, and a given value of ϕ will have a relation of up or down, but not of right or left, to itself; a complex (θ, ϕ) will have no spatial relation to itself. This fact is what we are trying to express when we say that it can only occur once in a given visual field.

If, now, a given quality, say a shade of colour C, exists throughout a region of the visual field, that means that it overlaps with many values of the pair of qualities (θ, ϕ). Since θ and ϕ are numerically measurable, we can define straightforwardly what we mean by a 'continuous' region in the visual field. Similarly we can define regions in tactual space. What we should commonly regard as a 'substantial' part of the whole W is any continuous region which is part of W. Any such region may be a 'this'.

When we say 'A is to the left of B', we may take 'A' to be the name of the complex consisting of given values of θ and ϕ together with all the qualities overlapping with both, while 'B' is similarly defined for other given values of θ and ϕ. Our statement is to be true if the A-value of ϕ is to the left of the B-value.

Thus in 'A is to the left of B' the whole W does not need to be mentioned. But if this sentence expresses a judgement of perception, there must *be* a whole W of which A and B are parts.

We may now reach a conclusion as to names. The primary names are those applying to such wholes as W, or to continuous regions which are parts of some W. Other names are derivative, and theoretically unnecessary.

It will perhaps help to make clear the scope of what has been said if we proceed to the construction of physical space-time. In this construction we necessarily assume the truth of physics.

Space-time in physics is elaborately inferential, and is

constructed largely by means of causal laws. It is assumed that, if there is a causal law connecting two events at different places in space-time, they are connected by means of a chain of events at intermediate places. The physical and physiological causation of percepts compels us to regard them as all in one region, which must be inside the percipient's head (not, of course, inside his or anyone else's percept of his head). The relation of compresence, which exists between percepts, may be supposed to exist also between any two physical events which overlap in space-time. A 'point' in space-time may be defined as a group of events having the following two properties: (1) any two of the group are compresent; (2) nothing outside the group is compresent with every member of it.

The ordering of points in space-time is by no means a simple matter, as Einstein has shown. It begins, historically, from the belief that every percept is 'of' some physical object, and that the order of the physical objects in physical space is correlated, somewhat roughly, with that of the corresponding percepts in perceptual space. The angular coordinates of stars in physical space are very nearly the same as those of their percepts in visual space. But the notion that a percept is 'of' a physical object turns out to be inexact, causal, and unreliable. The more exact determination of space-time order depends upon causal laws: e.g. the distance of Jupiter is calculated from observations which, assuming the law of gravitation, enable us to calculate how long light has taken to travel from there to us.

There is no need to pursue this matter further. The important points, for us, are two: that my perceptual whole W is, from the standpoint of physics, inside my head as a physical object; and that space-time whole and part is too elaborate and inferential a concept to be of much importance in the foundations of theory of knowledge.

CHAPTER 25

LANGUAGE AND METAPHYSICS

IN the present chapter I propose to consider whether anything, and, if so, what, can be inferred from the structure of language as to the structure of the world. There has been a tendency, especially among logical positivists, to treat language as an independent realm, which can be studied without regard to non-linguistic occurrences. To some extent, and in a limited field, this separation of language from other facts is possible; the detached study of logical syntax has undoubtedly yielded valuable results. But I think it is easy to exaggerate what can be achieved by syntax alone. There is, I think, a discoverable relation between the structure of sentences and the structure of the occurrences to which the sentences refer. I do not think the structure of non-verbal facts is wholly unknowable, and I believe that, with sufficient caution, the properties of language may help us to understand the structure of the world.

With regard to the relation of words to non-verbal facts, most philosophers can be divided into three broad types:

A. Those who infer properties of the world from properties of language. These are a very distinguished party; they include Parmenides, Plato, Spinoza, Leibniz, Hegel, and Bradley.

B. Those who maintain that knowledge is only of words. Among these are the Nominalists and some of the Logical Positivists.

C. Those who maintain that there is knowledge not expressible in words, and use words to tell us what this knowledge is. These include the mystics, Bergson, and Wittgenstein; also certain aspects of Hegel and Bradley.

Of these three parties, the third can be dismissed as self-contradictory. The second comes to grief on the empirical fact that we can know what words occur in a sentence, and that this is not a verbal fact, although it is indispensable to the verbalists. If, therefore, we are confined to the above three alternatives, we must make the best of the first.

We may divide our problem into two parts: first, what is implied by the correspondence theory of truth, in the measure in which we have accepted this theory? Second, is there anything in the world corresponding to the distinction between different parts of speech, as this appears in a logical language?

As regards 'correspondence', we have been led to the belief that, when a proposition is true, it is true in virtue of one or more occurrences which are called its 'verifiers'. If it is a proposition containing no variable, it cannot have more than one verifier. We may confine ourselves to this case, since it involves the whole of the problem with which we are concerned. We have thus to inquire whether, given a sentence (supposed true) which contains no variable, we can infer anything as to the structure of the verifier from that of the sentence. In this inquiry we shall presuppose a logical language.

Consider first a group of sentences which all contain a certain name (or a synonym for it). These sentences all have something in common. Can we say that their verifiers also have something in common?

Here we must distinguish according to the kind of name concerned. If W is a complete group of qualities, such as we considered in the last chapter, and we form a number of judgements of perception, such as 'W is red', 'W is round', 'W is bright', etc., these all have one single verifier, namely W. But if I make a number of true statements concerning a given shade of colour C, they all have different verifiers. These all have a common part C, just as the statements have a common part 'C'. It will be seen that here, as in the last chapter, we are led to a view which, syntactically, is scarcely distinguishable from the subject-predicate view, from which it differs only in that it regards the 'subject' as a bundle of compresent qualities. We may state what has just been said as follows: given a number of subject-predicate sentences expressing judgements of perception, such as 'this is red', if they all have the same subject they all have the same verifier, which is what the subject designates; if they all have the same predicate, the verifiers all have a common part, which is what the predicate designates.

This theory is not applicable to such a sentence as 'A is to the left of B', where 'A' and 'B' are names for two parts of my visual field. So far as 'A' and 'B' are concerned, we considered this sentence sufficiently in the last chapter. What I now wish to examine is the question: what, if anything, is common to the verifiers of a number of different sentences of the form 'A is to the left of B'?

The question involved is the old question of 'universals'. We might have investigated this question in connexion with predicates – say 'red is a colour', or 'high C is a sound'. But since we have explained the more apparently obvious subject-predicate sentences – e.g. 'this is red' – as really not subject-predicate sentences, we shall find it more convenient to discuss 'universals' in connexion with relations.

Sentences – except object-words used in an exclamatory manner – require words other than names. Such words, generically, we call 'relation-words', including predicates as words for monadic relations. The definition, as explained in Chapter 6, is syntactical: a 'name' is a word which can occur significantly in an atomic sentence of any form; a 'relation-word' is one which can occur in some atomic sentences, but only in such as contain the appropriate number of names.

It is generally agreed that language requires relation-words; the question at issue is: 'what does this imply as regards the verifiers of sentences?' A 'universal' may be defined as 'the meaning (if any) of a relation-word'. Such words as 'if' and 'or' have no meaning in isolation, and it may be that the same is true of relation-words.

It may be suggested (erroneously, as I think and shall try to prove) that we need not assume universals, but only a set of stimuli to the making of one of a set of similar noises. The matter is, however, not quite straightforward. A defender of universals, if attacked, might begin in this way: 'you say that two cats, because they are similar, stimulate the utterance of two similar noises which are both instances of the word "cat". But the cats must be *really* similar to each other, and so must the noises. And if they are *really* similar, it is impossible that "similarity" should be just a word. It is a word which you utter on certain occasions, namely, when there *is* similarity. Your tricks and devices' he will say, 'may seem to dispose of other universals, but only by putting all the work on to this one remaining universal, similarity; of that you cannot get rid, and therefore you might as well admit all the rest.'

The question of universals is difficult, not only to decide, but to formulate. Let us consider 'A is to the left of B'. Places in the momentary visual field, as we have seen, are absolute, and are defined by relation to the centre of the field of vision. They may be defined by the two relations right-and-left, up-and-down; these relations, at any rate, suffice for topological purposes. In order to study momentary visual space, it is necessary to keep the eyes motionless and attend to things near the periphery as well as in the centre of the field of vision. If we are not deliberately keeping our eyes motionless, we shall look directly at whatever we notice; the natural way to examine a series of places is to look at each in turn. But if we want to study what we can see at one moment, this method will not do, since a given physical object, as a visual datum, is different when it is seen directly and when it is far from the centre of the field. In fact, however, this makes very little difference. We cannot escape from the fact that visual positions form a two-dimensional series, and that such series demand dyadic asymmetrical relations. The view we take as to colours makes no difference in this respect.

It seems that there is no escape from admitting relations as parts of the non-linguistic constitution of the world; similarity, and perhaps also asymmetrical relations, cannot be explained away, like 'or' and 'not', as belonging only to speech. Such words as 'before' and 'above', just as truly as proper names, 'mean' something which occurs in objects of perception. It follows that there is a valid form of analysis which is not that of whole and part. We can perceive A-before-B as a whole, but if we perceived it *only* as a whole we should not know whether we had seen it or B-before-A. The whole-and-part analysis of the datum A-before-B yields only A and B, and leaves out 'before'. In a logical language, therefore, there will be *some* distinctions of parts of speech which correspond to objective distinctions.

Let us examine once more the question whether asymmetrical relations are needed as well as similarity; and let us take, for the purpose, 'A is above B', where 'A' and 'B' are proper names of events. We shall suppose that we perceive that A is above B. Now it is clear, to begin with a trivial point, that we do not need the word 'below' as well as the word 'above'; either alone suffices. I shall therefore assume that our language contains no word 'below'. The whole percept, A-above-B, resembles other percepts C-above-D, E-above-F, etc., in a manner which makes us call them all facts of vertical order. So far, we do not need a concept 'above'; we may have merely a group of similar occurrences, all called 'vertical orders', i.e. all causing a noise similar to 'above'. So far, we can do with only similarity.

But now we must consider asymmetry. When you say 'A is above B', how does your hearer know that you have not said 'B is above A'? In exactly the same way as *you* know that A is above B; he perceives that the noise 'A' precedes the noise 'B'.

Thus the vital matter is the distinction between A-first-and-then-B, B-first-and-then-A; or, in writing, between AB and BA. Consider, then, the two following shapes: AB and BA. I want to make it clear that I am speaking of just these, not of others like them. Let S_1 be the proper name of the first shape, S_2 that of the second; let A_1, A_2 be the proper names of the two A's, and B_1, B_2 of the two B's. Then S_1, S_2 each consist of two parts, and one part of S_1 is closely similar to one part of S_2, while the other part is closely similar to the other part. Moreover, the ordering relation is the same in both cases. Nevertheless, the two wholes are not very similar. Perhaps asymmetry could be explained in this way: given a number of A's and a number of B's, arranged in pairs, the resulting wholes fall into two classes, members of the same class being closely similar to each other, while members of different classes are very dissimilar. If we give the proper names S_3, S_4 to the following two shapes: AB and BA, then it is obvious that S_1 and S_3 are very similar, and so are S_2 and S_4, but S_1 and S_3 are not very similar to S_2 and S_4. (Observe that, in describing S_1 and S_2, we shall have to say: S_1 consists of A_1 before B_1, S_2 consists of B_2 before A_2.) Perhaps in this way it is possible to explain asymmetry in terms of similarity, though the explanation is not very satisfactory.

Assuming that we can, in the above manner or in some other, get rid of all universals except similarity, it remains to be considered whether similarity itself could be explained away.

We will consider this in the simplest possible case. Two patches of red (not necessarily of exactly the same shade) are similar, and so are two instances of the word 'red'. Let us suppose that we are being shown a number of coloured discs and asked to name their colours - say in a test for colour-blindness. We are shown two red discs in succession, and each time we say 'red'. We have been saying that, in the primary language, similar stimuli produce similar reactions; our theory of meaning has been based on this. In our case, the two discs are similar, and the two utterances of the word 'red' are similar. Are we saying the *same* thing about the discs and about the utterances when we say the discs are similar and when we say the utterances are similar? or are we only saying similar things? In the former case, similarity is a true universal; in the latter case, not. The difficulty, in the latter case, is the endless regress; but are we sure that this difficulty is insuparable? We shall say, if we adopt this alternative: if A and B are perceived to be similar, and C and D are also perceived to be similar, that means that AB is a whole of a certain kind and CD is a whole of the same kind; i.e., since we do not want to define the kind by a universal, AB and CD are *similar* wholes. I do not see how we are to avoid an endless regress of the vicious kind if we attempt to explain similarity in this way.

I conclude, therefore, though with hesitation, that there are universals, and not merely general words. Similarity, at least, will have to be admitted; and in that case it seems hardly worth while to adopt elaborate devices for the exclusion of other universals.

It should be observed that the above argument only proves the necessity of the word 'similar', not of the word 'similarity'.

Some propositions containing the word 'similarity' can be replaced by equivalent propositions containing the word 'similar', while others cannot. These latter need not be admitted. Suppose, for example, I say 'similarity exists'. If 'exists' means what it does when I say 'the President of the United States exists', my statement is nonsense. What I can mean may, to begin with, be expressed in the statement: 'there are occurrences which require for their verbal description sentences of the form "*a* is similar to *b*"'. But this linguistic fact seems to imply a fact about the occurrences described, namely the sort of fact that is asserted when I say '*a* is similar to *b*'. When I say 'similarity exists', it is this fact about the world, not a fact about language, that I mean to assert. The word 'yellow' is necessary because there are yellow things; the word 'similar' is necessary because there are pairs of similar things. And the similarity of two things is as truly a non-linguistic fact as the yellowness of one thing.

We have arrived, in this chapter, at a result which has been, in a sense, the goal of all our discussions. The result I have in mind is this: that complete metaphysical agnosticism is not compatible with the maintenance of linguistic propositions. Some modern philosophers hold that we know much about language, but nothing about anything else. This view forgets that language is an empirical phenomenon like another, and that a man who is metaphysically agnostic must deny that he knows when he uses a word. For my part, I believe that, partly by means of the study of syntax, we can arrive at considerable knowledge concerning the structure of the world.

INDEX

MORE ABOUT PENGUINS

Penguinews, which appears every month, contains details of all the new books issued by Penguins as they are published. From time to time it is supplemented by *Penguins in Print*, which is a complete list of all available books published by Penguins. (There are well over four thousand of these.)

A specimen copy of *Penguinews* will be sent to you free on request, and you can become a subscriber for the price of the postage. For a year's issues (including the complete lists) please send 30p if you live in the United Kingdom, or 60p if you live elsewhere. Just write to Dept EP, Penguin Books Ltd, Harmondsworth, Middlesex, enclosing a cheque or postal order, and your name will be added to the mailing list.

Note: *Penguinews* and *Penguins in Print* are not available in the U.S.A. or Canada

FUNDAMENTAL QUESTIONS
IN PHILOSOPHY
Stephan Körner

Here Stephan Körner, Professor of Philosophy at the University of Bristol, introduces the fundamental issues of philosophy to those who have not previously studied them. In a lucid appraisal of a constantly developing discipline he discusses the diverse problems which philosophers throughout the ages have attempted to tackle and the methods they have chosen to apply.

THE EUROPEAN MIND 1680–1715*
Paul Hazard

A fundamental change of outlook in every field of thought swept Europe between 1680 and 1715, forming a distinct watershed between modern thought and that of the ancient, medieval, and renaissance worlds. In this book Paul Hazard conveyed all the excitement – and much of the detail – of what he saw as the most significant single revolution in human thought: the birth of Newtonian science and of comparative religion, the impact of Descartes and Boyle, Newton and Locke, Spinoza and Leibniz; the creation of *our* world.

THE CONCEPT OF MIND*
Gilbert Ryle

Professor Ryle sets out to expose the myth of Descartes's doctrine of the separateness of mental and physical existences, an attitude still fundamental to much philosophical and psychological thinking today and based on an aversion to the mechanistic assumption that 'human nature differs only in degree of complexity from clockwork'.

'This is probably one of the two or three most important and original works of general philosophy which have been published in England in the last twenty years' – Stuart Hampshire in *Mind*.

* Not for sale in the U.S.A.